MW01193845

Terry Crist offers an
striving and find true
ing reminder that we
can run toward the grace and peace found in Jesus. This book is a
powerful guide for anyone longing to experience the healing and rest
their soul desperately needs.

—CRAIG GROESCHEL, founding and senior pastor, Life.Church;
   New York Times bestselling author

If we are going to run our race and finish our course, we must stop
running after the things that deplete and destroy us and find refuge and
rest in the only one who can strengthen and sustain us. In this book,
Terry Crist unpacks an important message for our time with vulnerability and transparency. This book offers much-needed wisdom for
fulfilling our purpose and flourishing in life.

—CHRISTINE CAINE, founder, A21 and Propel Women

Terry Crist invites us to step off the exhausting treadmill of striving
and into the rest found in Jesus. With profound insights from Scripture
and personal stories, he guides us to confront our pain and fears,
revealing that true peace is found only in God's embrace of grace. This
book is not just a theological treatise, it's a practical manual for spiritual
renewal. If you're weary from running in circles, this is your call to stop,
reflect, and discover the deep rest waiting for you in God's presence.
Embrace this journey; your soul will thank you.

—DR. DERWIN L. GRAY, cofounder and lead pastor, Transformation
   Church; author, *Lit Up with Love*

In a world where exhaustion has become the norm, our culture stands
on the brink of perpetual weariness. For those seeking to transcend this
cycle and find true rest, Dr. Terry Crist offers profound wisdom in this
book. His insights guide the reader from the depths of depletion to the
heights of spiritual vitality, urging us to pursue the good race that God
has set before us, rather than succumbing to the relentless rat race that
society often glorifies.

—DR. JEREMY DEWEERDT, lead pastor, CityFirst Church, IL and FL

If you're exhausted from the endless race of life, burdened by guilt, shame, or inadequacy, and longing to break free, this book offers the tools you need to find rest and refuge in the arms of God. He restores, renews, and lovingly gives us permission to stop running from it all. With biblical insights and practical guidance, Terry Crist reminds us that God meets us in our surrender. A timely message that will undoubtedly help you slow down to find the peace and healing you've been longing for.

—TAMMY TRENT, author; speaker; cohost, *Life Today TV*

Terry Crist has crafted a transformative work in *Now You Can Stop Running*, uncovering the pain, fear, and guilt that drive us to live at an unsustainable pace. With wisdom and compassion, he offers a clear path to healing and rest, inviting readers to find refuge in the unshakable reality of the grace of God. This timeless guide will become a companion for the journey for anyone longing to live with purpose, peace, and resilience!

—DR. DONNA PISANI, author, *The Power of Not Yet* and *Entrusted to Lead*

Profound yet practical! Few books tackle such weighty themes with this level of honesty and grace. Terry not only makes a compelling case for rest and soul care but also offers the rare gift of perspective, allowing us to see the patriarchs as they truly were: human, flawed, runners. Undiminished in their stature yet deeply relatable. We all run, and as this book so beautifully outlines, we've been running since the garden. Terry strips the shame from the run and gracefully points a weary generation toward where to run to. What a gift!

—REWARD SIBANDA, speaker; author, *How to Fast: Rediscover the Ancient Practice for Unlocking Spiritual Renewal*; pastor, Saddleback Church

Few people call us to live a deeper and more meaningful life with their presence. Dr. Terry Crist is one of those people. His new book is no different. It invites us to take off our running shoes so we can walk on holy ground. It shows us how to boldly choose the path of peace and experience God's presence. It teaches our souls how to breathe again so we can live the life God created us for.

—NAEEM FAZAL, lead pastor, Mosaic Church; author, *Ex-Muslim* and *Tomorrow Needs You*

Many of us have been habituated into a life of self-protection as a response to adversity. In other words, we learned to run away. But running from pain doesn't lead to transformation. In this latest offering, my friend Terry Crist gives us a durable path to healing and resilience. As you read, may your heart be reindexed toward wholeness.

—CHRISTOPHER COOK, author, *Healing What You Can't Erase;* podcast host, *Win Today with Christopher Cook*

The exhaustion in our culture is not because of a lack of grit. There is a devastating hunger, a malnourishment of the soul in those who said yes to following Jesus, but somewhere along the way strategy took the place of intimacy. Strategy does not invite us to look within and to remain searchable by the Spirit. Because of this, our depth is compromised, because depth requires introspection, repentance, and renewal. Terry's words in this book will resound the invitation to encounter God and commune with the presence of a restorative, healing, and personal God who saves us over and over again. It will be a balm to your soul.

—NOEMI CHAVEZ, lead pastor, Revive Church; cofounder, Brave Global

In today's society, we often take pride in our frenzied pace, feeling inadequate if we admit to having a slow day. We grow impatient at red lights, wish two-minute eggs could cook faster, and relentlessly avoid confronting our challenges, fears, and flaws. It seems we're always running—either toward something or away from it. In this book, Terry Crist draws wisdom from personal experience and Scripture to offer readers permission to pause—Selah—and embrace God's grace in the present moment. As Dallas Willard has profoundly stated, "Grace is not opposed to effort, it is opposed to earning." This book invites us to remove our running shoes, rest, and find peace at Jesus' feet.

—DR. SCOTT R. JONES, lead pastor, Grace Church; professor; former runner

NOW YOU CAN STOP RUNNING

ALSO BY TERRY CRIST

Loving Samaritans: Radical Kindness in an Us vs. Them World

NOW YOU CAN STOP RUNNING

FINDING THE REST YOUR SOUL DESPERATELY NEEDS

TERRY CRIST

ZONDERVAN BOOKS

ZONDERVAN BOOKS

Now You Can Stop Running
Copyright © 2025 by Terry M. Crist

Published in Grand Rapids, Michigan, by Zondervan. Zondervan is a registered trademark of The Zondervan Corporation, L.L.C., a wholly owned subsidiary of HarperCollins Christian Publishing, Inc.

Requests for information should be addressed to customercare@harpercollins.com.

Zondervan titles may be purchased in bulk for educational, business, fundraising, or sales promotional use. For information, please email SpecialMarkets@Zondervan.com.

ISBN 978-0-310-36702-4 (audio)

Library of Congress Cataloging-in-Publication Data

Names: Crist, Terry M., 1965– author.
Title: Now you can stop running : finding the rest your soul desperately needs / Terry Crist.
Description: Grand Rapids, Michigan : Zondervan Books, [2025]
Identifiers: LCCN 2024059297 (print) | LCCN 2024059298 (ebook) | ISBN 9780310366997 (trade paperback) | ISBN 9780310367000 (ebook)
Subjects: LCSH: Self-actualization (Psychology)—Religious aspects—Christianity. | Crist, Terry M., 1965–
Classification: LCC BV4598.2 .C683 2025 (print) | LCC BV4598.2 (ebook) | DDC 248.4—dc23/eng/20250216
LC record available at https://lccn.loc.gov/2024059297
LC ebook record available at https://lccn.loc.gov/2024059298

Published in association with The Bindery Agency, www.TheBinderyAgency.com.

Cover design: Micah Kandros
Cover illustration: Shutterstock
Interior design: Lori Lynch

Printed in the United States of America

25 26 27 28 29 LBC 5 4 3 2 1

To my firstborn grandson,
Asher Phoenix Crist:
May you never feel the need to run but always rest in
the unshakable truth that you are unconditionally loved
by the one who provides true and lasting refuge.
You are his, and that is enough.

CONTENTS

FOREWORD BY CHRIS HODGES

For years, I was running at a pace I thought was sustainable—until my body forced me to stop. Like many leaders, I had mistaken movement for progress and had to learn that strength isn't in striving but in knowing when to stop running.

The wake-up call came during a ministry trip to Australia, where I was teaching and preaching almost nonstop. I hadn't built in time to recover from the fifteen-hour flight, so I propped myself up with caffeine and pushed through the exhaustion. On top of the relentless pace, I was still grieving the recent loss of my father, and our church had just celebrated ten years—a milestone marked by God's faithfulness and the hard work of so many.

I was thoroughly enjoying my life, yet looking back, I now see that it was too full. God kept surprising me, and I had accomplished far more than I'd ever expected. Every part of my life was devoted to knowing him, serving him, and helping others experience Jesus' love. I was faithful in obedience—except in one unintended way: resting. And apparently, because I was overlooking the need for rest, it took a major crash to get my attention.

That crash came on the side of the road in Australia when I thought I was having a heart attack. My pulse raced higher and higher, I couldn't catch my breath, and my chest felt like it was caught in a vise. Forced to rest until I stabilized enough to return stateside, I didn't learn the cause until my doctor ran a battery of tests back home. It wasn't my heart, it was my nervous system. I had hit a breaking point, the culmination of running too hard for too long. My body could no longer function at the level of intensity that had become my default. I had to learn to rest.

You can outrun your past for only so long before exhaustion catches up with you. The harder you push, the farther you drift from the refuge your soul is desperate to find. Looking back, I see that I wasn't just physically depleted, I was spiritually running on empty. That's why I love this book by my friend Terry Crist.

Now You Can Stop Running is the book I needed long before my panic attack Down Under. With wisdom and compassion, Terry offers permission to change the way we view rest and instruction on how to incorporate it as an essential faith practice. He draws on his own seasons of busyness and self-reliance to show us how to walk by faith and experience soul rest in God. In sharp contrast to our culture of constant activity, Terry makes it clear that the only way he has grown in his faith is by learning to surrender more and to strive less.

Delving into God's Word with fresh insight, Terry reveals that the permission to rest we often withhold from ourselves has been not only given by God but wired into how he made us. Our creator designed us to "be still, and know that I am God" (Ps. 46:10) and rested on the seventh day to set an example for us (Gen. 2:2–3). Sabbath rest requires us to stop our striving in order to refresh our minds and bodies and to renew our spirits in him.

Jesus not only invites us to this same kind of soul rest but reminds us of its necessity: "Come to me, all you who are weary and burdened, and I will give you rest" (Matt. 11:28). When we follow his example and rely on his Spirit as the source for our lives, we discover we don't have to strive. "Take my yoke upon you and learn from me, for I am gentle and humble in heart, and you will find rest for your souls. For my yoke is easy and my burden is light" (Matt. 11:29–30).

Perhaps you don't need convincing that you need to prioritize rest. What you need is someone to help you realign your relationship with God and show you how to make rest part of your life. Terry offers ways to experience what you know you need but so often tend to overlook until you hit a wall of exhaustion, depression, or burnout. Please take it from me and don't wait until you crash before you realize the ongoing importance of rest. You don't have to work harder or go faster. You can surrender your cares to him and rest in his love, strength, and power.

I encourage you to read this book slowly and carefully, with the eyes of your heart. If fear keeps you running, let Jesus catch you. If spiritual fatigue has brought you down, let him lift you up. Like a slow, gentle hike through a sunlit wooded trail, this book refreshes the soul, nourishes the mind, and soothes the heart. As I read it, I found myself both challenged and encouraged, convicted and comforted.

I pray you experience the gift Terry offers here in ways that cause you to stop running and start resting. If you long to experience the rest your soul desperately needs, take a deep breath and know that you're in the right place. If you want to grow in your faith and know God more intimately, now is the time.

Now you can be still and know that he is God.

Now you can stop running and start resting.

—CHRIS HODGES, founding pastor, Church of the Highlands; author, *Out of the Cave* and *Pray First*

READER'S GUIDE

Welcome to *Now You Can Stop Running: Finding the Rest Your Soul Desperately Needs*. Far too many of us spend our lives running from things that hurt us or racing toward what we think will fulfill us. All of that running leaves us exhausted and disconnected from the source of life and peace. But there is hope. God is with you right here and now, offering refuge and rest for your soul. This book will guide you in reconnecting with him and his gracious provision for your deepest needs.

If you find yourself feeling restless and dissatisfied with your life, this book is for you. My prayer is that, positioned at the intersection of Bible study and soul care, it serves as both a guide and a trusted companion. Through stories of biblical characters who faced similar struggles, you will gain insights and practices that will nurture your spirit and lead you to the feet of Jesus. Here's what you can expect and how to engage with the material to make the most of your journey.

WHAT TO EXPECT

Biblical Exploration. Each chapter centers on a different biblical character who embodies the themes of running and seeking refuge. You will journey through the lives of Cain, Hagar, Jacob, Moses, Elijah, David, and many others. Their stories are rich with lessons about human frailty, divine grace, and the transformative power of encountering God.

Spiritual Practices. At the end of each chapter, you will find a spiritual practice designed to help you internalize lessons and apply them to your life. These practices are crafted to foster soul care, reflection, and a deeper connection with God. I encourage you to practice the ones related to why *you* run until you feel you have found refuge and rest in that area of your life.

Personal Prayers. Each chapter concludes with a prayer that ties together the chapter's themes. These prayers are meant to guide you in your conversations with God, offering words that reflect the struggles and hopes we all share. They are starting points for your own heartfelt dialogue with God.

HOW TO USE THIS BOOK

Take your time. This book is best experienced slowly and reflectively. Take your time with each chapter, allowing the stories and lessons to resonate deeply. Don't rush. Give yourself the time to absorb and reflect on the insights presented.

Engage actively. Interact with the material through the suggested spiritual practices. These are not just add-ons but integral parts of your journey. They are designed to help you move from understanding to transformation, from head knowledge to heart experience.

Reflect and journal. Consider keeping a journal as you read. Write down your thoughts, feelings, and any revelations that come to you. Reflect on the questions posed in the spiritual practices sections and document your prayers. This process will help solidify what you've learned and provide a record of your spiritual journey.

Be open to transformation. Approach each chapter with an open heart, ready to be challenged and changed. Allow these biblical characters' stories to speak into your life. Let the spiritual practices guide you into deeper intimacy with God. Embrace the prayers as expressions of your own spiritual longing.

Lead a group discussion. If possible, read this book with your community. Sharing insights and experiences with others can enrich your understanding and provide mutual support. Discuss the biblical characters, spiritual practices, and prayers. Learn from each other's perspectives and support one another in soul care.

In this book, you will find an invitation to spiritual refuge and rest grounded in the timeless truths of Scripture. May you discover the peace that comes from ceasing your running and resting in Jesus' loving arms. Happy reading, and may God bless you on this journey.

With grace and peace,
—TERRY CRIST

CAN'T STOP RUNNING

From Avoidance to Awareness

*"Come to me, all you who are weary and
burdened, and I will give you rest."*

—MATTHEW 11:28

I was born running.

In our family videos, captured on vintage film reels, I am barely in the frame because I'm in constant motion. Back then, everyone felt the need to perform for the camera—smiling, waving, mouthing words that couldn't be heard. I was the kid who couldn't sit still, a whirlwind of energy that refused to be restrained.

But as the years passed, I ran for other reasons too.

Running was my escape. From my earliest memories, the wind brushing my face and the pounding of my feet on the ground were more than just physical sensations. Running transcended sport; it was my release valve, my escape, and a metaphor for my life. Dissatisfaction fueled my running as I sought to distance myself from generational conflict, familial expectations, and even childhood trauma. It drove me toward an idealized future in which my life would finally make sense.

As I matured, running remained my steadfast companion. The challenges of school, the burden of parental expectations, and the ache of young love lost spurred me to keep running in the solitude of dawn or the stillness of evening. Sometimes it felt like escaping. Paradoxically, the very act of running that drove me from pain also taught me resilience, endurance, and mental discipline. As the saying goes, "What doesn't kill you makes you stronger." There were days when my legs felt like lead, my lungs screamed for air, and my heart pounded in my chest like a war drum. Yet I persevered. Each time I thought I couldn't go on, I remembered why I started: to outrun the shadows, to quiet the voices, to heal the pain.

Running also gave me space to reflect on deeper issues. I began to realize that just as I was running physically, I was also running spiritually. Running—both as a feet-on-the-ground activity and as an abstract concept—became an opportunity to wrestle with the questions stirring in my soul:

- What is the source of my inner compulsion to flee?
- Will I ever find a rest that endures?
- Is there a sanctuary in this world where peace resides?

As I wrestled with these questions, a deeper realization took shape within me: the greatest challenge we face is not the road we travel but the trauma we carry.

Over time, I realized I was carrying a heavy load of unresolved emotions as I ran. All the running in the world couldn't lighten that burden. No matter how much I tried to stay one step ahead of my struggles, I found that escape wasn't the same as healing.

This book is about what I found when I began to live in the light of that realization.

RUN FOR YOUR LIFE

I have this theory: we are all running either from or toward something—driven by hidden wounds, unmet needs, and holy longings. In this sense, running becomes a metaphor for how we distance ourselves from pain or pursue the desires of our hearts. These internal drives motivate us to act, to move, to leave, to search, to strive—all driven by a profound ache for something more.

Yet here lies the paradox: the harder we chase what we yearn for, the farther it seems to slip from our grasp. The pursuit demands more of us—faster, farther, longer—until we're trapped in an endless cycle. Instead of finding relief, we're left drained, exhausted by the very restlessness we were desperate to escape. From the cradle to the grave, life unfolds as a series of dashes—between risk and reward, brokenness and wholeness, chance and comfort, the known and the unknown. We run from the past, haunted by regrets and fears, and we run toward the future, compelled by the allure of what lies just beyond our reach. For most of us, running feels as natural as breathing. It's not a calculated act of cowardice but an instinctive act of survival. At its core, it's a testament to our yearning for refuge and rest.

> WE RUN FROM THE PAIN OF YESTERDAY TOWARD THE HOPE OF TOMORROW.

We run from the pain of yesterday toward the hope of tomorrow.

This spiritual and emotional running reveals itself in countless ways: in our avoidance of deep fears, unhealed wounds, and unmet longings; in impulsive choices and racing thoughts; in our hesitation to build meaningful connections. It surfaces in our addictions, restless habits, and the neglect of our souls' deeper needs.

But what if there's more to it?

What if we're not just running away but also running *toward*? What if, beneath the surface, our pursuit isn't for something but for *someone*—one who invites us to rest from our striving and find refuge in him? If such a being exists, then our running is transformed. It's no longer an exercise in futility but a journey toward the peace, safety, and wholeness our souls were made to experience.

As Augustine observed, "Thou hast made us for thyself, O Lord, and our heart is restless until it finds its rest in thee."[1] Ultimately, the restlessness and weariness we feel find their rest in Jesus.

Throughout this book, we'll explore the concept of running similarly to how Paul Tournier uses the term *place* in his groundbreaking work *A Place for You*. Tournier, a renowned Christian physician of the twentieth century, considered a place to be more than a physical location. He saw it as a metaphorical and relational space where we find opportunities for growth, healing, and self-discovery.

His pastoral-therapeutic approach helped patients discover their places in the world, spaces where they could deeply connect with others and with God, leading to a more integrated and authentic life. For Tournier, a place can be anything that makes us feel at home: a house, a comfortable suit, a beloved book, a typewriter, a song, a spot in nature, or even a comforting memory.[2]

These are all places within time and space, each offering a sanctuary for the soul.[3]

Similarly, running to distance ourselves from what hurts us and to pursue what we think will fulfill us can take many forms: an urgent sprint, a careful retreat, or, paradoxically, even a standing still in quiet inner defiance. In the folksy wisdom of Willie Nelson, "Still is still moving to me."

Running is an act of resistance, pushing back against life's constraints and challenges. Rest, on the other hand, is the act of surrender.

The Bible is filled with stories of people who ran not just from physical danger but from emotional, spiritual, and existential crises. Hagar ran from the trauma of being used as a surrogate and of being abused by the one who enslaved her. Jacob fled from family dynamics. Moses fled after killing an Egyptian. David spent years evading King Saul's wrath. And Esther rose from obscurity in a race against the clock to save her people from genocide. These figures embody the complexity of our urge to run, driven by guilt, fear, duty, and sometimes a sense of inadequacy or to fulfill a higher calling.

> RUNNING IS AN ACT OF RESISTANCE, PUSHING BACK AGAINST LIFE'S CONSTRAINTS AND CHALLENGES. REST, ON THE OTHER HAND, IS THE ACT OF SURRENDER.

But for every story of a biblical character running from someone or something, there's a story of their finding rest, facing their fears, surrendering their wills, embracing their healing, and accepting their missional calling. Hagar returned to give birth to her child after receiving the assurance of having been seen by God. Jacob stopped running from Esau after making peace with his identity. Moses went back to lead his people to freedom.

David, after years of running from an abusive mentor, finally became a king after God's own heart.

Their stories bear witness that you can stop running too.

The same God who loved and guided Jacob, Moses, Hagar, and David walks alongside us today. He is not a God of empty promises or false hopes. His rest is genuine, and the refuge he provides is safe and secure.

What are you running from?

What deprives you of tranquility and leads you to seek refuge?

What causes that aching dissatisfaction in your soul?

It's okay if you don't know the answers. We are often too close to our own lives to see bigger patterns or discern deeper meanings. That's why we need spiritual companions, people to journey through life with us and offer the much needed perspective and insight we crave.

Many Christians don't realize that heroes of our faith can serve as fellow sojourners, a running club of sorts. As we immerse ourselves in their stories, we can learn much about ourselves. The answers they discovered may be just the balm we need to soothe our troubled hearts.

In the pages ahead, we'll explore the theme of running woven throughout the Scriptures. In the stories of those who ran before us, we will hear echoes of our own footsteps. Along the way, we will discover why we run and how to slow down enough to find the fulfilling, authentic, spiritually rich life we seek. To stop running is not to cease progress but to confront what we've been fleeing and to find rest for our souls.

THE RUNNER'S MIND

Running begins deep in the soul long before the feet start to move. In the moments before a race, runners enter a state of heightened readiness: muscles tensed, hearts pulsing with anticipation, and lungs expanding in preparation, all synchronized in the silent countdown. Then the crack of the starting pistol ignites this poised energy, transforming internal preparedness into external action. This auditory trigger flips a switch in the brain, propelling the body forward and turning potential energy into kinetic energy as the race begins.

The same principle applies spiritually and emotionally as our souls react to the pain we experience, often without our even realizing it.

Through my own experiences and in ministering to others, I've witnessed how deeply our emotional state affects our physical well-being. Often our impulse to run stems from two issues: the trauma response and cognitive dissonance. These forces, frequently operating beyond our awareness or control, significantly shape the trajectory and quality of our lives.

One of the most common reasons we run is to escape the pain of the past, a key aspect of the trauma response. Memories of abuse and pain can be overwhelming, causing us to instinctively avoid confronting them. The fear of reexperiencing emotional distress, coupled with feelings of shame or guilt, or the belief that facing these memories won't lead to any positive outcome, often drives us to flee from our past.

It hurts to remember, so we try our best to forget. But our minds don't just create new monsters, they also remember former monsters in horrifying detail.[4] Regardless of how hard we try to ignore them, suppress them, or replace them with new memories, our minds keep a careful record of past trauma.

We repeatedly opt for evasion rather than transformation. Avoidance is a behavioral pattern in which we deliberately steer clear of situations, thoughts, or feelings that might trigger emotional discomfort. Initially this strategy offers a temporary escape, granting us momentary relief from distressing feelings. This immediate alleviation makes avoidance tempting, turning it into a recurring tactic in our attempt to navigate discomfort. But avoidance only makes matters worse over time.

The long-term effects of avoidance include stunted personal growth and delayed emotional healing. Avoidance accumulates unresolved issues as problems that are ignored do not simply disappear but often grow in magnitude.

Chronic avoidance can significantly impact mental health. It is closely linked to anxiety disorders, depression, and stress-related ailments. When we consistently avoid facing our fears, we fail to develop healthy coping mechanisms. This lack of coping skills can make us more vulnerable to mental-health issues.

Avoidance can manifest in various forms, such as procrastination, denying or minimizing problems, substance abuse, and withdrawal from social interaction. These behaviors can have far-reaching implications. In personal relationships, avoidance can lead to communication breakdowns and unresolved conflicts. Professionally, it can hinder performance and productivity as essential tasks are perpetually postponed.

Avoidance is rooted in fear—fear of physical harm, emotional discomfort, or psychological distress. But refusing to face our fears only makes them stronger. The more we avoid something, the more intimidating and overwhelming it becomes, reinforcing the fear and increasing the need to avoid it.

Avoidance is a temporary shelter; acceptance is a permanent home.

Finding rest means acknowledging the reasons behind our running and embracing Jesus, who transforms our desperate flight into a movement toward wholeness and refuge in his embrace.

Acknowledging and addressing avoidance behaviors is essential to accepting God's provision of refuge and rest. This process begins with awareness—recognizing our avoidance patterns, identifying what triggers them, and understanding their impacts on our lives. The next step is to confront the avoided situations, thoughts, or feelings. This approach is often used in cognitive-behavioral therapy, and although I am not a counselor, I believe there is value in finding one who is grounded in Scripture. Such support can be instrumental in learning to confront our issues head-on rather than perpetually sidestepping them.

AVOIDANCE IS A TEMPORARY SHELTER; ACCEPTANCE IS A PERMANENT HOME.

Many of us lack the emotional tools or support systems to effectively work through past trauma. Without the right resources and guidance, facing painful memories can be overwhelming. Consequently, evasion and denial might appear to be appealing, albeit temporary, solutions for coping with intense emotions. The lack of a supportive network can lead us to disconnect from our past experiences, continuing a cycle of avoidance and emotional repression.

Denial only prolongs the journey.

Boarding the train of denial can be tempting, leading us farther away from doing the necessary work to be at peace. In doing so, however, we entrench our feelings. Our minds run in patterns shaped by past experiences and present fears. We run in circles, bound by our own stories, each revolution an attempt to outrun yesterday, hoping to find a foundation in faith where we can finally rest and be at ease.

Facing the past is a formidable task. It demands the courage to confront difficult emotions and the willingness to redefine one's understanding of oneself and one's story. It requires us to unpack the baggage we have carried for so long and explore our innermost struggles. This process can be daunting because it challenges our established narratives and calls into question the foundation of our identity. No wonder many of us run to avoid it.

THE RUNNER'S FOOTSTEPS

In addition to the trauma response, cognitive dissonance is the second issue lying at the heart of our propensity to run. Cognitive dissonance is a state of mental discomfort caused by conflicting beliefs, attitudes, or behaviors. We may believe we are strong, confident, and rooted in our faith, but a painful memory or challenging emotion makes us feel weak, timid, and doubtful. When confronted with painful memories or feelings, we may experience an inner conflict that drives us to seek escape or denial as a means of alleviating this discomfort. So instead of examining the reason for the conflict, we try to escape it.

It's like trying to dance to your favorite 1980s ballad while someone plays the bagpipes off-key. *Are they ever on-key?* It's much easier to cover our ears and run away than to sort through the discordant sounds and find the melody.

Our emotional triggers—those silent alarms that set us off on yet another sprint—are echoes of a deeper dissonance. We run from the pain of the past, the uncertainty of the present, and the fear of the unknown future. We flee from the haunting echoes of regret, the burdens of unnamed shame, the weight of the unmet expectations of those we love, and the heavy cloak of judgment we fear will settle on our shoulders if we ever dare to stop. Yet we are also running toward something—a glimmer of hope, a promise of healing, and the prospect of a brighter tomorrow.

In the following pages, we will explore the connection between running and resting as we uncover why we run, what we're running from, and who or what we're running toward. Our lives are a synthesis of movement and stillness, action and

reflection, work and play. The interplay between these opposing forces shapes our perceptions of ourselves and our world. By
understanding this interplay, we gain insights into our humanity
and spiritual journey, showing us how these different parts of our
lives are connected.

As we run, we must ask ourselves what we are running toward.
Is it the temporary shelter of our earthly identity, worldly pursuits, pleasures, and accolades, or the eternal stronghold of a life
built on the cornerstone of Christ? Ultimately it is not so much
about the race but about meeting the one who stands at the finish
line, who has been with us at every twist and turn in the path.

We must discern the *true* destination.

In our pursuit of refuge, we will encounter the allure of false
security—temporary havens that offer fleeting solace but fail to
provide lasting peace. These illusory sanctuaries entice us with
promises of quick fixes and instant relief, yet they only conceal
the wounds that need healing. Discerning between true refuge
and false security is essential if we hope
to find lasting rest.

The dangers in our destinations lurk
disguised as the security we seek. We run
toward mirages of happiness in the form
of success, relationships, and material
gain only to find ourselves more driven
than before. Refuge is found not in these
but in the oasis of our relationship with
the one who is our ultimate sanctuary.

> THE DANGERS
> IN OUR
> DESTINATIONS
> LURK DISGUISED
> AS THE SECURITY
> WE SEEK.

God is the only finish line who provides safety and sanctuary,
meaning and purpose, refuge and rest. The writer of Proverbs
assures us, "The name of the LORD is a fortified tower; the righteous run to it and are safe."[5] Seeking shelter from anything less
than God will bring us only disappointment and disillusionment.

No one else is strong enough to save us. No king is mighty enough to protect us.

Temporary emotional escapes, whether through substance abuse, busyness, or pleasures, offer brief relief from our internal turmoil. But these short-term fixes come with hidden dangers, often leading to more destructive cycles of dependence, disillusionment, and emotional pain. By looking at the pitfalls of these temporary escapes, we see how avoiding our emotional and spiritual struggles can block our paths to wholeness.

I want to warn you about another false refuge: the mirage of a "successful life." Many, driven by other people's expectations, dedicate their lives to chasing this ideal, which, although defined variously—career milestones, wealth, familial ideals, achievements—uniformly promises fulfillment. While ambition and the achievement of goals are commendable, the misconception lies in equating success with ultimate satisfaction.

This idea is a carefully curated myth in our culture. The core of our yearning isn't merely success, it's the meaning and purpose we anticipate these accomplishments will bestow upon us. Yet there's a disillusioning twist: attaining a goal rarely quenches our thirst for fulfillment. Instead, the goalpost is continually moved farther, transforming our pursuit into an endless journey in which each summit only unveils the next peak waiting to be climbed.

This is the ache we all carry, isn't it? The gnawing sense that no matter how far we go or how much we achieve, there's still something more we long for—something deeper, richer, truer. As C. S. Lewis writes, "There have been times when I think we do not desire heaven but more often I find myself wondering whether, in our heart of hearts, we have ever desired anything else."[6] It's not just heaven as a place that we're yearning for; it's the presence of God, the sanctuary of being fully known and completely at rest in him. This is what our restless hearts are running toward, even when we're not aware of it.

TRAVELING LIGHT

Much like an ultramarathon, life is not about how fast we run but how lightly we travel. The "race is not to the swift,"[7] as Ecclesiastes reminds us, but to those who persevere. The journey is about finding your pace, understanding your rhythm, and appreciating moments of respite along the way, however brief they may be. It's about seeking God and finding him in the beat, pause, step, and stride.

Eventually we all must slow down. Some may resign themselves to lives of exhaustion and quiet desperation, as Thoreau aptly described.[8] Some may lose hope of finding rest or experience a loss of zeal and passion. Even if the impulse to flee fades over time, this is not genuine refuge and rest. Rest is more than merely ceasing to run.

Ultimately my restlessness found refuge in Jesus. His redemptive work on the cross addresses our deepest longings for refuge and rest. In him, we discover that our past wounds can be healed, our present anxieties can be calmed, and our future can be secured. His grace turns our desperate running into a journey toward the very things our hearts most long for.

By understanding the motives for our running, we uncover the unmet needs, hidden wounds, and holy longings within us, unraveling the profound yearnings of our hearts.

Slowly, we learn to discern between true refuge in God and the false security of the world. This empowers us to distinguish between fleeting respites and enduring healing, guiding us toward restoration and wholeness.

In the chapters ahead, we'll explore a tapestry of biblical

wisdom and some pastoral insights as we join the race with others who have gone before us. Together, we'll uncover how a relationship with Jesus can guide us through our past pain, give meaning to our present struggles, and illuminate our path forward with hope. Rather than repeating past cycles of brokenness, we will discover a renewed wholeness and authenticity to carry with us into the future.

This book is your invitation to find refuge and rest. Let it guide you to a finish line where you will discover not just respite but sanctuary—resting in the boundless love of God.

COMING HOME

Begin your day by orienting your soul to what God has planned for you. He has good plans and purposes and has gone before you into every second that awaits you. Before the daily rush begins, carve out a sacred space where your spirit can breathe. Open the Scriptures—whether through reading or listening—and allow the words to seep into your heart. Don't rush. If you're already in a rhythm, continue with what works for you. If not, consider starting with something simple and manageable, like a daily reading from the *Once-a-Day Bible* or *The One Year Bible*.

Pause and linger. After you've absorbed the Word, sit quietly. Let the truths you've encountered resonate within you. Allow them to settle into the soil of your soul, nourishing you for the day ahead.

Breathe with intention. Close your eyes and breathe slowly. Inhale deeply, welcoming the gift of life that God has graciously given you. As you exhale, release the tension, the worries, the distractions that cling to you. This isn't about emptying your mind but about becoming fully present, aware of the breath that sustains you and the Spirit of God who breathes life into you. In these quiet moments, recognize that you are being held, loved, and guided.

PRAYER

Heavenly Father, guide me in the quiet stillness of your presence, where I can face my tendencies to avoid and escape. Help me cultivate a heart of awareness, open to the truths you reveal and the lessons you teach me each day. Grant me the courage to confront my fears and anxieties with faith instead of fleeing them. Teach me to embrace every challenge as an opportunity to grow closer to you, trusting that your grace is sufficient to transform my fears into pathways of peace. In Jesus' name, amen.

CHAPTER 1

RUNNING NOWHERE
From Guilt to Grace

> *"When you work the ground, it will no longer yield its crops for you. You will be a restless wanderer on the earth."*
>   *Cain said to the LORD, "My punishment is more than I can bear. Today you are driving me from the land, and I will be hidden from your presence; I will be a restless wanderer on the earth, and whoever finds me will kill me."*
> —GENESIS 4:12–14

I remember the first time I heard the message of grace. I mean *really* heard it.

I was eighteen years old.

That might not sound remarkable, but by all rights, I should have encountered the beauty of grace much sooner, considering my background. My dad was a pastor, and I grew up in a church pew. My parents took me to church within the first week of my life; I attended three times a week from that point onward. No one in our home ever asked, "Are we going to church?" because it was a nonissue. We were going early and staying late—every single service.

By age three, I had memorized my first Scripture, and at six, I dedicated my life to Jesus. And as I knelt in prayer before a makeshift altar, I had a profound encounter with the Holy Spirit.

As I age, my appreciation for my upbringing deepens. The foundation it provided, the values it instilled, and the sense of direction it imparted have been invaluable.

Although my spiritual life was at the forefront of my parents' concerns, we were entrenched in a legalistic framework. Our faith was governed by a stringent set of rules underpinned by the belief that God's approval was contingent on strict adherence to a holiness code defined in the Old Testament. We were led to believe that God was easily disappointed in us; therefore, our relationship with him was fragile. It could be interrupted and disconnected because of any sin we committed at any time. We believed that salvation could be gained and lost and regained and lost and regained and lost, so we could never be sure that our souls were secure in God. And perhaps worst of all, we exhibited all the characteristics of people who believe that God is an angry deity who needs to be constantly appeased.

To be fair, these weren't explicitly stated messages; rather, they were the undercurrents of our religious environment. When sermon after sermon paints a picture of condemnation, when every altar call compels you to seek the reassurance of your salvation, and when the specter of hell is tied to every misstep, you form a perception. Gradually, your confidence in God and in your salvation are undermined, and you are left with a sense of insecurity in your relationship with him.

Writing this book has forced a lot of personal reflection, as you will see in the coming chapters, and it required me to recall some of my earliest memories of feeling that God was disappointed in me. I was just seven or eight years old when one of my cousins exposed me to pornography for the first time, and everything in me went, "Wow!" But as hours passed, that wonder turned into a deep unease, and I was sick to my stomach.

Guilt descended on me.

Shame washed over me.

Conviction stirred within me.

Condemnation weighed heavily on me.

Worst of all, I was overwhelmed by the thought that God was angry with me for something that had been shown *to* me.

This episode began a pattern in my younger years and into my teens. It was a cycle of passionately seeking God, followed by moments when I felt I had let him down, leading to a cascade of guilt, shame, and the looming sense of his displeasure. These experiences, rooted in my earliest memories, profoundly shaped the cycle of my spiritual life, creating a constant striving for holiness and a fear of falling short.

All that took place while attending church three times a week, reading and memorizing Scriptures, and trying to live a good Christian life. I never walked away from God. I never *backslid*, as some Christians call it. My love for God was constant and abiding, yet the sense of his dissatisfaction lingered.

Tragically, their own relentless sense of disappointment proved too burdensome for many of my childhood friends. Overwhelmed by the weight of their perceived failures, they chose to distance themselves from their faith, finding it less painful to turn away from God than to grapple with the constant feelings of guilt and shame.

Maybe you know this feeling? There is no shame quite like the type related to our spiritual lives. This is where we are most vulnerable and where the enemy of our souls whispers his lies the loudest.

You're a hypocrite.
You aren't good enough.
You're unworthy of grace.
You don't pray and read your Bible enough.
If you were a real Christian, you would _____ .

This shame-based experience is far more widespread than you might think. Not long ago, I encountered a man who had been absent from our church for some time. When I mentioned that I had missed him, his wife spoke up and said, "He feels guilty for something he did; that's why he hasn't been attending church." He flushed, and I thought, *What is it that we don't understand about God and the beauty of his church that drives us into the shadows of shame instead of inviting us into the light of grace, where we find forgiveness and freedom?*

Only when I graduated from high school, went off to college, and visited a little nondenominational charismatic church did I find people who loved God and lived free from legalism. By then, I had attended approximately 2,808 church services, not to mention numerous revivals, conferences, and youth camps. I had memorized a lot of Scripture and devoted many days to fasting and prayer. I had rededicated my life to God more times than I could remember. Despite all this, the message of grace had somehow eluded me. Perhaps that's why I am fixated on grace now—I'm making up for lost time. More important, I don't want you to endure even a single day in an environment ruled by judgment, condemnation, and shame.

> YOUR SALVATION IS LESS FRAGILE THAN RELIGION WOULD HAVE YOU BELIEVE.

Your salvation is less fragile than religion would have you believe.

In fact, it isn't even fragile at all.

The believer is secure in the love and blood of Jesus, and nothing can pluck you from his hand.[1]

TURNED INWARD

Guilt feels like a nocturnal emotion, a shadowy companion that slips in while the world sleeps. You might run fast enough to escape its grip by day, yet as dusk settles and the world quiets, guilt emerges from the shadows, unbidden and insistent. It whispers deceptions and distortions, half-truths, and outright lies, speaking with a voice that claims to know you better than anyone else, even God.

The burden of unresolved guilt can affect our emotional reserves and even our physical posture; over time, our heads bow and our shoulders slump, a physical manifestation of inward submission. Saint Augustine, the bishop of Hippo, and later Martin Luther described sinful humanity as *incurvatus in se*, leading a life "curved in on itself."[2] Sin and its accompanying burden of guilt weigh heavily on the soul, serving as a torturous reminder of the past, an oppressive weight that's almost too heavy to bear.

Have you heard those whispers in the darkness?

Have you carried those lies into the light of day?

Has the weight of unresolved guilt turned you inward?

Do you find yourself running nowhere?

I've had the unfortunate experience of running nowhere in hotel gyms all over the world, looking through the window at the beautiful landscapes of world-class cities. When time allows, I take to the streets, but more often than not, I find myself on a treadmill going nowhere, running like a human hamster.

You might know that feeling too—the sense of exhausting yourself, of giving everything but feeling like you're getting nowhere. Reasoning with guilt is just as frustrating: you exert all your emotional energy, your legs burn, and your breathing grows labored, yet you remain stationary, trapped in a cycle of motion without progress. Each step reminds you of your confinement, the landscape unchanged, the distance covered merely a number on a screen. This ceaseless running symbolizes the struggle with guilt and shame—an endless journey on a path that leads nowhere, a race against yourself, your past, your perceived irredeemability.

For anyone who has felt stuck on guilt's relentless treadmill, my experience resonates with stark reality. It's here, in this cycle of self-reproach, that grace emerges as a beacon of hope. Grace offers a way of escape, interrupting the endless loop of guilt, presenting a pathway forward that leads toward a light of freedom from shame.

Cain was intimately familiar with the whispers of guilt, feeling its weight on his shoulders and an acidic burn in his stomach. This never should have happened. He knew better. God had warned him of his vulnerability to sin, surfacing the contents of his heart before he had risen to violence against his brother. His rebellion had cost both him and his brother their lives.

Cain's story begins with promise but unfolds into one of the earliest recorded examples of guilt and grace. Esteemed Old Testament scholar Walter Brueggemann warns against trivializing this account, noting, "It contains so many layers of meaning that attempted explanations are likely to hinder and miscommunicate rather than illuminate."[3] Despite this complexity, the story deserves our attention and effort to understand, especially if we hope to confront our own struggles with guilt.

As we study the Scriptures to understand the mindsets of the biblical characters we will run alongside, we must acknowledge the limits of our perspective. Our insights are pieced together from the fragments of their stories, and any attempt to apply modern mental-health diagnoses to these ancient figures is inherently flawed. The language and framework we use to discuss our emotional lives have evolved, and it's impossible to diagnose anyone who lived in the past with absolute certainty.

As a pastor, my goal isn't to diagnose but to recognize behavioral patterns that might resonate with our own. My focus is on the spiritual insights these stories can provide, not on clinical analysis, which goes beyond my training. One thing I'm certain of is that almost everyone experiences guilt. That's why it's worth including Cain in our running club. He has a lot to teach us. If we explore the complexities of his story, we just might find answers to what troubles our souls.

FOOTSTEPS OF CAIN

The life of Adam and Eve's firstborn son unfolds in the nascent world, where every action sets a precedent. When Cain was born, his mother was so amazed that she exclaimed, "With the help of the LORD I have brought forth a man."[4] Later, Cain was enveloped in the "family business," following in his father's footsteps as a farmer, a tiller of the soil.

His brother, Abel, had a different arrival into this world. Eve uttered no shouts of joy or astonishment at Abel's birth. Strangely, although he is only the second person born to the human race, his birth announcement reads like a banal footnote in history: "Later she gave birth to his brother Abel."[5] If ever there was "an heir and a spare," it was Cain and Abel.[6]

Cain was the firstborn, and his name landed with the force of his entrance into the world. He was named *qayin* (from the verb *qanab*), which means "get, create, or beget." When Eve declares, "I have *qanab* a man," she is telling us she has accomplished something significant and is proud of it. With the promise of a coming redeemer still ringing in her ears, it is possible that she thought she had birthed the Messiah.[7]

As the secondborn son, Abel was received without fanfare and was expected to take his place quietly in the familial order. Much later, the laws of inheritance would be created and codified; the firstborn son inherited the land and his father's business, and the second would stand behind him quietly and dutifully. This enabled a family to maintain their land holdings instead of dividing them with each generation.

The relationship between Cain and Abel worsened as they established themselves in their vocations. Cain dedicated himself to tilling the earth, a pursuit requiring patience and resilience. His identity seems closely tied to his role as a cultivator of the land, a provider of sustenance.

Following Adam and Eve's disobedience, God punished Adam, saying, "Cursed is the ground because of you; through painful toil you will eat food from it all the days of your life."[8] Cain lived in the daily reminder of the curse and might have gleaned satisfaction from providing for his father by tilling the very soil Adam had forfeited his right to steward.

Abel chose shepherding instead of farming, and he thrived despite the lack of a role model, mentor, or even a clear idea of what his vocation entailed. Perhaps this is when Cain's jealousy began, as he observed his brother's success in contrast to his own struggles. It is also likely that Abel's work caused him to clash with Cain when his flocks grazed in Cain's garden. Though he was the favored son, Cain seems to come up short in his own mind.

This set the stage for a deep-seated sibling rivalry fueled by Cain's growing sense of inadequacy and craving for acknowledgment. Tension mounted within Cain. He felt unfulfilled and unaccepted. Something was missing in his life, something that

Abel already had. Cain was consumed by striving, reaching, and searching for that elusive something more.

Cain's inner turmoil culminated in a moment of religious offering. Both brothers presented their gifts to God, but only Abel's offering was looked upon with favor. The Bible does not tell us why God preferred Abel's offering over Cain's gift, but what is clear is that God had criteria for the offerings, and Cain did not follow them. This rejection of Cain's offering was not just a moment of divine preference but a mirror reflecting Cain's deepest fears and insecurities. He perceived it as a reflection of his worth and value, exacerbating his feelings of jealousy and rejection.

We can imagine some notions swirling in Cain's mind: Didn't God notice how hard he worked? Why did everything come so easily to Abel? It wasn't fair. Compared with his brother, Cain always seemed to come up short. This perceived inequality, mixed with the toxic guilt of failing to please God, made him furious.

Throughout Cain's story are clues that his anger had likely been brewing long before it exploded in fratricide.

Cain was born after Adam and Eve were expelled from Eden, and he lived in the shadow of what had been lost. While he toiled and sweated to cultivate the land, he could gaze back at the abundant Eden, a constant reminder of what his parents once enjoyed. Think of how that must have felt! This view must have stirred a yearning deep within him—a desire to reclaim, rebuild, and restore what had been lost, though he might not have been fully aware of this inner turmoil. Like many of us, Cain was driven by an undefined need, an insatiable ache, a missing piece he could not locate. He knew he was angry, but he didn't understand the root of his emotion. This lack of self-awareness was his undoing.

Similarly, when we fail to engage in self-reflection or to develop self-awareness, we risk perpetuating cycles, patterns, and habits of brokenness. We react instinctively rather than choosing our actions deliberately, living our lives by default rather than by design. This mode of living can easily lead us into trouble, replicating Cain's tragic trajectory. By understanding the importance of self-awareness and taking time for introspection, we can break free from these cycles and choose a path that leads to a healthier, more intentional life.

God knew Cain was wrestling with caustic, intense emotions. Looking at Cain with great love, God warned him about the dangerous path his anger was leading him down, saying, "Why are you angry? Why is your face downcast? If you do what is right, will you not be accepted? But if you do not do what is right, sin is crouching at your door; it desires to have you, but you must rule over it."[9]

This divine intervention was a gracious, loving act, offering Cain a chance to pause, reflect, and choose a different path. He could have looked into his heart and sought forgiveness, but he refused to do the necessary work of evaluating and releasing his pain. Perhaps by this time, guilt, shame, insecurity, and jealousy were so deeply embedded in his heart and mind that he did not know how to let grace in.

In his wildly popular work, *Twelve Rules for Life: An Antidote to Chaos*, psychologist Jordan B. Peterson gives a possible explanation for Cain's refusal to heed God's warning: "The last thing you want to hear if your life has turned into a catastrophe and you take God to task for creating a universe where that sort of thing was allowed, is that it's your own damn fault, and that you should straighten up and fly right, so to speak, and that you shouldn't be complaining about the nature of being. But that is the answer he gets."[10]

That certainly seems to be how Cain interpreted God's intervention. In this way, Cain followed his parents' example of misinterpreting the word of God. Adam and Eve took God's warnings about the Tree of Life as an expression of selfishness, thinking he wanted to keep the good fruit for himself. Cain heard God's warnings as just more blame and shame. Neither Cain nor his parents seemed to remember that God's nature is love.

That loving nature is demonstrated through Jesus' redemptive act on the cross. While Cain struggled under the weight of guilt and shame, Jesus offers us a transformative grace that lifts these burdens. His sacrifice breaks the cycle of condemnation, inviting us into a relationship where guilt is replaced by forgiveness and shame is overcome by unconditional love.

Through Jesus, we are reminded that God's love seeks to redeem and restore, not condemn.

His words are expressions of love.

His actions are manifestations of love.

He is always moving toward us in love.

This perspective of Christ's redemptive love reshapes our understanding of guilt and grace. It offers a pathway to healing that Cain tragically missed but that remains open to us today.

Instead of leaning into God's love, Cain moved deeper into anger and hate. He felt wronged by God, wronged by his parents, wronged by his brother, Abel, wronged by his lot in life. Any suggestion that he had work to do or that the situation was his fault only infuriated him further.

Over time, toxic emotions can morph into destructive actions.

Before I write another paragraph, I want to assure you that you *can* stop running. You *can* find refuge and rest for your soul. Throughout this book, as we examine why we run, I want you to also explore a deeper issue: *why* you can stop running. Who do you need permission from to offload your anger, pain, and disappointment? Who do you need to hear say, "Welcome home. You belong here just as you are"?

Unable to direct his rage at God, Cain turned his anger toward his brother, enticing him into the field where he committed the ultimate betrayal. What followed mirrored the aftermath of Adam and Eve's transgression: God sought Cain, offering him a chance for confession. Yet Cain exhibited no remorse, sealing his fate. The repercussions of his deed were severe and enduring. Confronted by God, Cain was burdened with a curse—a nomadic existence, estranged from the fertile ground he had tended, forever haunted by his action. His past was inescapable, his former life irretrievable, his path irreversible.

Running doesn't make us softer; the miles, years, and experience only make us harder.

Cain learned, just as his parents did, that sin leads to separation from God. Yet both were also offered God's grace even after they sinned. Just as God gave Adam and Eve clothes to cover their nakedness, he provided Cain with protection, some sort of a mark "so that no one who found him would kill him."[11]

Jewish and Christian theologians have long speculated over what the mark was, and although we don't know, the most satisfying conception for me is that God inscribed the tetragrammaton, the four-letter name of God (YHWH), on his forehead, reaffirming his familial connection with Cain.[12] Regardless of what it was, it was an act of lovingkindness, signifying, "Cain is still my kid." Thus, we see a pattern emerging of how God interacts with us in our sin: loving us, calling out to us, urging us to pick the better way, and still offering us compassion even if we choose to turn away.

> RUNNING DOESN'T MAKE US SOFTER; THE MILES, YEARS, AND EXPERIENCE ONLY MAKE US HARDER.

Many of us may have grown up with the idea that God is angry with us, judging us, and always ready and waiting to call down fire and brimstone upon us. Sadly, the church has reinforced this poor theology by heaping guilt on top of guilt and failing to be the reservoir of God's grace. God does not want anyone to be crushed by the emotional weight of guilt and shame. He is always moving toward us with love and grace.

GUILT AND GRACE

Omar is one of those veterans who carries the stories of combat etched into the lines on his face. He was an Iraqi interpreter, "a terp" as they are called, who served the US military during some of the most dangerous missions in Iraq in the early 2010s.

Most Sundays, he shows up at church carrying the weight of trauma not just on his shoulders but in the depths of his soul. You can see it in his eyes. We've had a few conversations about his love for America and his gratitude for being relocated here after his tours of duty even as others are still waiting to be granted asylum.

One Sunday as I was preaching about the extravagance of God's grace—his unmerited favor—Omar caught my attention. That doesn't happen often in a large auditorium, but for some reason, it was as if there were no one in the room but the two of us. I watched him take a deep breath; he's a big, barrel-chested man, and he seemed to inhale all the oxygen in the room. Then I saw him repeatedly wiping his eyes with the back of his hand.

Afterward he approached me, his usual reserve replaced by raw openness. For the first time, he shared snippets of his story—not just the heroics but the horrors, the gut-wrenching decisions that saved lives yet stole his peace. I saw something different in his eyes, hearing him recount the moments that haunted his existence. That morning, God's grace came rushing into the dark corridors of his memory, offering him refuge from the torment.

There is nothing like hearing the message of grace for the first time and discovering that it is your way off the treadmill of guilt, shame, and condemnation.

DEFINING THE TERMS

We would benefit from distinguishing between four intertwined words: *guilt, shame, conviction,* and *condemnation.* Let's examine each more closely.

Guilt arises when we recognize that we've acted against our values or moral standards. It's an acknowledgment of doing something wrong, serving as an internal alarm that prompts discomfort and, ideally, a course correction.

Despite its uncomfortable nature, guilt can serve as a powerful motivator for positive change. When experienced in a healthy measure, it encourages reflection and accountability, prompting us to make amends and learn from our mistakes. This process fosters personal growth and even strengthens our relationships with others by demonstrating our commitment to doing the right thing. By interpreting guilt as a signal for self-improvement, we can transform it into a catalyst for personal transformation. Guilt should drive us to our knees in repentance, where we receive God's grace, which is the power to change our behavior.

Shame, on the other hand, extends beyond actions to affect our sense of self. It's not just feeling wrong about something we've done, it's feeling that we, as persons, are fundamentally flawed or unworthy. Shame is debilitating, leading to secrecy, withdrawal, and a diminished sense of self-worth, often hindering personal growth and healing.

Brené Brown, an acclaimed author, professor, and social worker, defines shame as "the intensely painful feeling or experience of believing that we are flawed and therefore unworthy of love and belonging."[13] Notice her precise wording. The mistake isn't in believing we are flawed, because we all are. To be human is to be flawed. The mistake is in believing that because we are flawed, we are unworthy of love and acceptance.

This misbelief can be rooted deeply in our hearts and influence our behavior and relationships. Shame thrives in secrecy, silence, and judgment, often preventing us from seeking the absolution we need. It convinces us that we must hide our behavior to be accepted, which only deepens our sense of shame.

Christopher Cook shares his journey through shame in *Healing What You Can't Erase*. He writes, "Shame sinks its teeth deeper than addressing behavior and goes right to attacking identity. Where guilt says, 'You made a mistake and need to clean up your mess' (that's obviously healthy!), shame says, 'You are a mistake.'"[14]

Shame is toxic; it whispers lies about your essential identity from the earliest of days when well-meaning but misguided authority figures reprimanded you by saying, "Shame on you." These lies can become a distorted mirror in which we view ourselves, shaping our actions and interactions with the world in ways that reinforce this negative self-view, ultimately hindering our ability to see and live out our true worth and potential.

The intertwining of guilt and shame is common, and most of us have felt it. As Daniel DeWitt explains, "When you violate God's laws, you feel guilt. But that emotion is quickly, nearly simultaneously, joined by shame. Guilt says, 'You did something wrong.' Shame says, 'That's why you need to hide. You're no good. You deserve to live in darkness. Come with me; I'll lead the way.'"[15] This powerful interplay between guilt and shame can profoundly influence our actions and self-perception, leading us on a path where concealment feels like the only option and our sense of self-worth is deeply compromised.

Guilt may trigger our instinct to flee from the light, but shame fuels our flight into the shadows of condemnation.

In the classic 1980s movie *The Mission*, the waterfall scene is one of the film's most visually striking and symbolically significant moments. This scene occurs when the main character, Rodrigo Mendoza, played by Robert De Niro, undergoes a profound personal transformation. Mendoza, a former slave trader and mercenary, is burdened with the weight of past sins, represented by a heavy net filled with armor and weaponry that he drags behind him.

As part of his penance, Mendoza is tasked with climbing up a steep and treacherous waterfall while carrying this heavy load. The journey up the waterfall is arduous, symbolizing Mendoza's struggle with guilt and his quest for redemption. His companions, Jesuit priests working to convert the indigenous Guarani people to Christianity, watch as he painstakingly makes his ascent. The turning point in the scene comes when Mendoza reaches the top of the waterfall, exhausted and at the end of his strength. In a decisive moment of grace and forgiveness, one of the Guarani, whom he once enslaved, cuts the rope binding Mendoza to his heavy burden, sending it plummeting down the falls. This act signifies Mendoza's release from his sins and the weight of shame he carries.

> SHAME CHAINS YOU TO THE PAST; GRACE RELEASES YOU INTO THE FUTURE.

Shame chains you to the past; grace releases you into the future.

So many of us strive to mend what has been broken, to fill voids we've carried from our earliest days, driven by unseen wounds and unmet needs. We are running ourselves ragged, attempting to restore what we believe is missing. But in Jesus, we find our rest, our refuge, and the realization that what we're searching for has been right beside us all along. God invites us to stop running, hiding, laboring, and striving and instead to trust that his grace is sufficient, allowing our souls to rest in him. Rest is not just a place, it is a person.

Unlike guilt and shame, *conviction*, particularly in a biblical context, is the work of the Holy Spirit stirring the conscience following sinful behavior.[16] This feeling might manifest as a subtle internal prompt indicating we've done something wrong or as a persistent heaviness on our hearts indicating something is wrong. Sometimes a conviction might arise when we suddenly recall a biblical principle we've violated or a Scripture that speaks directly to our actions.[17] The Holy Spirit's work in conviction highlights wrongdoing and motivates a genuine desire to change and grow. Conviction is about moving forward, offering a pathway to amend our ways and live closer and more faithfully to God.

Finally, *condemnation*, unlike conviction, offers no redemptive path forward. It's the feeling of being irredeemably judged, carrying a weight of disapproval that provides no escape or solution. Condemnation can trap us in a state of perpetual guilt and shame, stifling spiritual growth and fostering a cycle of negative self-reflection and despair. It overwhelms us to the point that we just quit trying to please God.

CONDEMNATION VERSUS CONVICTION

Guilt and shame can lead to despair, but there is a better way facilitated by the Holy Spirit, who convicts and convinces us of who we are and what God has provided for us through the cross. Conviction is the better way; it's a gift, a divine resource. Conviction flags our wrongdoings so grace can lead us to repentance and renewal. Rather than estranging us from God, conviction gently calls us to draw closer, embrace the forgiveness we've received, and experience renewal in his presence.

Condemnation and conviction emanate from different sources, serve different purposes, and elicit different responses, yet both affect our relationship with God. Distinguishing between condemnation and conviction can mean the difference between being trapped on a treadmill of hopelessness and finding the path to peace and joy. Have you ever felt a sense that you have done something wrong and need to repent or make amends? That's conviction. Have you ever felt a sense that you have done something wrong but, for some reason, can't repent or make amends? That's condemnation.

Condemnation comes down hard on the conscience like a judge's gavel on a sounding dock, issuing a sentence without hope for parole. It conveys the message that the verdict is in and the sentence cannot be changed. Conversely, conviction brings about spiritual growth and transformation. It invites and even nudges us toward confession, repentance, and the opportunity for forgiveness and reconciliation.

Condemnation instills fear, creates a sense of distance, and fosters judgment, discouraging us from approaching God. Thankfully, we are assured that "there is now no condemnation for those who are in Christ Jesus, because through Christ Jesus the law of the Spirit who gives life has set [us] free from the law of sin and death."[18] If we are in Christ, we are liberated from condemnation. This means the voice of shame is wrong about us. When we grasp this truth, we can reject the despair that condemnation tries to heap upon us and embrace the gentle persuasions of the Holy Spirit.

The good news is that God always provides a way out of guilt and shame. Christ's redemptive work on the cross offers a solution. When Jesus died, he took on our guilt and bore our shame, providing us with the opportunity to be reconciled to God. This divine act of love transforms our instinct to run away into an invitation to run toward God. Instead of fleeing from our sins, we can embrace the forgiveness and grace that Christ offers. Through his sacrifice, we are defined no longer by our mistakes but by the new life he grants us. Jesus invites us to lay down our burdens and find our refuge in him.

Guilt describes what we've done; grace defines who we can become. When we trust Jesus for our salvation, we become the "righteousness of God" in Christ.[19] Understanding, embracing, and moving toward righteousness is the antidote to condemnation. When we feel condemned, we become preoccupied with our sins, a state called "sin consciousness," which causes us to hyperfocus until sin is all we see.[20]

While the Holy Spirit leads us toward paths of righteousness and reminds us that we are in Jesus, we must choose to focus on what brings us life, not death. Even at his lowest point, Cain was offered an opportunity to alter his course. Redemption is always within reach, but we must stretch out our hands to grasp it. Cain's refusal to seize the grace to change led to a life marked by regret and isolation.

> GUILT DESCRIBES WHAT WE'VE DONE; GRACE DEFINES WHO WE CAN BECOME.

I wonder how Cain's story would have been different had he chosen humility and repentance instead of anger and revenge. While he doesn't have the chance to rewrite his story, we can still write our own.

None of us are too far gone.

None of us are beyond the hope of redemption.

None of us are outside the scope of God's love.

Just as every treadmill comes equipped with a stop button—a kill switch—to interrupt the never-ending cycle, so too does grace provide the means to halt the unending cycle of shame and condemnation. Rest comes when we release our guilt and embrace God's grace, finding peace in forgiveness and freedom from the cycle of shame and condemnation.

Embracing grace is the first step on our journey, and it's never too late to start.

COMING HOME

Begin by acknowledging the guilt that may linger in your heart. Guilt, though often a signal that something is amiss, is not meant to be a permanent state. Take a moment to sit quietly and think about the areas where guilt has taken hold. Allow yourself to feel its weight, but remember you are not meant to carry this burden indefinitely.

Invite God into this space of guilt with a heart of repentance. As you reflect, speak openly to God about how you have sinned, fallen short, or strayed from his will. In this moment of confession, remember that God is not distant or punitive, he is near, ready to forgive and eager to restore you.

Embrace the freedom from condemnation that is yours in Christ. As you rise from this time of reflection, choose to walk in the freedom that grace provides. Let go of the guilt that has held you back and step into the newness of life that God offers. When guilt tries to return, remind yourself of the truth: you are not condemned; you are loved, forgiven, and free.

Make personal confession to God a regular practice in your spiritual life. Each time guilt arises, return to this place of repentance and grace. Let it be a reminder that your identity is defined not by your mistakes but by God's unending love and mercy. Over time, you will find that the pull of guilt weakens and the power of grace grows stronger, leading you into a deeper experience of God's freedom and peace.

PRAYER

Lord of Mercy, thank you for your unending grace covering all my faults. Help me to release my guilt and embrace the grace you freely offer. Let your spirit of forgiveness permeate my heart, teaching me to forgive myself as you have forgiven me. Remind me daily of your love, which does not keep a record of wrongs but renews and restores. Let this knowledge mold me into an instrument of your grace, extending mercy to others. In Jesus' name, amen.

CHAPTER 2

RUNAWAY THOUGHTS

From Trauma to Resilience

"Your slave is in your hands," Abram said. "Do with her whatever you think best." Then Sarai mistreated Hagar; so she fled from her.

The angel of the LORD found Hagar near a spring in the desert; it was the spring that is beside the road to Shur. And he said, "Hagar, slave of Sarai, where have you come from, and where are you going?"

"I'm running away from my mistress Sarai," she answered.

—GENESIS 16:6–8

On my forty-fifth birthday, I stood in the ruins of Port-au-Prince, Haiti, witnessing the aftermath of a disastrous 7.0 M_w earthquake. The epicenter, sixteen miles southwest of the capital, left nearly 300,000 dead, as many injured, and about 1.3 million homeless, deprived of essentials like shelter, water, food, and sanitation. Within two weeks, fifty-two aftershocks of 4.5 M_w or greater compounded the trauma.

Ten days earlier, horrifying images on the news had motivated me to act; I couldn't just watch and pray. I quickly assembled a relief team of pastors experienced in humanitarian work, aid workers, medics, and combat veterans for security. After gathering supplies, we set off. Our journey began with a flight to the Dominican Republic, followed by a slow, challenging trek over the mountains into Haiti. The roads, congested with people fleeing and others providing help, made our journey three times longer than usual.

Upon reaching Port-au-Prince, the tragedy struck with overwhelming force. The city was in ruins, a stark landscape where buildings were reduced to rubble. The capitol building, reminiscent of our own, was demolished, its majestic domes tilted off their foundations. The air was dense with the pungent smell of death. Amid the wreckage, bloated human remains bore silent witness to the disaster. The sights, sounds, and smells will remain with me for a lifetime, and it took months after my return home to sleep without nightmares.

Even more visceral than the destroyed buildings were the images of traumatized Haitians stumbling through the streets covered in white dust. Precious image bearers moved like actors in a zombie movie, stripped of privacy and dignity. Residents had no choice but to perform their most private acts in public.

Throughout our two-week mission, we encountered horrific conditions while providing aid to those who couldn't return to the safety of their homes, as we soon would. When our mission drew to a close, we focused on one last endeavor—a visit to an orphanage that had yet to receive assistance. With most of our supplies distributed, we assembled our final care package and left our belongings with the pastors who hosted us.

Our journey took us through the dusty, demolished streets of Port-au-Prince to the city's outskirts, where we faced an unexpected challenge. The narrow dirt roads were impassable for our fifteen-passenger bus. Adjusting our plan, we contacted the orphanage to send a smaller vehicle to retrieve three of our team members, ensuring the delivery of our aid. I remained with the others.

Before long, desperate men pleading for food and supplies encircled our bus. We had nothing to offer; our resources were gone. The tension escalated quickly, the atmosphere becoming dangerous. With the food riots of the past two weeks at the forefront of my concern, I cautiously moved forward, opened the bus door, and raised my voice above the clamor: "I'm sorry, but we have given everything away. We don't have any food or supplies left, but if you tell me your story, I will film you and share it with my community."

These meager words, a poor offering in the face of such immense need, had a powerful effect. The crowd immediately quieted down and waited patiently as I made my way from person to person, looking into their eyes and recording their stories of heartbreak and loss.

I discovered something that day.

Our fundamental needs extend far beyond food, water, and shelter. At our core, we yearn for connection—to be seen, heard, and acknowledged. We need someone to bear witness to our pain. Amid our deepest despair, a listening ear becomes invaluable.

We were not made to bear trauma alone.

> WE WERE NOT MADE TO BEAR TRAUMA ALONE.

TRAUMA TRAVELS

Trauma is an invisible traveler, weaving its way through the fabric of our lives. Its presence is unmistakable, etched in the lines of the faces we encounter on city streets, reverberating through conversations around dinner tables, and even making an appearance in schoolyards. It lurks behind the practiced smiles of those masking their inner turmoil with a veneer of happiness. Unresolved trauma knows no boundaries; as it follows us, it defies the passage of time and the strength of our willpower. No matter how far or fast we run, trauma is a relentless companion that journeys with us across geographical and generational landscapes.

Trauma transcends boundaries of culture, race, and creed and binds us all in a shared experience, as most of us have encountered it in some form or another. Those who know it for what it is, who can identify and name it, speak a universal language of suffering and resilience. Their stories of trauma passed down through generations, like painful family heirlooms, remind us of the need for healing and redemption, breaking the chains of generational sin and pain.

According to mental-health professionals, there are three types of trauma: acute, chronic, and complex.[1] Acute trauma comes from a single event, such as a car accident or a natural disaster, shaking our sense of security and emotional balance. Chronic trauma stems from prolonged exposure to adverse situations, such as persistent bullying or ongoing domestic violence, where the impact deepens over time. Complex trauma involves continuous exposure to deeply distressing events, such as sexual abuse or enduring neglect, leaving profound emotional scars. Each type of trauma—acute, chronic, and complex—has unique effects on the brain and body that significantly influence our mental health and healing journey.

Research shows that trauma can alter brain structures, especially those involved in memory, emotion, and decision-making. For instance, the hippocampus, which is connected to learning and memory, can shrink, while the amygdala, which handles emotions, can become overactive, leading to heightened anxiety and emotional responses. Trauma also disrupts neurotransmitters, the brain's communication chemicals, causing depression, anxiety, and mood swings. This disruption can impair cognitive functions, making it hard to concentrate and make decisions.

The body also bears long-term consequences of trauma. Continuous stress-response activation releases hormones such as cortisol and adrenaline, leading to wear and tear on the body (allostatic load), increasing the risk of chronic conditions such as heart disease and diabetes. A weakened immune system makes a person more prone to illness, and symptoms such as chronic pain and digestive issues highlight the deep connection between trauma and physical health.

Trauma travels from the brain to the body, from the past to the present, and from one generation to the next. Even among people of faith. The biblical principle of generational blessings and consequences seems to be embedded in our very DNA.

Intergenerational trauma is becoming increasingly recognized by mental-health professionals, showing how traumatic experiences can affect not only those who directly encounter them but also their descendants.[2] Trauma can cascade like a Niagara Falls of pain and suffering through generations, impacting those who were not exposed to the original event. This type of trauma is often observed in communities that have faced significant adversity such as war, genocide, or severe social injustice, altering the behavioral and emotional patterns of subsequent generations.[3]

Studies reveal that intergenerational trauma can manifest in various ways, including psychological symptoms, behavioral changes, and even biological markers. For example, descendants of Holocaust survivors exhibit unique stress-response patterns, attested by epigenetic research suggesting that traumatic exposure can result in inheritable genetic changes.[4] Similarly, research within Indigenous communities, particularly those that have endured the traumas of colonization and cultural displacement, shows heightened incidences of mental-health disorders, indicating a lineage of pain passed from one generation to the next.[5]

Addressing intergenerational trauma requires a well-rounded approach that includes prayer, therapy, community support, and facing the traumatic event. It's important to tackle trauma as both a personal experience and a shared legacy. Taking care of our emotional health is vital, not just for our own sakes but also for our children, our communities, and the world around us.

FOOTSTEPS OF HAGAR

Trauma is a universal human experience, yet it disproportionately impacts the young and the vulnerable, as we see in Hagar's story. Hagar's Egyptian identity in a Hebrew society positioned her on the fringes, exacerbating her vulnerability. As a bondservant to Abram and Sarai, Hagar was subject to the whims and dictates of her mistress, with little room for autonomy. Her situation was further complicated by prevailing gender dynamics, which diminished her status and agency even more. While a valued part of the household, Hagar was, essentially, property.

Hagar's personal identity was lost amid her roles as an outsider, a servant, and a vessel for another's legacy. The Bible doesn't tell us about Hagar's life before she joined Sarai and Abram, but we know she was somehow uprooted from her home and enslaved. It's likely she was acquired by Abram during his interactions with the Egyptian pharaoh, as a purchase, a gift, or part of a diplomatic exchange—a common practice among ancient Near Eastern rulers.[6]

I wonder whether Hagar saw herself as "the other" before she was taken to a foreign land. Did she identify as a slave before she came into Sarai's possession? Had she ever viewed her body as merely the carrier of another person's hopes and dreams? Perhaps Hagar had a completely different sense of self before she was possessed by those who enslaved her.

The power imbalance between Hagar and her mistress was a powder keg, and Sarai's desperation was a spark. Longing for a child she couldn't conceive, Sarai faced social pressure and the weight of a divine promise: Abram was to father a great nation. How could this be if Sarai remained childless?

In response to this dilemma, the customs of the time presented a harsh solution: forced surrogacy. When a woman couldn't bear children, it was acceptable for her servant to take her place. Driven by a desire to uphold her status and meet the expectations set upon her, Sarai chose this path for Hagar, compelling her to conceive with Abram, thereby intertwining their fates in a complex web of ambition, duty, and social inequity.[7]

Sarai's strategy yielded immediate results but also triggered unforeseen repercussions. Her status as the principal wife became jeopardized once Hagar conceived Abram's child, ascended in stature, and began to despise Sarai for her behavior.[8] Consumed by insecurity, Sarai mistreated Hagar even more.[9] Hagar absorbed the abuse, shouldering the trauma until the burden became unbearable. Finally, driven by despair, she fled from the place she called home.

Hagar saw no other option but to run.

Perhaps you've felt that way too. Under pressure to deliver something more than we can produce, we all find it easier to run. Fleeing often seems like the path of least resistance.

It's easier to run than to live under the weight of comparison.

It's easier to run than to face the consequences of failure.

It's easier to run than to confront limitations.

It's easier to run than to navigate guilt and shame.

It's easier to run than to stay and rebuild the ruins of hopes and expectations.

The problem with running is that it rarely turns out as we imagine when we pack our bags.

Hagar faced a harsh reality in the wilderness, a place as empty and barren as the void she felt inside. Surrounded by desolation, she experienced loneliness, rejection, and abandonment. It was at this nadir of her despair that an angel of the Lord manifested, providing solace, guidance, and the assurance of a lasting legacy.[10]

The vulnerable one had a heavenly protector offering refuge for her soul.

In this moment, Hagar was not only acknowledged but empowered. Her story shifted from one of mere survival to one marked by divine intervention. The angel told Hagar to name her son "Ishmael, for the LORD has heard of your misery."[11] Ishmael means "God hears." The name Ishmael, a constant reminder of God's attentiveness, served as a beacon of hope in Hagar's ongoing journey, a testament to the fact that her cries were not cast into an abyss but heard by the divine. In response, Hagar "gave this name to the LORD who spoke to her: 'You are the God who sees me,' for she said, 'I have now seen the One who sees me.'"[12]

> THE PROBLEM WITH RUNNING IS THAT IT RARELY TURNS OUT AS WE IMAGINE WHEN WE PACK OUR BAGS.

Did you catch that?

I invite you to read the beginning of that quotation of Scripture again.

Hagar "gave this name *to the* LORD."

This young, traumatized runaway slave experienced such a manifestation of God's kindness that she took the audacious step of naming him. He became not only the God of Abraham, known as YHWH, but also her personal deity, "the One who sees me."[13] And God received this gesture. In a moving act of gratitude, she named the nearby spring "Beer Lahai Roi," which is translated "well of the Living One who sees me," forever marking the place of her divine encounter.[14]

Revelation born on the darkest and loneliest part of your journey will not only define you, it will also determine how you see and name God.

HE SEES YOU

Hagar's story is a beacon for anyone hiding in the shadows of trauma. It serves as a testament to the notion that even in our deepest loneliness and despair, there is a presence who recognizes and validates our struggle, a presence who *sees* us. Isn't that what we all long for? Understanding that we are never truly alone, even when our paths lead us through a desolate wilderness, can be a source of immense comfort and strength, guiding us toward refuge and rest.

Just as the angel of the Lord came to Hagar, we should rest in the knowledge that God moves toward us in our struggle. He sees our suffering and joins us on our journey. This is one of the central tenets of Christianity, but one easily forgotten. God sent his son, Jesus, to join us in our suffering by becoming one of us. And when Jesus returned to heaven, he promised to always be with us, even until the end of the age.[15] He sent the Holy Spirit to live within us, our counselor and friend who will never leave us alone.[16]

God's choice to include Hagar's story in the Scriptures, rather than omit it to cast Abram and Sarai in a more favorable light, speaks volumes about his commitment to those marred by pain and trauma. By choosing not to omit the complex and uncomfortable moments leading up to Isaac's birth, God demonstrates a profound understanding of our need to see him engaging with the human experience.

This acknowledgment of our fallibility, struggles, and burdens —whether personal or passed down through generations— underscores the importance of facing our reality with honesty and humility. When we confront and acknowledge our struggles, rather than hiding them, we open ourselves to growth and healing. God's engagement with human frailty shows us that our flaws and hardships are not barriers to his love but opportunities for deeper connection and transformation.

WHO YOU ARE

Trauma will threaten your identity, either by reducing you to something *less* than or by redefining you as something *other* than. Regardless of how smart or successful you are, trauma can make you feel small, insignificant, and ignorant. It makes you question who you are down deep in your soul.

Trauma may have a way of eroding, reducing, or altering our sense of self, yet at the core of our being, particularly as children of God, is an unalterable truth. We are sons and daughters of the king of the universe. This identity resonates with the deepest, truest, unshakable parts of our souls. When we remember our identity as God's children, every other part of our identity falls into place. If we know that God loves us, is for us, and calls us his own, then we can find the courage to face whatever comes our way.

Hagar remained with Abram and Sarai (now called Abraham and Sarah) for another fourteen years until they finally had their son, Isaac. We do not know what those years were like for Hagar and whether she was subjected to further trauma or abuse. The Bible picks her story back up when Isaac is born. The arrival of

Isaac, the heir to Abraham's legacy, toppled Ishmael's position within the family. Seeing that Ishmael was threatened by her new baby, Sarah banished Hagar and her son from the household.

Once more, Hagar sought refuge in the wilderness, but this journey was even more traumatic because she was accompanied by Ishmael.[17] Imagine the fear and despair that enveloped her as she stumbled out into the desert, knowing what awaited them there. As their meager supplies diminished, their circumstances grew increasingly bleak.

Ishmael, no longer a child but a teenager, was acutely aware of their dire predicament. He had become so weak that Hagar had to carry him, and he could not get back up after she set him down. Amid this despair, a gut-wrenching moment unfolds: Hagar, overwhelmed by anguish, places Ishmael under a bush, distancing herself to within a bowshot, just far enough away from her son's distress not to hear his suffering. There, in the vastness of the desert, she sobs, lamenting the imminent loss she cannot bear to witness. She utters one of the saddest lines in her story. Hagar says, "I cannot watch the boy die."[18]

In this moment of despair, God hears Ishmael crying and intervenes.[19] He speaks from heaven, assuring Hagar that he has not forgotten her and that he has made full provision for her well-being and her son's future. Then God shows her a wellspring of water. The well symbolizes the life-giving force of hope and renewal in the midst of despair. God saves Hagar and Ishmael, and Scripture says the Lord was with Ishmael.[20]

SOMETIMES WE NEED TO HEAR THE WHISPERS OF GOD'S PROMISES, EVEN IF WE'VE HEARD THEM BEFORE.

Sometimes we need to hear the whispers of God's promises, even if we've heard them before.

Hagar's journey, marked by both hardship and divine intervention, concludes with the beginning of a new chapter in her life. Even then, her body must have borne not only the stretch marks of Ishmael's birth but also the trauma of what she'd experienced. As we've learned in recent years, the body always keeps score.

THE BODY KEEPS SCORE

Our understanding of trauma has deepened significantly over the past decade or so, largely thanks to insights from experts like Dr. Bessel van der Kolk. In his immensely popular 2014 book, *The Body Keeps the Score*, van der Kolk describes a theory of how trauma embeds in our nervous systems and becomes trapped there. He explains that trauma is not merely a past event but a persistent imprint on our minds, brains, and bodies, affecting our ability to process and respond to the present.[21] This new perspective highlights that trauma fundamentally alters the mind and brain's function, impacting our thoughts, perceptions, and even ability to think.

Van der Kolk's insights resonate deeply with my own experience with trauma. For years, I kept my sexual abuse a closely guarded secret, letting shame silence my voice until the pain became too great to ignore, manifesting as panic attacks.

Although I've alluded to my story in public settings, typing these words isn't easy.

Though I was a preschooler at the time, I can recall the details with remarkable clarity. Equally unforgettable is the moment I told my father what I had endured.

The perpetrator, a member of our extended family, was navigating his own complex struggles, shaped by wounds of rejection and childhood trauma. When I shared my experience with my parents, my father rose to my defense and confronted him. That moment is etched in my memory like deep lines scratched in glass—but for all the right reasons. I had been seen and heard.

And then we did what families did in that era: we never discussed it again.

It was as though we had all conspired to bury the pain, clinging to the hope that silence might somehow erase the haunting memories. Yet no matter how deeply I tried to suppress them, the memories would resurface, unbidden and unrelenting, and when they did, I ran.

After Judith and I married, I finally found the courage to share my experience of being abused with her. It was one of those sacred, soul-baring conversations that define the intimacy of a marriage—the kind where the most hidden parts of a life are brought into the light.

Judith held me close as the weight of my words settled between us, and together, we wept. In sharing my pain, I experienced a cathartic release, as though the grip of those memories loosened. Judith offered what I needed most: reassurance, unwavering support, and the kind of love that sees the broken places and chooses to stay.

But again, we did what families in that era often did: we never discussed it again.

For decades, the memory lay dormant, scarcely crossing my mind, until one day, without warning, it all came flooding back. This time, there was no running away.

The memories were triggered during an especially stressful season of ministry. Following a merger with another church, my responsibilities increased dramatically, and the pressures of leadership multiplied. Amid the demands of shepherding a growing community, the weight of expectations, and my battles with insecurity and self-doubt, the unresolved trauma from my past broke through my consciousness. The memories were relentless and tormenting, a constant whisper from the shadows, and I couldn't shake the sense that the enemy was exploiting them to destroy me.

I couldn't outrun the trauma anymore; it had been traveling with me all along, locked deep within my mind and body, waiting for the right moment to resurface.

Trauma is a persistent presence on our journey through life, even though we are unaware of it most days. It lurks in the shadows of our existence—a silent traveler, invisible yet influential. It waits, biding its time, and steps out only occasionally, but with devastating impact. When it does emerge, it's not a mere reminder of past events but a force that can shake the foundation of our present reality. It manifests in sudden, unexpected ways, intruding into our daily lives and reactivating emotions and sensations we thought were long buried. These resurgences aren't just echoes of the past, they're vivid, potent recollections that can trigger emotional and physical responses as intense as the original experience.

Confronting the memories meant taking a difficult step—one long overdue. I had a heart-to-heart conversation with my parents about the abuse, the first one in my adult life. It was undoubtedly hard for them as we confronted the painful past together. And then I did something I should have done decades earlier: I reached out for help. I found a professional counselor whose name, coincidentally, is Grace.

Grace.

How appropriate that the very message that set me free from a performance-based, religiously legalistic upbringing was also represented in a way that embodied freedom from shame.

Grace extended to me the compassion I needed, but she did more than just empathize; she offered me the hope of healing and some tools to work with. Over time, through our conversations,

I began the challenging work to recover my sense of self apart from what had happened to me. It wasn't easy to stop running and commit to the interior work, but I finally resolved to face my trauma head-on rather than continue to suppress it.

One thing I have learned in my trauma-recovery journey is that the fruit of the Spirit is a marker of resilience. As I found healing from trauma, I discovered a greater capacity for love, joy, peace, patience, kindness, goodness, faithfulness, gentleness, and self-control. It was as if the burdens of trauma had been lifted, allowing the Spirit to work more freely in my life, producing fruit that had long been stifled. This was a powerful sign that God was facilitating my healing process, and it reminded me why seeking healing and resilience is so important. God longs to see us whole and holy, healthy and healed.

True rest involves facing our trauma and trusting God to heal our wounds and provide a sanctuary for our weary souls.

RUN, FORREST, RUN

Last year I had a fascinating discussion with a Bulgarian filmmaker at a small restaurant in Rome. He was making a documentary about Pope Francis and unity in the church, but our conversation turned to Christian films and how they mostly feel shallow and contrived.

"Do you know the greatest movie of all time?" he asked in broken English, tilting his head as if to say, "Don't get this wrong."

Of all time?

In every genre?

In every language?

Uh, I'm not sure. You tell me.

Without a moment of hesitation, he earnestly declared, "*Forrest Gump.* It's what every movie wants to be."

Run, Forrest, run.

That iconic line is not merely cinematic flair, it's a powerful expression of our desire to flee from pain. Forrest begins his journey running from the trauma of bullying, and he keeps on running for three years, two months, fourteen days, and sixteen hours as the movie chronicles his every step. But Forrest can't keep running forever. One day he stops and unceremoniously declares, "I'm pretty tired. Think I'll go home now."

Following our conversation, I watched the film again, and that line struck a chord deep within me. Running from trauma is exhausting. I ran for decades, and it left me empty, lonely, and riddled with insecurity despite my accomplishments.

Maybe there comes a moment when we just decide, "I'm pretty tired. I think I'll go home now."

I hope you're considering that option as you read this. I promise you this: home is not just a place but a state of being, a sanctuary in time and space. In Jesus, there exists a refuge so powerful and enduring that it can sustain you through your most traumatic times. It's a sanctuary where your deepest fears and pains can be confronted and healed, a place where you're not just recognized but truly known and loved.

THE PATH TO HEALING AND RESILIENCE IS PAVED WITH THE COURAGE TO FACE THE DAUNTING SHADOWS WE OFTEN RUN FROM.

If this is that moment, lean into home, whatever that is and wherever that may be, and embrace it wholeheartedly. The path to healing and resilience is paved with the courage to face the daunting shadows we often run from. Your journey might have begun with trauma, but by God's grace, you will experience rest for your soul.

COMING HOME

Each morning, ground yourself in the Word by reading aloud a selection of Scripture that speaks to resilience and divine support. Choose passages that remind you of God's unwavering presence in times of trauma, verses that echo his promises of protection, strength, and faithfulness.

Let these words be your spiritual armor. As you read, allow the Scriptures to resonate deeply within you, affirming your faith and fortifying your spirit. These daily affirmations aren't just words, they're declarations of trust in God's ability to carry you through even the darkest valleys.

Reframe your perspective with each verse. As you immerse yourself in these promises, shift your focus from the scars of past trauma to the strength and recovery God offers. Let his Word be the lens through which you view your life, reminding you daily that your resilience is rooted not in your own strength but in his unshakable support.

PRAYER

Father, you are my refuge and strength, an ever-present help in times of trouble. Help me to hold on to your promises as I navigate the effects of trauma. Strengthen my heart with the resilience to rise above my circumstances, fortified by your enduring love and power. Let each day renew my hope, and may I know that you are with me, healing and restoring my brokenness. May your peace guard my heart and mind, anchoring me during storms. In Jesus' name, amen.

CHAPTER 3

RUNNING FROM YOUR SHADOW

From Insecurity to Approval

When Rebekah was told what her older son Esau had said, she sent for her younger son Jacob and said to him, "Your brother Esau is planning to avenge himself by killing you. Now then, my son, do what I say: Flee at once to my brother Laban in Harran.

—GENESIS 27:42–43

Every person is born connected to a family, which has a complex web of history, expectations, and unspoken rules that shapes us in profound ways. Our families mold us, not just in the visible traits we inherit but in the unseen psychological imprints that influence our choices, behaviors, and even our sense of self. Within this familial bond, we experience our most intense joys and deepest pains. Our families can be sources of immense support and love, but they can also be the origin of our profoundest disappointments, instilling fears and insecurities that we carry throughout our lives.

Think back to when you laughed your deepest authentic laugh.

Think back to when you cried bitter tears of sorrow.

Was it related to some joyful or painful experience in your family?

When you grow up in a family marked by rejection and insecurity, the impact lingers, weaving uncertainty into every aspect of life. These insecurities become shadowy companions, always present, pushing you to seek validation, acceptance, and a place where you belong.

But there is hope beyond these shadows that shape our identities. Amid our deepest insecurities and fears, there exists a love that seeks to validate our existence. Through Jesus' redemptive work, we find the approval our hearts yearn for. His sacrifice on the cross is the ultimate affirmation of our worth, silencing the voices of insecurity and fear. Through his redemptive work, we are defined no longer by our failures or the approval of others but by his unchanging love. This divine approval liberates us from the relentless pursuit of validation, grounding us in the unshakable truth that we are beloved children of God.

> REST IS FOUND IN SHEDDING OUR INSECURITIES AND SEEKING GOD'S APPROVAL, UNDERSTANDING THAT WE ARE ALREADY FULLY KNOWN AND LOVED BY HIM.

Rest is found in shedding our insecurities and seeking God's approval, understanding that we are already fully known and loved by him.

Recognizing the influence of our family's history is the first step toward sorting the healthy from the unhealthy, deciding what to carry into our future as a gift to the next generation. It's about acknowledging where we've come from, understanding how it has shaped us, and choosing how we move forward. This journey is about finding a lasting rest—one that honors our past but refuses to be constrained by it.

No one understands that longing better than Jacob did.

FOOTSTEPS OF JACOB

Biblical scholar Robert Alter describes Jacob's father, Isaac, as "the most passive of all the patriarchs," noting that the only action he initiates in the Bible is to pray about his wife's barrenness.[1] Isaac wasn't even present at his betrothal to Rebekah, relying instead on a surrogate to arrange the marriage.[2] This passivity continued throughout his marriage and deeply affected his relationships with his sons.

In contrast, Jacob's mother, Rebekah, was anything but passive. From our first glimpse of her in the Scriptures, she stands out as confident, engaging, assertive, and adventurous. Yet as her story unfolds, a more devious side emerges, characterized by deception and manipulation.

When Rebekah was pregnant, God told her that she would give birth to twins and that the older would serve the younger. Esau was born first, with Jacob grasping his heel, a detail reflected in Jacob's name, which means "he grasps the heel," a Hebrew idiom for "he deceives."[3] From birth, Jacob was marked as a deceiver, a trickster, and he struggled with this label throughout his life until God finally changed his name.

In ancient cultures, a name was far more than a mere label; it encapsulated a person's identity, destiny, and role within the community. This profound significance of names is why God often renamed individuals at pivotal moments in their lives, marking a transformation or a new beginning. We first witness this in Genesis when God promises to make Jacob's grandfather Abram ("exalted father") the patriarch of many nations and renames him Abraham ("father of a multitude").[4] This practice of renaming to signify spiritual victory or transformation continues throughout the Bible, culminating in Revelation, where Jesus declares, "To the one who is victorious, I will give . . . a white stone with a *new name* written on it, known only to the one who receives it."[5]

> IN JESUS, WE RECEIVE OUR NEW NAMES, OUR NEW FAMILY, OUR TRUE AND ESSENTIAL IDENTITIES.

In Jesus, we receive our new names, our new family, our true and essential identities. This identity as a child of God, this approval from our heavenly Father, is ultimately what frees us from our insecurities.

But the process is rarely as easy or quick as we want it to be.

Jacob wrestled with insecurity throughout his life. His name was a constant reminder of his perceived deceitfulness, and he bore the heavy burden of his parents' favoritism.[6] Isaac favored Esau, proud of his elder son's hunting prowess and ready to bestow upon him the blessings and rights customarily reserved for the firstborn. Meanwhile, Rebekah favored Jacob, conspiring with him to manipulate Isaac into giving him the blessing instead. Perhaps Rebekah's actions were influenced by the prophecy she received during her pregnancy. Regardless, the favoritism shown by both parents sowed the seeds of a volatile and damaging sibling rivalry between Jacob and Esau.

Jacob's spiritual formation—or malformation—was significantly shaped by the dynamics within his family. At times, he must have felt like an outsider among them—unloved, undervalued, unseen, and unaccepted.

Perhaps you've felt that way too.

We all desire to be seen, heard, and unconditionally loved. We long to show our true selves and be accepted for who we are. This need for acceptance and affirmation from those we love isn't a luxury, it's a necessity. But when our families fail to provide this sense of belonging, it can leave a void we spend our lives trying to fill.

This search for validation often spills over into other areas of our lives. We look for approval and understanding from friends, colleagues, and even strangers, trying to make up for the support we missed at home. The lack of family affirmation can lead us to constantly seek approval, hoping to find the sense of worth and identity that our family didn't provide.

Recognizing this gap within ourselves is the first step toward resolving these deep internal conflicts. Becoming aware of the distance between who we are and who we are called to be opens the door to transformation. Instead of chasing after the fleeting approval of others, we can begin the inner work of aligning our identities with God's truth. This shift in focus allows us to move from a place of striving for external validation to resting in the assurance of God's unchanging love and acceptance. And it helps us form genuine and fulfilling relationships.

Jacob's life was defined by a facade, always striving to prove his worth and value, endlessly compensating for something he felt was missing. For most of his life, he lived in the shadows, far from being the person he was created to be.

Like Jacob, many of us carry unhealed wounds that shape our stories. If we don't receive what we need from our parents in a safe, loving, and secure environment, we often spend our days feeling insecure, constantly trying to make up for what we lack.

The journey toward healing and self-acceptance requires us to confront these painful family memories and dynamics, a necessary step to break cycles of dysfunction and forge a new path. And the moment we stop running from our insecurities and find the courage to face our family wounds, we begin to discover the approval and rest we've longed for.

FAMILY CONNECTIONS

Family systems theory, developed by psychiatrist Murray Bowen, views the family as an interconnected emotional unit in which each member's thoughts, feelings, and actions are intertwined. No individual can be fully understood in isolation; the dynamics of the entire family shape each person's identity and behavior.[7]

Once again, I'm not a therapist, and I don't think it's possible to diagnose biblical characters with complete accuracy. Yet looking at Jacob's story through the lens of family systems theory helps us appreciate his story's complexity. It might explain why Jacob ran from home, fled from Laban, and spent twenty years running from his brother, Esau.

Might it explain your running too?

Unmet needs within a family drive us to seek what is missing in other relationships, and some of those relationships can be even more unhealthy. Take, for example, a young lady who doesn't receive healthy affection from her father and how that fact can shape her identity and drive her into unhealthy sexual behaviors. Or consider a young man who feels as if he is always competing with his mother for validation, leaving an aching void in his soul that shapes his sense of worth.

Any therapist studying Jacob's story would immediately point out Rebekah's unhealthy role in the family. Her favoritism toward Jacob and the pressure she applied to her husband to manipulate his blessing show us a deeper problem. Rather than encouraging open communication and individual differentiation, Rebekah opted for deceit to ensure Jacob received the family blessing.[8]

It was Rebekah's idea for Jacob to imitate Esau and trick his father into giving him the blessing of the firstborn son. This plot reveals her anxiety about the family's future and her fear that the divine promise that the older would serve the younger might not be fulfilled. Her intervention in her sons' lives seems successful in the short term but sets off a chain of damaging events.

Rebekah's actions contributed to her losing touch with her beloved son for many years. When Esau learned Jacob received his blessing, he threatened to kill him.[9] So at his mother's insistence, Jacob fled for his life, the first of many times he chose to run rather than face his problems head-on.[10] Jacob's journey away from his family can also be seen as an attempt to distance himself from the emotional intensity of his family system.

In family systems theory, there's a concept called "emotional cutoff."[11] This is when someone tries to manage unresolved family issues by cutting a family member out of their lives. It's a reasonable explanation for the rift between Jacob and Esau. Instead of facing what he did or trying to make things right, Jacob ran away and tried to cut Esau out of his life.

Can you relate? Have you ever needed to distance yourself from a relative to maintain your emotional well-being? Perhaps you've stepped away for a time—or even longer—because it seemed impossible to preserve a healthy sense of self while remaining close.

I've been there.

I know what that feels like.

And I know why sometimes it is necessary.

Even Jesus had family dynamics, and (at least in my reading

of the Gospels) there were moments when he had to separate himself so he could remain focused on his mission.[12]

When we view Jacob's story through the lens of family systems theory, we see generational patterns at play. Yet we must tread carefully not to impose a modern psychological framework too rigidly onto this ancient narrative. Jacob's story is more than an exploration of emotional health; it's a rich and complex story of survival, deceit, and divine destiny, rooted in the cultural context of birthrights and blessings.

Jacob's flight from home after deceiving his brother, Esau, can't be reduced to something as simple as an emotional cutoff. His departure wasn't about safeguarding his emotional well-being, it was a desperate act to save his life. Esau, more than just a hurt sibling, was a wronged heir, furious and dangerous enough to pose a real threat. Jacob didn't leave for self-care, he ran because his betrayal had placed him in mortal danger, with far-reaching consequences in their world.

Jacob's role in his family's dysfunction was active, not passive. He participated in a broader narrative of generational brokenness that had been unfolding since long before his time. The favoritism shown by Isaac and Rebekah wasn't an isolated incident, it was part of a much larger saga of wounds and divine promises that shaped their family's destiny, and he perpetuated their dysfunction.

Despite his efforts to distance himself, Jacob could never fully escape the shadow of his family's dysfunction. His deception of Isaac and betrayal of Esau followed him throughout his life, influencing his relationships and choices for years. The repercussions of Rebekah's actions reverberated through Jacob's life, teaching him difficult lessons about trust, betrayal, and the complexity of human connections.

Jacob's story illustrates how profoundly the family shapes an individual's development and destiny. The wounds and lessons we inherit from our families do not disappear when we leave home; they travel with us, influencing our actions and decisions. Jacob's journey reminds us that even when we try to escape our pasts, we remain entangled in their webs.

Jacob was seventy-seven years old when he deceived his father and took his brother's blessing.

Did you process that?

He was seventy-seven years old and still wrestling with issues related to his identity.

This incident reminds us that the wounds and patterns of our childhoods still influence our actions, no matter our age. But Jacob's story also shows that it's never too late to confront those patterns, seek reconciliation, and find a path forward that breaks the cycle of brokenness.

If you're in your twenties, thirties, or forties, I urge you to do the hard and holy work of resolving your family-of-origin issues now so you can enjoy the rest of your life. Stop running from the pain of your past and seek resolution within your soul. And if you're in your fifties, sixties, or seventies, know that it's never too late to find refuge and rest.

We cannot simply outrun the issues rooted in our family of origin. Instead we must outgrow them by developing our character and spirit in alignment with Jesus' teachings. We must devote ourselves to becoming more like Jesus than we are like our ancestors. And the glorious irony is that the more we become like Jesus, the more we become our new selves, our "true selves, [our] child-of-God selves."[13]

Understanding our family dynamics can feel like unraveling a tangled knot of memories, pain, and confusion. It's not easy work, and it's tempting to throw our hands up and walk away. But we can't because trauma, dysfunction, and family dynamics travel with us. There's no escaping them. The harder and farther we run, the more stubbornly they cling to us.

Some Christians describe these dynamics as generational curses and labor fervently in prayer to break them. Over the past thirty years, my thinking on this has evolved. While I still believe in generational patterns, I now see the work of the cross as the simple but sufficient solution for our souls' freedom. Jesus redeemed us from the curse of the law and of sin and death.[14] When we surrender to his grace, trust him for our salvation, and rest in his finished work, we are made new and free.[15]

But new beings still have the agency to follow old patterns.

In his family systems theory, Bowen calls these generational patterns the "multigenerational transmission process." In essence, it means that each generation passes something on to the next. No matter how old you are, it's important to consider what legacy you want to leave for those who follow. It's not about what your obituary will say. The real question is what story your children's lives will tell about you.

In facing this question, remember that no parent is perfect. We are all human, and so are our children. We all try to shape our children's values, morals, and character while also still shaping our own. This is challenging work, but by the grace of God, it is possible.

THE RELATIONSHIPS THAT WORK ARE THE ONES WE WORK ON.

The relationships that work are the ones we work on.

The best gift you can give your children and future generations is your own healed and healthy soul. Time spent pursuing your healing is an investment in your family, your community, and everyone you encounter. You've likely heard that hurting people hurt people, and wounded people wound people. If you're hurting or wounded, don't pass that on to the next generation.

Investing in your healing stops generational trauma and is one of the most valuable gifts you can offer.

A friend of mine once received the gift of therapy from his kids for Christmas. He wasn't offended, he was grateful. It wasn't a passive-aggressive hint but a beautiful expression of their love for him and their desire for his health and wholeness. They wanted the best for him and encouraged him to invest in his healing.

When your family's messy past feels overwhelming, remember that our earthly families don't get the last word. We have a heavenly Father, a perfect parent who invites us into a relationship in which he is sufficient to provide what we lack and redeems the years we have wasted.

IMPERSONATION

One recurring aspect in Jacob's story is his continual dissatisfaction with himself and his attempt to impersonate someone else. He was overlooked by his father, manipulated by his mother, rejected by his brother, cheated by his father-in-law, and married to a woman he didn't love.

The thread that tied every event together was a sense of feeling unloved, unworthy, and inadequate.

Consider the moment when Jacob pretended to be Esau to secure his father's blessing. He altered his appearance, dressing up in his brother's clothes and tying hairy goat skin to his arms to gain his father's acceptance.[16] He believed he was unworthy, so he assumed his brother's identity just to get his father to bless him.

Even though Jacob succeeded in receiving his father's blessing, he still lacked his father's favor. It seems to me that he probably wanted the favor more than he wanted the blessing. He wanted his father to accept him and love him just as he was. This gnawing insecurity drove Jacob's ruthless, naked ambition.

Jacob also struggled to prove his worth to his uncle Laban. After fleeing from Esau, Jacob went to stay with Laban. First, he tried to prove he was worthy of marrying Laban's daughter Rachel. But Laban tricked him into marrying Leah instead.[17] So Jacob had to work another seven years to prove he was a worthy husband for Rachel. Throughout his time with Laban, Jacob's worth, ability, and integrity were questioned and challenged over and over again.

After many years of working for Laban and enduring deceit and changing work conditions, Jacob decided to leave stealthily with his family and possessions.[18] This departure, while strategic, also shows Jacob running away from a difficult situation with his father-in-law rather than dealing with it. He just didn't see himself as someone who could face a problem and find a solution. Running was easier than exposing his vulnerability and insecurity.

From his earliest days, Jacob believed he had to be someone else to succeed. Many of us fall for the same lie at some point in our journeys, spending years chasing others' success instead of finding our own paths.

Sadly, we live by comparisons, we die by comparisons, and we repeatedly believe the lie that who we are is not enough.

When you surrender to the wonder and beauty of Jesus, you discover that you are complete in him, and that is more than enough.[19]

You are chosen.

You are accepted.

You are unconditionally loved.

You have nothing to prove.

SHADOW PUPPETS

The defining moment of Jacob's life came during his return to Canaan. At the river Jabbok, he wrestled with a mysterious figure throughout the night, a struggle that was both physical and spiritual.[20] The description of Jacob wrestling alone until dawn offers a glimpse into his transformational journey. This event, detailed in Genesis 32:22–32, has sparked extensive analysis regarding the identity of the enigmatic "man" Jacob contends with. Common interpretations suggest this figure was a divine messenger, an angel, or even a prefiguring of Jesus. Yet there is also room to speculate that Jacob was grappling with his internal demons.

The presence of a man in the story, despite Jacob's being solitary, raises intriguing questions. This struggle could symbolize the internal battle between Jacob's virtuous aspirations and his deceptive qualities. We all have mixed motivations and imperfect aspirations—our highest selves and base instincts. Sometimes they even keep us tossing and turning all night, losing sleep to the battle within.

When Jacob realized he could not win, he asked the man to bless him. That's when Jacob received a new name, Israel, which means "he struggles with God." This renaming signifies his transformation from a schemer who struggled with his shadow to one who struggled with God and prevailed.

We often experience spiritual growth in our shadowy struggles, in which we wrestle with both God and our sense of self.

Like Jacob, we all have constructed superficial identities that battle with our true identity found in Christ. We all have another nature, a false self, that we wrestle with. The term *false self* was popularized by twentieth-century spiritual writers and theologians who sought to describe the persona we adopt in response to our environments, our experiences, and the expectations of others.

This concept isn't named in Scripture but aligns with the outcome of the fall, when humanity's identity was distorted by sin. The false self is essentially a mask, a constructed identity that thrives on approval, success, power, and material possessions. It's armor worn to protect against the vulnerability of being seen and known in our imperfections. We see it in the plastered-on smile for a selfie and in the way we highlight only our successes on social media.

Clinical psychologist and author David Benner references this instinct to present a false self to others and even to God when he writes, "Everything within me wants to show my best 'pretend self' to both other people and God. This is my false self—the self of my own making. This self can never be transformed because it is never willing to receive love in vulnerability. When this pretend self receives love, it simply becomes stronger, and I am even more deeply in bondage to my false ways of living."[21]

This facade stands as a barrier to transformation. It's a shield against vulnerability, deflecting genuine connection and love. When this counterfeit self is acknowledged or praised, it doesn't lead to our growth; instead, it entrenches us further in a life that's misaligned with our authentic selves. This false self thrives on the applause and approval of others, yet it leaves us feeling empty because it's a version of us that isn't real.

The allure of this pretend self is reinforced by many streams of popular psychology and even some strands of Christian spirituality, which often focus on self-improvement. This approach, while seemingly beneficial, can inadvertently bolster our false selves because it aligns with the belief that we must constantly become better versions of ourselves through our own efforts. Yet this path often leads us away from the unpolished beauty of our true selves, masking our need for transformation and the accepting embrace of love.

Imagine the freedom of dropping that facade, of no longer needing to sustain the exhausting performance of being someone you're not. Envision the liberation that comes with embracing your true self, with all of its imperfections and raw edges, and presenting that self to God and others. This is where transformation begins—not in perfecting our pretend selves but in offering our real, unvarnished selves to the transformative power of love.

As Brené Brown says, "Vulnerability is not winning or losing; it's having the courage to show up and be seen when we have no control over the outcome. Vulnerability is not weakness; it's our greatest measure of courage."[22] By acknowledging our resistance to vulnerability, we can challenge it, peel away the layers of pretense, and reach for something genuine. It's a journey of unmasking, of moving away from the constructs we've clung to and stepping into the light of authenticity. This process isn't just about self-discovery, it's about freeing ourselves from the chains of our own making, allowing us to live more fully in the truth of who we are and who we are meant to be.

Though the Scriptures do not use the term *false self*, they articulate the contrast between living in the flesh (false self) and living in the Spirit (true self). Paul's letters, particularly his letter to the Galatians, contrast the works of the flesh with the fruit of the Spirit, highlighting a dichotomy between a life led by our lower desires and one led by our identity in Christ.[23] Jesus' teachings also confront the false self, particularly in his criticism of hypocrisy and his call to deny ourselves and take up our crosses.[24] These passages challenge us to shed our false identities and embrace a life characterized by spiritual authenticity.

For centuries, Christian mystics and theologians have delved into the journey from the false self to the true self as a central aspect of spiritual growth. Thomas Merton, a Trappist monk and spiritual writer, described the false self as the accumulation of our ambitions, fears, and illusions, a self that must die if we are to live in God.[25] Henri Nouwen similarly spoke of the spiritual life as a movement from the illusion of control to the realization of God's unconditional love for our innermost self.[26] These perspectives underscore that the false self is a barrier to intimacy with God and others, thriving on pretense and the illusion of self-sufficiency.

The path from the false to the true self involves recognizing and renouncing the lies we tell ourselves about our identities and worth. As David Benner writes, "We do not find our true self by seeking it. Rather, we find it by seeking God. For as I have said, in finding God we find our deepest and truest self."[27]

Our truest self is not a self-made or self-discovered identity but one that is received from God. It is the self that is rooted in Christ, created in the image of God, and redeemed by Christ's sacrifice. This identity is characterized by freedom, peace, and the fruit of the Spirit.

The journey away from the false self toward the true self is not without challenges. It requires the courage to face our brokenness and the humility to accept God's grace. It confronts the cultural narratives that equate value with achievement, success, and the accumulation of wealth. For followers of Jesus, this

> OUR TRUEST SELF IS NOT A SELF-MADE OR SELF-DISCOVERED IDENTITY BUT ONE THAT IS RECEIVED FROM GOD.

work implies a radical trust in God's vision for our lives, a willingness to be led by the Spirit rather than by ego or societal expectations.

The false self is sustained by the fear of vulnerability and the belief that our true selves are not enough. But the gospel message assures us that in our weakness, God's strength is made perfect.[28] Embracing this truth allows us to live with openness, honesty, and a willingness to be transformed by God's love.

Following his mysterious wrestling match, Jacob suffered a hip injury, a lifelong reminder and perhaps a symbol of his ongoing struggle with his false self. Then he began his new life with his new name, Israel. He had wrestled with God and lived to tell the tale.

The day after his life-defining wrestling match, Jacob encountered Esau for the first time in twenty years. I wonder how many times Jacob worried about what would happen if he ever saw Esau again. Did he replay the scenarios over and over again, imagining what Esau would say and crafting the perfect retort? With all those years of built up fear and anger and anxiety, how was he able finally to approach him peacefully?

Jacob was able to face Esau because he was a changed man. Knowing he had God's approval allowed him to lay down the exhausting insecurities that defined his life. He stopped running from himself, from his fears, from the wounds of his past. He found a place of refuge and rest. From that place of peace, he could finally face his brother.

The reconciliation of Jacob and Esau reminds us of the power of forgiveness and the possibility of reconciliation, even in the most fraught relationships. Reconciliation extends beyond mere forgiveness, touching on the need to face our inner shadows. Only when we have found healing and peace within ourselves can we extend what we have received to others.

I find it telling that after Jacob's mysterious wrestling match and the healing of his family wounds, the Scriptures intermittently revert to calling him Jacob, hinting at his continual internal conflict. Even the heroes of our faith felt the tension between their old natures and their new selves throughout their lives. Even after encountering God, imperfections remain. Even with a new name, Jacob was still himself.

Despite his encounters with God, Jacob continued to be

caught in a tug-of-war between his true self and the shadow that tried to restrain him. There is a troubling scene near the end of Jacob's life that we often gloss over. It's not the topic of many sermons or discussed in many books, but it tells us something about our shared humanity. Even after his remarkable and successful life and powerful encounters with God, Jacob confessed to Pharaoh that he was dissatisfied with his life, describing it as short and difficult.[29]

Jacob's statement is both comforting and unsettling. Part of me wonders, "If this pillar of faith and great man of God felt unfulfilled, what hope is there for me?" But when I reflect on my own dark days, imperfections, and ongoing struggles and see evidence of God's faithfulness at work, I find renewed hope. I realize I don't need to feel insecure about my shortcomings.

My God loves me.

My God approves of me.

My God is with me and for me now and always.

And the same is true for you.

The work of the cross addresses the false self by exposing and dismantling the illusions we construct about our identity apart from God. The false self is built on the shifting sands of human achievement, societal validation, and personal ambition. At the cross, Jesus reveals the futility of these pursuits by willingly taking on the ultimate form of human failure and disgrace. In his crucifixion, he strips away the masks we wear, laying bare the reality that worth and identity are found not in what we do or how others perceive us but in our value as God's beloved children.

The cross also addresses the false self by demonstrating the depth of God's unconditional love and grace. The false self thrives on the notion that we must earn love and approval through our efforts. But Jesus' sacrifice turns this idea on its head.

God gives us his love freely and abundantly. We don't earn it. We *can't* earn it.

This act of grace invites us to let go of our striving and self-made identities and embrace the truth that we are fully accepted and *cherished* by God. The cross calls us to rest in the assurance that our true selves are rooted in this divine love, liberating us from the relentless pursuit of external validation.

Finally, the work of the cross empowers us to live out of our true selves by inviting us into a transformative relationship with Jesus. In his death and resurrection, Jesus forgives our sins and imparts his new life to us. This new life challenges and redefines our understanding of who we are. As we identify with his death, we are called to put to death our false self with its self-centered desires and fears.[30] As we identify with his resurrection, we are invited to embrace our new identity in Christ, one marked by humility, love, and a sense of belonging to God's family. This transformation, rooted in the work of the cross, allows us to live authentically and freely as the people God created us to be.

In embracing this transformative journey, we find refuge and rest for our souls. It is here, in the shadow of the cross, that we are reminded of the depth of God's love and the freedom found in surrender. Anchored in his grace, we step into the fullness of our true identity, unburdened by the weight of the world and rooted in the unchanging truth that we are cherished, redeemed, and made whole in him.

COMING HOME

Set aside a sacred time each week to engage in reflection through journaling. Begin by writing about the parts of yourself that you struggle to accept, those areas in which insecurity takes root. Don't shy away from these shadows; instead, bring them to the light, acknowledging their presence without judgment.

Respond to these entries with the truth of Scripture. Beside each confession, write out verses that speak of God's unwavering acceptance and boundless love for you. Let these Scriptures serve as a gentle yet powerful reminder that you are deeply known and fully loved, just as you are.

This journaling practice isn't merely about self-examination, it's about healing. By bringing the hidden parts of yourself into the light of God's truth, you allow his love to begin the work of restoration. After journaling, spend time in quiet prayer, bringing your reflections before God. Ask him to help you accept these aspects of yourself, to heal the wounds that feed your insecurity, and to draw you closer to the fullness of his love.

PRAYER

Gracious God, illuminate the shadows of my insecurities and bathe them in your light of truth. Help me to see myself as you see me—valuable, chosen, and loved. Erase my cravings for human approval as I learn to find my worth in you alone. Strengthen me with the courage to accept all parts of myself, relying on your approval above all others. May this newfound security transform how I interact with others, fostering relationships built on love and acceptance. In Jesus' name, amen.

CHAPTER 4

RUNNING IN CIRCLES

From Anger to Acceptance

*When Pharaoh heard of this, he tried to kill Moses,
but Moses fled from Pharaoh and went to live in
Midian, where he sat down by a well.*

—EXODUS 2:15

Damien is one of the most likable people you could meet,
radiating warmth, compassion, curiosity, and exceptional
thoughtfulness in every interaction. He is an active and empathic
listener, making those around him feel seen and heard. He
embodies kindness, often going out of his way to perform acts
of generosity, like bringing donuts for his colleagues or crafting
handwritten notes of encouragement.

But beneath his friendly exterior lies a stark contrast.

Damien harbors a cauldron of secret rage.

Rather than manifesting in loud outbursts, his anger brews
quietly. You see it in small signs: a tightening around his eyes
when he is annoyed or a smile that doesn't quite reach his eyes

after a slight irritation. His suppressed frustration also manifests in his obsessively organized desk, on which every item is meticulously positioned, a symbol of his desire for control in a chaotic world. His intensity is evident when he grips his pencil too tightly, frequently breaking the tip. When faced with frustrations, he retreats inward, distancing himself from the world and those around him.

Damien has always been known as the quiet one, the type who avoids conflict at all costs. Yet beneath the surface of his calm exterior is a simmering anger that he can never quite explain. He feels it most acutely when he perceives that others are taking advantage of him, or when he witnesses what he considers to be unfair treatment of others. Though he rarely voices his frustrations, these moments ignite something within him, a sense of injustice that he can't shake off. This anger is not explosive, it is a slow burn, an underlying tension that occasionally bubbles up in unexpected ways. Damien doesn't realize that his anger is signaling a deeper issue, a perception that something is fundamentally wrong, both in his world and within himself. And he lacks the tools to translate that anger into anything constructive. Instead it often leaves him feeling more isolated and conflicted.

Damien's anger, though suppressed, is a signal, an alarm alerting him to something deeper, something wrong in his world. But without the tools to understand or address it constructively, he often lets this anger fester, leading to isolation rather than resolution. Like many of us, Damien struggles to navigate the fine line between acknowledging his anger and letting it consume him.

Anger in itself isn't a sin, it's an emotion. Like any emotion, it can swing from useful to destructive in the blink of an eye. Unlike other emotions, anger doesn't exist in a vacuum; it manifests in response to situations or experiences that cause emotional discomfort.[1]

Unprocessed anger drives us to act—to lash out or flee, to attack or hide.

We live in an era saturated with anger and resentment, when frustration intensifies every sphere of life—from conflict in traffic and altercations on airplanes to vitriolic exchanges on social media and in countless daily interactions. Our time is one when the flames of anger expand inexorably, fueled by injustices, misunderstandings, and the spread of misinformation. In this furnace the urge to escape, to run from the inferno threatening to consume our lives, is overpowering. We long for a haven, a refuge from the storm of conflict raging around us.

> UNPROCESSED ANGER DRIVES US TO ACT—TO LASH OUT OR FLEE, TO ATTACK OR HIDE.

But where do we seek refuge?

What place is safe from rage?

A recent poll conducted just before the COVID-19 pandemic revealed a jarring reality: 84 percent of individuals sensed a heightened level of anger among Americans compared with previous generations. This perception, captured as the world teetered on the edge of widespread lockdowns, suggests frustration and discontent simmering beneath our daily interactions.

The surge in collective anger can be attributed to many factors: deep-rooted social and economic disparities breeding resentment, political polarization tearing at the fabric of our communities, and the echo chambers of social media exacerbating division. Also, the pandemic added layers of stress and uncertainty to an already volatile emotional landscape. Environmental concerns and an overwhelming focus on negative news only serve to fan the flames of discontent.

Anger is nothing new; it is as ancient and primal as original sin. We saw its destructive force in the story of Cain and Abel, and now we will explore its other expressions in the life of Moses.

FOOTSTEPS OF MOSES

Moses' story starts with someone else's anger. Pharaoh was angry at how rapidly the Hebrew population was growing.[2] So he made an edict to kill all newborn Hebrew boys.[3] In this dark and terrifying time, Moses was born. His beginning was marked by a desperate act of preservation when his Hebrew mother placed him in the Nile to save him from Pharoah's deadly decree.[4]

Throughout his life, Moses experienced eruptions of anger. Even as God called him from a burning bush, worked miracles, and provided him power and purpose, anger simmered under the surface.

I think Moses was angry subconsciously because he couldn't do anything about his circumstances until he came of age, and even then, his agency was limited. He felt powerless as a youth, suffered from a lack of control and, later, a loss of agency. Many roots bear the fruit of anger, but none are more pervasive than the roots of lacking agency, losing control, feeling powerless, and facing injustice.

Anger arises when we see injustice perpetrated against ourselves or those whom we love. When we fail to channel it in a constructive way, it becomes something else, something ugly, sinful, and destructive.

Though more people currently seem to suffer from the anger associated with feeling powerless than I can recall in my lifetime, this is nothing new. We have seen it all through history.

Moses experienced a lack of agency from his earliest days, beginning when his mother, in a bid for his safety, placed him among the bulrushes. Although he was adopted into Pharaoh's palace and raised with privilege, this very privilege further complicated his sense of identity and control. He was caught between two worlds: the royal upbringing that afforded him status and education, and the world of his biological family—and people—who were suffering under oppression. His mother's menial role within the palace, coupled with the contradictions of his life, only deepened his internal conflict. When he witnessed the harsh reality of his people's suffering, Moses reacted impulsively in a fit of rage, killing an oppressor.[5] This act, far from being a display of power, underscored his feeling of powerlessness. His subsequent rejection by his own people when he attempted to stand up for them only deepened his sense of ineffectiveness, prompting his flight to Midian.[6]

Even when God called upon him to serve as a divine spokesperson, Moses was plagued by a sense of inadequacy. He questioned his ability and worthiness to undertake such a monumental task. This pattern of external circumstances dictating his path highlights a recurring theme in Moses' life: his limited personal agency. Significant moments in his journey are marked by a sense of not being in control of his own destiny.

Even after gaining agency through his divine assignment at the burning bush, Moses lost it again when he came down from Sinai and saw the people worshiping a golden calf. Upon seeing the people's idolatry and revelry, Moses, in a moment of anger and dismay, threw down the tablets he was carrying and shattered them at the base of the mountain as if to say, "These people won't keep this law anyway."[7] This act symbolized the Israelites' breach of the covenant they had just made with God. Later God instructed Moses to chisel out two new stone tablets and bring them up the mountain, where God rewrote the Ten Commandments.[8]

Moses also lacked agency when he struck the rock twice to bring forth water in the incident at Meribah.[9] This event occurred when the Israelites were wandering in the desert and came to the wilderness of Zin. The people, lacking water, quarreled with Moses and Aaron, expressing their distress and regret for leaving Egypt. God instructed Moses to take the staff and, in the presence of the assembly, speak to the rock to bring forth water. But Moses, possibly frustrated by the people's complaints, struck the rock twice with his staff instead of speaking to it as God had commanded. Water gushed out, providing relief to the Israelites, but God saw Moses' action as an act of disobedience and a lack of trust. As a consequence, God told Moses and Aaron that they would not bring the community into the land he had given them.

Yet despite Moses' anger and imperfections, he is still one of the most powerful, influential, and revered leaders of our faith. Learning about Moses' anger and then realizing that God still loved him, led him, and did great things through him fills me with hope that we can learn how to handle the challenges of this age of anger. If we can understand where Moses' anger came from and how he worked through it, maybe we can learn to navigate our own volatile emotions.

Anger is the alarm that signals injustice, but acceptance is the sound that introduces peace.

Like Moses and Damien, many of us grapple with anger that we can't always justify or fully understand. This anger is often a signal, an alarm alerting us to perceived injustice, whether real or imagined. But recognizing the alarm isn't enough; it's just the first step. To move forward, we must discover the key that unlocks peace. Acceptance, though challenging, is that key. It is through acceptance that we can transcend our anger, finding the path to resolution and lasting rest.

MOUNTING TENSION

If we want to understand Moses' anger, we have to go all the way back to when he was rescued from the Nile by Pharaoh's daughter. From that moment on, he was raised as an Egyptian prince in the halls of power and prestige. He was educated and sophisticated and had unlimited wealth and opportunity. He probably spoke multiple languages, was versed in mathematics and astronomy, and had the greatest pleasures in Egypt at his fingertips.

Moses' upbringing within the Egyptian royal palace starkly contrasted with the plight of his Hebrew kin, who endured the harshness of slavery. Surrounded by luxury and privilege, Moses experienced freedoms unknown to his brethren, who were silenced, powerless, and forced to work in backbreaking conditions. This disparity likely fueled his inner turmoil, intensifying his sense of injustice and anger. Imagine the tension building within him, akin to a rubber band stretched to its limits until, inevitably, the pressure becomes too great and it snaps.

Throughout his journey, Moses grappled with internal conflicts, particularly regarding his identity and role in God's plan. If Moses had embraced acceptance of himself—acknowledging his roots, his fears, and his limitations—this self-acceptance could have mitigated his anger and frustration. Such acceptance is pivotal for us as well. When we acknowledge and embrace our complexities and contradictions, we pave the way for a more peaceful inner life. This acceptance doesn't negate the desire for growth but allows us to operate from a place of understanding and compassion toward ourselves, reducing internal conflict and fostering peace amid life's tumult.

Moses' life was a tapestry of uncontrollable events—from his birth in a Hebrew family during a time of oppression to his unexpected calling by God. Acceptance of these circumstances could have eased his emotional turmoil. Similarly, when we confront situations beyond our control, recognizing and accepting what we cannot change is crucial. Doing so liberates us from the chains of frustration and anger, enabling us to focus our energy on what we can influence.

When Moses witnessed an Egyptian taskmaster abusing an Israelite slave, his anger erupted. Trying to fix one act of violence, he committed another, killing a slave master for beating a slave.

Rather than face his transgression, Moses started running.

Moses' decision to flee to Midian after killing the Egyptian was a simplistic, impulsive response to a complex situation. It also launched Moses into his life as a long-distance runner. In this first flight, Moses went to the land of Midian, seeking refuge from his guilt and the consequences of his actions. This act exemplifies his inclination to evade conflict and escape the challenges that come with accountability.

> IN THE WILDERNESS OF OUR LIVES, WE OFTEN FIND OUR TRUEST SELVES NOT BY RUNNING FROM CHALLENGES BUT BY FACING THEM HEAD-ON.

In Midian, Moses adopted a humble life as a shepherd and eventually married Zipporah. Their family lived simply, in contrast to his former life in Pharaoh's court. Moses' time in Midian, away from Egypt and his people, can be interpreted as a period of introspection and spiritual growth. It is also possible that Moses battled internal wounds, questioning his identity, actions, and the path ahead. The spiritual journey often involves confronting such internal conflicts, where one's reasoning can either lead to further entrapment in self-justification or pave the way for spiritual awakening and alignment with a higher purpose.

In the wilderness of our lives, we often find our truest selves not by running from challenges but by facing them head-on.

Moses' encounter with God in the form of a burning bush at Mount Horeb was a turning point. The burning bush was more than a call to Moses, it was a divine invitation to break free from the cycles of doubt and fear. This experience laid bare Moses' lack of agency and tendency to run, forcing him to face both God and himself. This is when Moses stopped running long enough to listen, reflect, wrestle with his lack of agency, and confess his struggles to God.

When God called Moses to free his people, Moses' immediate response was to throw out a bunch of excuses. His initial reluctance, citing his lack of eloquence and feelings of being an outsider, shows how he was battling his tendency to run. He wanted to avoid the monumental task in front of him. Despite a divine mandate and the promise of divine support, Moses repeatedly tried to evade responsibility. Imagine how different his story and the story of our faith would be if Moses had walked away. What if he had convinced himself that the whole vision was merely a figment of his overactive imagination?

Thankfully, this time, Moses did not run. He stayed and talked out his concerns with God, bringing his fears and worries into the open instead of letting them continue to fester within him.

This encounter with God revealed just how deep Moses' lack of agency went. In Exodus 3:11, Moses questions his ability, saying, "Who am I that I should go to Pharaoh and bring the Israelites out of Egypt?" Moses is telling God how unqualified he is. In his mind, he is a nobody. He throws out multiple excuses, citing his failures and inability. This self-doubt leads to prolonged negotiations with God as he attempts to transfer the burden of leadership elsewhere.

Moses must have felt like an impostor long before impostor syndrome was a thing.

Impostor syndrome refers to a pattern of self-doubt and feeling like a fraud despite achievements and capabilities. Moses, despite being raised as an Egyptian prince, still identified as an Israelite and carried the burden of his people's suffering. This conflict between his privileged upbringing and his true identity likely contributed to his feelings of inadequacy and the belief that he was not fit to fulfill the role of a leader.

In the midst of Moses' insecurity, God reassured Moses by giving him two strong promises: the promise of his presence and the promise to bring Moses back to the very spot where he was standing. God told Moses he would be with him now, and he would see him through whatever came next.

God also equipped Moses through a personal revelation of his divine identity and ultimate authority. Nothing is more empowering than that. To know God is to be empowered to do his will. A revelation of God is the foundation for all power and authority. Knowing that God was with him empowered Moses to finally accept the mission as his reluctance turned into resolve.

From running in fear to leading with faith, Moses' journey is a testament to the transformative power of confronting our deepest fears.

LOOPS AND CYCLES

In Moses' excuses and questions at the burning bush, we see him battle through impostor syndrome. Once he laid out all of those fears and doubts, he was able to break through the negative cognitive and emotional loops that had held him captive for far too long.[10] Whereas previously he may have given in to his doubts and fears, this time he pushed through to the other side.

A cognitive loop is a pattern of thoughts and beliefs producing intense feelings that reinforce those thoughts and beliefs, leading to a cycle that consumes energy and hinders progress. Many people suffer from painful cognitive loops, such as thinking, "There is something wrong with me," "No one will ever love me," or, "I am a failure." These thoughts lead to painful emotional loops of despair and defeat.

Thankfully, it is possible to break these patterns. The first step toward freedom from a cognitive loop is cultivating self-awareness. We must first recognize and acknowledge that we are caught in a cycle. Instead of condemning ourselves for being in this state, we must accept it as part of our present experience. This acceptance can ease the pressure and intensity of the loop. So the initial step to breaking an emotional loop is to stop resisting it. This is often challenging because the thoughts and emotions can be deeply painful. Our instinct is to push them away, but progress comes when we pause, take a breath, and notice what is happening within us.

Next we have to choose to break the pattern. This could mean engaging in an activity that shifts our focus or challenges the thoughts that are fueling the loop. A great tip to guide us during this time is to stay connected to our bodies and the physical sensations arising from them. We can take a few deep breaths, paying attention to how the air moves in and out of our noses and what it feels like as our lungs rise and fall. Paying attention to the body helps prevent us from getting lost in our thoughts once again.

After the emotional energy is released, we can explore our thoughts with curiosity. Ask yourself questions to understand their validity and truth. Don't judge them or start fighting them again. Simply look at them and ask, "Is this true? Am I a failure? What is the evidence of that? Is there any evidence that I'm not a failure?"

Many other strategies can help break the loop of negative thinking. These include journaling, physical exercise, mindfulness, grounding techniques, creative outlets, and relaxation techniques. We will cover one of them in greater depth at the end of this chapter. As we deal with these loops, we need to practice self-compassion. Breaking them is not easy, but as Moses shows us, it is possible.

Even after Moses broke through his cognitive and emotional loops to accept God's assignment at the burning bush, he continued to deal with moments of anger. Like all of us, Moses was a work in progress with perfection forever out of reach. Yet he was growing in faith and learning to rely on God more each day. Though his anger could have grown into more and more explosive outbursts, he instead leaned more and more into his meekness.

MEEK AND ANGRY

The Bible describes Moses as the meekest man on the face of the earth,[11] but not the mildest. The term *meek* in contemporary English often carries connotations of submissiveness, timidity, or lack of strength. In the biblical context, meekness is a virtue that represents something much more complex. Understanding this description in its historical and cultural context provides insights into how Moses overcame his anger.

In the biblical context, meekness is associated with humility, gentleness, and a reliance on God rather than one's own strength. It does not imply weakness; rather, it suggests strength under control, the ability to submit one's will to God, and a disposition of patience and compassion toward others. Meekness is a quality of character that enables us to endure adversity and opposition with patience and without resorting to harshness or violence.

When the Bible refers to Moses as the meekest man, it highlights how he led with humility. Despite his significant role in leading the Israelites out of Egypt and mediating the covenant between God and his people, Moses did not assert his own authority. Instead he consistently acknowledged his dependence on God, seeking his guidance and help every step of the way.

Moses faced considerable challenges, including opposition from within his community and the daunting task of confronting Pharaoh. His meekness is reflected in how he patiently persisted in the face of these challenges, trusting in God's timing and power rather than resorting to his own. If Moses had rigidly clung to his own plans and desires, then he would have been a lot angrier. Instead we see him slowly learning to accept God's call and trust in God's timing.

Although anger and gentleness may seem like opposite demeanors, Moses demonstrated both. Like all of us, Moses had a multitude of jumbled emotions and mixed motivations.

We see Moses' gentle and forgiving spirit when he is wronged by his own people. His intercessions on behalf of the Israelites, asking for God's mercy instead of judgment, underscore his compassionate and meek nature.

Meekness in Moses' case also involved having immense power and authority at his disposal but choosing to exercise it according to God's will. This is exemplified by his encounters with Pharaoh, when he acted as God's instrument, and in his leadership in the desert, when he led with a servant's heart.

Moses' meekness is not about weakness but about the power of character, the strength of spirit to submit to God's will, and the ability to lead and serve with humility. This biblical portrayal of meekness invites a reevaluation of the virtues that define leadership and strength, suggesting that the greatest leaders are those who lead not by might or by power but by a spirit of humility and reliance on God.

Moses' meek nature was a healthy and helpful counterbalance

to his anger. A prideful person is more prone to angry outbursts than someone who is humble. If you struggle with anger, start leaning into meekness. This could look like submitting your plans to God every day. You could make a regular practice of praying for others, even (and especially!) those you don't understand or who don't agree with. As you rely more on God and accept his ways, you will see how he calms your anger and lengthens your fuse.

JESUS, THE NEW MOSES

Throughout Jesus' life, people were often confused about his identity. Some thought he was Elijah, while others said he was Jeremiah. Herod was even afraid he might be a resurrected John the Baptist. Certainly Jesus was a powerful prophet like Elijah, a truth teller like Jeremiah, and a baptizer like John, but of course, he was much more than that too.

Jesus was the Son of God and the fulfillment of the law and the prophets. Comparing him to the prophets who came before reveals a lot about Jesus and God's plan for the world.

As Christians living a world away from the time and place the Scriptures were written in, the connection between Jesus and Moses may easily pass us by. But to first-century readers, especially a Jewish audience, there were many obvious correlations. If you look closely, you will see that the first four chapters of Matthew are an overlay of the first few chapters of Exodus. Here we see the same scenes in Moses' and Jesus' lives, including the massacre of the firstborn, the flight from Egypt, and the journey into the wilderness, where they were tempted.

This is purposeful. Matthew is telling his readers that the story of Israel is reaching its fulfillment. Jesus is the new and final Moses, leading everyone into the promised land. What God has been doing throughout all time is coming to a pinnacle in the person and work of Jesus.

But there is one important difference between Moses' and Jesus' stories. After being tempted in the wilderness, Moses went up on a mountain to hear the word of God. Then he brought that word back down to the people. The people were not even allowed to touch the mountain. They had to stay far away from God and wait for Moses to bring them the law.

But after Jesus was tempted in the wilderness, he preached the Sermon on the Mount. He brought people up onto a mountain to hear the word of God directly from God. Jesus was speaking as the new mosaic Messiah, delivering a new messianic Torah, which had a new way to live, a new way to be as the people of God, and a new way to flourish.

Moses' law was God's word coming down; Jesus' kingdom was God lifting us up.

The Sermon on the Mount stands in the place that the law did on Mount Sinai, not as a mere substitute but as its eschatological fulfillment. "For the law was given through Moses; grace and truth came through Jesus Christ."[12] Jesus is not being presented as just another Moses, he is the Messiah who fulfills everything Moses set out to accomplish and more—not just for Israel but for all humanity.

Just as Moses led the people toward a flourishing land called Canaan, Jesus will lead God's people into a greater Canaan—a flourishing place called the kingdom of God—and into an eternal home in the age to come.

There is another important difference between Moses and Jesus. Moses struggled with rage against his feelings of powerlessness and injustice. Jesus, the new and final Moses, showed us what righteous anger looks like. Before I qualify how that applies to us, let's look at the story.

All four gospels record the story of Jesus' clearing the temple, and each one gives helpful clues into righteous anger. In Mark's gospel, we read that Jesus went into the temple, looked around, and decided it was too late to do anything. So he went back to Bethany with the disciples for the night before returning to the temple the following day.[13]

This important detail is often left out of the story. Jesus assessed the situation and chose not to express his anger when it flared within him. Perhaps he wanted to take time that night to talk to God about it or pray about what he should do. Either way, Jesus' clearing the temple was not the rash act of an enraged man. It was an intentional action to serve a godly purpose.

In Matthew's gospel, we learn that right after Jesus cleared the temple, "the blind and the lame came to him at the temple, and he healed them."[14] Jesus cleared the temple and then served the poor, alleviated the pain of the suffering, and shared God's love with people on the margins of society. His clearing of the temple made a way for the marginalized to come into God's presence.

The gospel of Luke gives us greater insight into Jesus' emotional state before clearing the temple. Luke writes about Jesus looking out over Jerusalem and weeping over the people. Jesus longed to bring them peace but knew that they would not accept him. He foresaw pain in their future, and it made him cry. Jesus' anger came from sorrow over the suffering of his people.[15]

Later, in John, we read that when Jesus was clearing the temple, his disciples remembered the words of the psalmist: "For zeal for your house consumes me."[16] Colin Brown defines zeal as "the passionate readiness for service which allows itself to be controlled by the will of God."[17] Jesus stood poised and ready to serve God and do his will; he was anything but furious.

According to what we see demonstrated by Jesus, righteous

anger looks like weeping over what makes us angry and waiting on God's guidance about whether, how, and when we should act. Righteous anger is rooted in sorrow for the suffering of others and a passionate readiness to serve God. The end of righteous anger is to make a way for the marginalized and suffering to experience more of God's love. Righteous anger is not about expressing rage on God's behalf.

RIGHTEOUS ANGER?

One of the most insightful and comprehensive essays I've read on righteous anger is "The Myth of 'Righteous Anger': What the Bible Says About Human Anger," by Jeffrey Gibbs. In it, Gibbs challenges the notion that anger can ever be righteous when it is expressed through anyone other than God. He writes, "There is a place for anger, and for vengeance. But it does not belong to the disciples of Jesus; that prerogative belongs to God alone.

As I heard someone say long ago, vengeance is too dangerous a weapon to be placed into the hands of sinners. This contrast is consistent with how anger is portrayed, described, and mentioned in both the Old and New Testaments. Anger belongs to God, not to humans—and especially not to the disciples of Jesus. Anger is dangerous and quickly leads to sin. So close is this connection that at times, being or becoming angry is simply equated with sin. That is a remarkable truth and should be restated because no other emotion receives that sort of attention in the New Testament. The connection between 'being/becoming' angry on the one hand and actually sinning on the other hand is so close that most of the time, Jesus and the apostles simply equate anger with sin."[18]

Gibbs is right about the predominant New Testament view on anger: it is presented as a clear and present danger, and we are warned against giving place to it.[19]

So what about righteous anger? As shocking as this may seem, the Scriptures don't specifically advocate righteous anger—anger that doesn't lead to sin or require repentance afterward—as a norm for Christians. This observation is particularly interesting given that many Christians often justify their anger as righteous anger.

Brant Hansen writes persuasively about this in his book *Unoffendable*: "The thing that you think makes your anger 'righteous' is the very thing you are called to forgive. Grace isn't for the deserving. Forgiving means surrendering your claim to resentment and letting go of anger. Anger is extraordinarily easy. It's our default setting. Love is very difficult. Love is a miracle."[20]

Later Hansen adds, "Let's face it: we're positively in love with 'taking stands' that cost us absolutely nothing. We even get to be fashionable in the process. We get to think we're involved, doing something, and if we're angry, we get to say, 'My anger is righteous anger.' And since it's 'righteous' anger, it stands to reason that we're actually more righteous than the people who aren't angry like we are!"[21]

Maybe we describe our anger as righteous because we are trying to justify harboring and expressing it. The problem, though, is that the Scriptures never describe our anger as anything close to righteous.

Dietrich Bonhoeffer, the German pastor and theologian, believed too that the idea of our own righteous anger is foreign to the Scriptures. In *The Cost of Discipleship*, he makes it clear: "Jesus will not accept the common distinction between righteous indignation and unjustifiable anger. The disciple must be entirely innocent of anger, because anger is an offence against both God and his neighbour."[22]

How do we stand against injustice without being motivated by righteous anger? There is a better way: love.

The wrath of man does not produce the righteousness of God.[23]

EMBRACING ACCEPTANCE

When considering acceptance as an alternative to anger, it's important to clarify what acceptance entails. It doesn't mean tolerating conditions within ourselves that oppose Jesus' teachings and practices. Acceptance here is not about accommodating what's wrong or unjust, it's about choosing a different, more constructive way to confront these things.

We are called to engage in the hard and holy work of changing the world using the same methods and means as Jesus did. We love our neighbors, we forgive our enemies, and we change the world by serving it. Instead of yielding to anger, we're encouraged to embrace a more effective approach grounded in love.

The alternative to anger leads to rest as we accept God's sovereignty over our lives, let go of anger, and find peace in his will, which enables us to stop running in circles.

Consider Moses' struggle with acceptance on every level of his life. He refused to identify as the son of Pharaoh, was reluctant to accept God's call to lead, resisted God's timing, and disobeyed God's instructions in moments of frustration. His repeated inclination toward anger highlights the difficulties of acceptance. Moses' journey underscores the human challenge of surrendering our wills to God's, reminding us that this struggle is neither new nor uncommon.

In contrast, Jesus exemplifies perfect acceptance, aligning himself entirely with his Father's will, even when it leads to the cross. His example teaches us that accepting challenging or unwelcome circumstances requires trust in God's presence in our struggles, and trust in his promises, his plans, and his timing.

Jesus' life and death illustrate that acceptance is rooted in an unwavering faith in God's goodness and sovereignty.

How can we embrace this level of surrender and acceptance?

This is an invitation to trust in God's plan, even when it's challenging, and to respond to life's difficulties with love and service, not anger. This shift changes us and can transform the world around us. By embracing acceptance, we open ourselves to the peace and strength that come from God, allowing us to navigate life's trials with grace.

Embracing acceptance is not about passive resignation but about aligning our lives with God's will and ways. A surrendered life results in a peaceful spirit, a contented heart, and the lightness of spirit that comes from trusting God. In this surrender, we find personal transformation and the ability to bring the hope of Jesus into a world running in circles.

COMING HOME

As the day winds down, create a space where you can enter into the release of forgiveness. Find a quiet spot and take a few deep breaths and remember the forgiveness you have found in Jesus. Begin by considering the faces of those who have wronged you, including your own. Let them come to mind without force, allowing them to arise naturally from your day.

Imagine holding each person in the light of God's love. As you do, mentally extend forgiveness to them. You might say something like, "I release you from the pain you caused me. I choose to let go of my anger and hold you in God's light." Allow this act of forgiveness to be gentle yet intentional, knowing that this is a process, not a one-time event.

Let this practice be an act of healing. Visualize your anger and pain dissolving into the light, being replaced by peace and acceptance. Notice the weight lifting from your heart. As you repeat this practice over time, feel the emotional burdens lightening, making room for the peace that surpasses understanding.

PRAYER

Lord of Peace, calm the storms of anger in my heart and replace them with your spirit of acceptance. Teach me the power of forgiveness and of releasing resentment to embrace peace. Guide my reactions to reflect your patience and understanding, helping me to navigate conflicts with grace and wisdom. Instill in me a heart that seeks reconciliation and unity rather than division and discord. May your love be the anchor that keeps me from drifting into anger. In Jesus' name, amen.

CHAPTER 5

RUNNING ON EMPTY
From Exhaustion to Renewal

Elijah was afraid and ran for his life. When he came to Beersheba in Judah, he left his servant there, while he himself went a day's journey into the wilderness. He came to a broom bush, sat down under it and prayed that he might die. "I have had enough, LORD," he said. *"Take my life; I am no better than my ancestors."*

—1 KINGS 19:3–4

There is a type of exhaustion that goes beyond the usual weariness of our busy lives. We all have been tired and overwhelmed during times of intense stress, such as studying for an exam, moving to a new home, losing a job, or preparing for the birth of a child. Yet this type of exhaustion is a weariness that transcends the physical and reaches into the core of our being, engulfing our souls and refusing to let go.

Everywhere I go, everyone I see looks exhausted.

Tired to the bone.

Weary in the soul.

The weight of the world seems to have settled upon our collective shoulders, and we struggle to carry on under its burden. This weariness is a societal malaise, reflecting the challenges and uncertainties of our era.

We are bombarded with information, expectations, and demands. The relentless pace of life, constant connectivity, and the flood of news and opinions leave us perpetually drained. Caught in a never-ending cycle of productivity and consumption, we find it difficult to escape the grip of our obligations.

This exhaustion is not merely physical or mental, it is a weariness of the spirit, a fatigue that erodes our sense of purpose and vitality. It disconnects us from the things that once brought joy and fulfillment. In the face of such exhaustion, mustering the strength to confront each day's challenges, let alone to envision a brighter future, can seem impossible.

EXHAUSTION IS THE SOUL'S CRY FOR REST.

Exhaustion is the soul's cry for rest. We find this rest when we cease striving and place our unreserved trust in God, allowing him to renew our strength and restore our spirits.

Elijah's story offers timeless wisdom on overcoming weariness and despair. His journey through the wilderness reflects our own struggles, providing insight into the human spirit and offering lessons on finding refuge and rest.

Even prophets need to pause to find strength in stillness.

FOOTSTEPS OF ELIJAH

The life of the biblical prophet Elijah is filled with remarkable events and powerful encounters with God. One of the most significant episodes is his flight from Queen Jezebel. This moment shows us his vulnerabilities and the faith and resilience that define his prophetic journey.

Elijah, whose name means "Yahweh is my God," emerged as a prominent figure in the northern kingdom of Israel during the reign of King Ahab and his queen, Jezebel. Jezebel was a Phoenician princess who introduced Israel to the worship of the Canaanite god Baal, leading Israel away from the worship of Yahweh. Her influence was marked by the promotion of idolatry and persecution of Yahweh's prophets, which set the stage for Elijah's dramatic appearance.

The confrontation between Elijah and Jezebel reached its pinnacle after the prophet's stunning victory on Mount Carmel. At the time, Israel was experiencing a severe drought, a divine consequence of its idolatry and departure from Yahweh. In a dramatic showdown, Elijah challenged the prophets of Baal to a contest, calling upon the God of Israel to send fire from heaven to consume a sacrificial offering. The prophets of Baal failed in their attempts, but Elijah's prayer was answered with a miraculous display of divine power, leaving no doubt about the supremacy of Yahweh.[1]

Elijah's victory should have prompted national repentance and the restoration of Yahweh as the sole God of Israel, but Jezebel's response was anything but repentant. Instead, she sent a message to Elijah, vowing to have him killed within twenty-four hours.[2] Her threat triggered an emotional and psychological response in the prophet.

That was when he started running.

Elijah is the most intense runner in the Bible. Initially, he ran seventeen miles from Mount Carmel to Jezreel. The Bible records that he ran *faster than the King's chariots*.[3] When Elijah reached Jezreel, he "was afraid and ran for his life."[4] This time, Elijah ran all the way down to Beersheba, which is about one hundred miles to the south. Then he left his servant behind and ran another day's journey into the desert. At this point, Elijah had run between 150 and 200 miles, exhausting himself.

This ultramarathon didn't come after weeks of preparation, rest, and carbo-loading. Elijah had just been through an intense confrontation with false prophets during a prolonged period of drought and fasting. It is no wonder that after all that running, he sat down under a broom bush and prayed the prayer of the truly and utterly exhausted: "I have had enough, LORD."[5] The Bible records that he was so weary and distraught that he wanted to die.

Elijah was running on empty. Giving up seemed to be his only option. He had done too much too quickly with too little respite. He had nothing left to give. So many of us fall into this trap. We push our bodies and our souls to their absolute limits. Our pace is not sustainable. We forget that life is a marathon, not a sprint.

Running a ministry is a marathon, not a sprint.

Leading a family is a marathon, not a sprint.

Building a career is a marathon, not a sprint.

After running multiple marathons, Elijah was weary and in need of nourishment and rest. He was a human being who needed sleep and food to fuel his body. His spiritual status as a prophet with the ability to call upon God's power did not exempt him from the necessity of meeting his physical needs.

We can pour out only what we've been filled with; renewal requires us to stop and receive.

This is why it is vital that we remain focused on what Jesus, our heavenly marathon runner, came running from the ends of the universe to bring us: life eternal and abundant. If we don't recognize our spiritual exhaustion brought on by the presence of sin and death in the world, we will never turn to him for eternal refreshing.

Being aware of our souls' exhaustion often requires first acknowledging our physical exhaustion. A tired body often houses a tired soul.

During stressful times, we ignore our basic needs. If you are anything like me, the busier you get, the more you pretend your body does not need sleep. It is easy to sacrifice an hour or two of sleep for an hour or two of work. But we can do this for only so long until the damaging effects creep in. After we've neglected sleep, healthy eating is often the next thing to go. And we all know that being tired and hungry is a toxic combination.

> WE CAN POUR OUT ONLY WHAT WE'VE BEEN FILLED WITH; RENEWAL REQUIRES US TO STOP AND RECEIVE.

Just as a car needs fuel, our bodies require sleep and food. Some of us are better at ignoring these needs than others. I have noticed there are two types of people: those who feel their car is empty when the tank is half full and those who think their tank is still full when the *E* light comes on. In our household, we call these two types Terry Crist and Judith Crist. While I am quick to find a gas station when my gauge hits the halfway mark, my lovely wife will wait until the last possible moment to refuel.

Once, during a scorching Phoenix summer, I posted on social media a snapshot of my dashboard, which showed it was a sweltering 118 degrees outside. Judith saw my post and decided to have some fun. She took a picture of her dashboard, which registered 120 degrees. Then our social-media feeds blew up! Judith hadn't noticed that her photo also captured her low-tire-pressure warning light, brightly illuminated, and the fact that she had only six miles of gas left. It turned out people were far less interested in the record-high temperatures than they were amused by her blissful unawareness of the warning lights on her dashboard.

Elijah, much like Judith, neglected the warnings his body and spirit were desperately signaling until he sought refuge under the broom bush. In this moment of vulnerability, divine intervention, through an angel's simple directive—"Get up and eat"—roused Elijah, offering sustenance and a reminder to heed his internal warning signals.[6]

Just think about that message for a moment. God sent an angel to feed Elijah and then tuck him into bed. Compare that with all the other times that angels appear throughout the Bible. As messengers of God, they usually share words of prophecy or fight epic battles, but this time an angel was deployed to share practical advice and physical provision. God cared that Elijah was tired and hungry. He saw Elijah's exhaustion, and he offered him rest. Elijah ate and returned to sleep.

Again the angel appeared. Again there was no prophecy and no summons to battle. Again there was bread, water, and advice, except this time, there was also a word of compassion: "The journey is too much for you."[7] God knew that Elijah was a human being with human limits. When he saw Elijah's exhaustion, he didn't chastise him for being weak or try to coax him into doing more. Instead, he told him to eat, drink, and rest. God showed Elijah love and compassion, and this is what restored him.

The healing power of the angel's message revealed that Elijah's exhaustion went beyond the physical. Not only did he need food and water but Elijah needed to know God saw him, cared for him, and was with him.

Just as Elijah found solace and strength in divine compassion, the same holds true for us. In moments of exhaustion and despair, we are not invisible. We are seen, understood, and cherished. The same care that reached Elijah under the bush extends to us, offering rest, renewal, and the gentle reminder that we are never alone.

Elijah was physically, emotionally, and spiritually drained right down to the core of his being. Even though he had just claimed a miraculous victory on Mount Carmel, the nation's spiritual condition remained unchanged. Elijah likely experienced disappointment and despair over the persistent idolatry and the lack of repentance among the people of Israel. He had done everything possible, but it still didn't seem enough.

Receiving the angel's provision of food, water, and encouragement gave Elijah the strength to get up and travel another forty days and nights, hopefully at a much slower pace.

UNDERSTANDING BURNOUT

Psychology Today recently pointed out that the average American man is ten times more likely to suffer burnout than his father and twenty times more likely to suffer burnout than his grandfather.[8] Burnout is a real and widespread problem. The term *burnout* was coined with the advent of the Space Age, and it was meant to describe the state a rocket is in when it runs out of fuel. Today it represents a state of physical, emotional, or spiritual depletion.

Burnout manifests as chronic stress characterized by physical and emotional exhaustion, a growing sense of cynicism and detachment, and a troubling feeling of ineffectiveness and lack of accomplishment. This condition doesn't ambush you overnight; instead, it deflates you gradually, like a slow leak, until you struggle to function effectively. Despite its stealthy approach, burnout sends subtle signals from our bodies and minds that something is amiss. By staying attuned to these signs, we can identify and address burnout, intercepting it before it fully takes hold, preserving our well-being and efficacy.

Physical depletion can be the most prominent and jarring sign of burnout, but it is far from the only indicator that it is time to slow down. Another sign that we are in danger of burning out is when we isolate ourselves from family, friends, and leaders.

The tireder we are, the more we need to lean on those around us for support. But often we do the opposite.

When Elijah headed toward burnout, he isolated himself. His servant was with him on the one-hundred-mile run to Beersheba, but then he left his servant there and traveled another day by himself. His servant had been his companion for many years. Why did Elijah abandon his support system at this critical moment? This is what many of us do when we get overwhelmed.

We push others away.

We isolate ourselves.

We pretend we can do it all on our own.

Unfortunately, being alone is often enough to push us over the edge when we are teetering on the brink of burnout. In those moments of stress and pressure, we need godly relationships more than ever. As Scripture reminds us, "Two people are better off than one, for they can help each other succeed. If one person falls, the other can reach out and help. But someone who falls alone is in real trouble."[9] God made us to be in a community where other believers can support us when we are exhausted and in need of soul care.

Another sign that we are in danger of burnout is when we let comparison fuel a sense of failure. When Elijah was under that broom bush, he said, "Take my life; I am no better than my ancestors."[10] In his deepest, darkest despair, Elijah compared himself with his ancestors. Maybe there was a time when he thought he would rise above the mistakes of the generations that came before him. He was on track to be a successful leader and an influential man of God, but in that moment, he doubted everything. All of his efforts seemed useless as he allowed negative self-talk to frame his outlook.

When we are depleted, it is easy to be hard on ourselves. It is easy to speak harshly to ourselves and play the soundtrack of despair in our souls. We tell ourselves, "I can't do it. I don't have it. I won't make it. I will never have enough. I can't measure up. My best is not good enough. I just can't catch a break." We are headed for burnout when we allow that soundtrack to play on repeat.

Comparison is a losing game because it leads to pride or despair.

If we compare and we win, we fall into the trap of pride. If we compare and come up short, we fall into the trap of despair. Either way, we lose.

Along with leading us to compare ourselves with others, burnout also makes us devalue the significance of our work. Regardless of our successful work, we begin to feel that our efforts to better our families, make a difference in our communities, or change the world don't matter.

> COMPARISON IS A LOSING GAME BECAUSE IT LEADS TO PRIDE OR DESPAIR.

In Elijah's despair, he looked back on his work for the Lord and felt like a failure because the Israelites were still far from God.[11] Elijah had done everything right. He had followed God's lead and preached his word, putting all his effort and strength into the work. But in the end, nothing changed. All of his hard work made no difference at all. The Israelites continued worshiping idols, and Elijah blamed himself.

Every pastor knows this feeling. Every parent knows this feeling. We rack our brains, wondering what we could have done differently. We question everything, wondering whether we heard God's direction right in the first place. We imagine that a better pastor, parent, or person could have achieved a better result.

At the heart of this self-doubt is the dangerous belief that we can control other people's actions. The truth is that we are not responsible for anyone's actions but our own. This is especially true for how people respond to God's Word. I am not responsible for my wife's response, my kid's response, or my church's response. Those things are out of my control. If I think I should be able to control everyone around me, I am just setting myself up for burnout.

Finally, when Elijah was burned out and exhausted, he exaggerated his problems and minimized his resources. Elijah felt that he was the only God-honoring person left, but we know that wasn't true. In the midst of his struggles, he had lost all perspective. He focused so much on his problems that they were all he could see. They grew in his mind until they blocked everything, including his resources. Even though Elijah had seen God's power on display, he didn't think God could save him.

Suppose you are physically depleted, isolating yourself, comparing yourself with others, devaluing your work, and exaggerating your problems. In that case, there is a good chance you are heading toward burnout or are already there.

Burnout can lead to some dark and terrible places. We cannot ignore or gloss over the fact that when Elijah was curled up under that broom bush, he wanted to die. He was distraught. He was suicidal. If you are in that place right now, please put down this book and call a loved one, a pastor, a counselor, or 988, the national suicide and crisis hotline. Your life is precious. Your burned-out, exhausted thoughts are lying to you. Things can and will get better. You just have to take the brave step of reaching out for help.

OVERCOMING BURNOUT

Ultimately, Elijah moved forward out of burnout. As we read, this process started with God meeting Elijah's physical needs and telling him to sleep and eat. After that practical intervention, Elijah had enough strength to travel forty days and nights to Horeb, the mountain of God.

Elijah's flight can be seen as an act of divine guidance. While he initially headed south to Beersheba, he eventually changed direction to journey to Mount Horeb, also known as Mount Sinai, the very place where God had appeared to Moses centuries earlier. This suggests that Elijah's flight was not solely an escape from danger but a journey of spiritual renewal and an encounter with God.

After Elijah traveled to Mount Horeb, God asked him what he was doing there. Of course, God knew, but he gave Elijah the chance to verbalize what was happening in his mind. God knew Elijah needed to get his destructive thoughts out into the open, where they could be healed.

In response, Elijah let loose a stream of bitter complaints, soul-crushing pain, and the harshest negative emotions you can imagine. He didn't hold back. He didn't try to make it sound palatable. He didn't pretend he was fine. He vented his frustrations fully. When Elijah finally ran out of words, God didn't respond with disappointment or chastisement. He didn't say, "I expect more from my prophets!"

> DON'T BE AFRAID TO EXPRESS YOUR RAW, MESSY, IMPERFECT FEELINGS TO GOD. HE IS LISTENING.

God wasn't angry with Elijah's imperfect emotions. Instead, he listened.

What if God asked you the same question today: "What are you doing here?" What emotions are you keeping inside that are desperate to come out? It is essential to face your frustrations and pour them out to God. Talking about your feelings is the first step to learning how to manage them.

Don't be afraid to express your raw, messy, imperfect feelings to God.

He is listening.

Once Elijah had fully expressed his frustrations, he refocused on God's voice. God commanded him to stand on the mountain before the Lord. Here is where one of the most epic scenes of the Bible unfolds: "Then a great and powerful wind tore the mountains apart and shattered the rocks before the Lord, but the Lord was not in the wind. After the wind there was an earthquake, but the Lord was not in the earthquake. After the earthquake came a fire, but the Lord was not in the fire. And after the fire came a gentle whisper. When Elijah heard it, he pulled his cloak over his face and went out and stood at the mouth of the cave."[12]

Elijah witnessed powerful natural phenomena—an earthquake, a fire, and a mighty wind. These were reminders of God's might. Elijah felt powerless, and God was revealing his power. Elijah felt alone, and God was revealing his presence. Elijah was frightened of the future, and God was demonstrating his ability to handle whatever may come.

Then God spoke to Elijah softly, gently, and kindly. God met Elijah right where he was and spoke directly into his pain. I imagine these gentle words were like a healing salve on Elijah's burned-out soul.

This season of burnout ended when God gave Elijah a new assignment. He told him to go find three people and anoint them for ministry. God didn't want Elijah to feel alone anymore, so he gave Elijah a team to work with him. God was encouraging Elijah to get back out there. God's love was not contingent on Elijah being productive for the kingdom, but God knew that Elijah would feel better moving forward with a renewed purpose.

God loved Elijah when he was huddled under the broom bush, ready to die, just as much as God loved Elijah when he was calling fire down from heaven and defeating the prophets of Baal.

Elijah didn't need to earn God's love. God loved Elijah for who he was, not what he did. God loves us like that too.

ELIJAH AND JESUS

From the top of Mount Carmel, where Elijah defeated the prophets of Baal, you can see Mount Tabor, where Jesus' transfiguration, centuries later, occurred.

A few years ago, I camped out one night at the base of Mount Tabor under the glow of a full moon. I was leading a group of trekkers on a four-day hike from Nazareth to Capernaum. As the moon rose across the valley, it bathed the mountain in silver light, transforming the landscape into a vision of ethereal beauty.

As I settled in, my thoughts went to a significant moment in the Gospels—the transfiguration of Jesus witnessed by three disciples atop that very mountain. Jesus stood there flanked by two titans of Jewish history: Moses and Elijah. Under a celestial cloud that shone with divine light, they appeared in a vision that linked past and future, earth and heaven.

The symbolism is rich. Moses, the giver of the Law, and Elijah, the embodiment of the Prophets, stood as pillars of Jewish faith. Their presence alongside Jesus at the transfiguration served as a divine endorsement, bridging the testament of the Old with the promise of the New.

When the voice of God from the heavens declared, "Listen to him!" it was not merely an instruction but a declaration. This moment signaled that Jesus was not just a continuation of what had come before, he was its culmination. Through Jesus, the Law and the Prophets find their fulfillment and a new covenant is revealed—a path not away from tradition but rooted in it, yet leading toward a horizon of renewed faith and understanding. This narrative arc from Moses and Elijah to Jesus symbolizes a divine passage from the foundational laws and prophetic visions of the Old Testament to the transformative gospel of love and salvation in the New Testament.

The disciples never forgot what happened that day on the mountain; no doubt this was the intended outcome. John wrote in his gospel, "We have seen his glory, the glory of the one and only Son."[13]

Elijah's story did not end with his exhaustion; instead, it ended with God's glory and his bearing witness to the Messiah on that mountain.

Elijah's story is a powerful reminder that burnout and exhaustion do not define us, and tiredness is not a sin. God does not judge us or chastise us for being overwhelmed. Instead, he longs to offer rest for our souls.

God calls out, "Come to me, all you who are weary."[14] And if, like Elijah, we are too weak to make our way to God, he meets us where we are in an exhausted heap under the broom bush. He tells us to sleep and eat. He listens to our frustrations. He reminds us of his power and might. He restores us and helps us find our purpose once again.

COMING HOME

Commit one day each week to a Sabbath rest, when you do no work and instead spend the day in rejuvenation through activities that restore your soul. These activities might include reading, walking in nature, or engaging in hobbies that you love but usually don't have time for. The Sabbath is a biblical principle designed as a gift from God to provide rest and renewal for our busy lives. Regular observance of a day of rest can help prevent burnout by ensuring we have time to recover from the week's demands.

PRAYER

Renewing God, when I am weary and burdened, lead me to your rest. Refresh my spirit with your renewing energy and inspire me with new strength each day. Help me recognize the signs of burnout and set boundaries that preserve my health and spirit so I can serve you and others with joy and vitality. May your wisdom guide my decisions, allowing me to find balance between work and rest. In Jesus' name, amen.

CHAPTER 6

RUNNING HOT AND COLD
From Anxiety to Worship

Saul sent men to David's house to watch it and to kill him in the morning. But Michal, David's wife, warned him, "If you don't run for your life tonight, tomorrow you'll be killed." So Michal let David down through a window, and he fled and escaped.

—1 SAMUEL 19:11–12

Michael seemed like the complete package: rugged good looks, an athletic build, and a quick wit. As a Division 1 athlete with a 3.9 GPA, he excelled both on the field and in the classroom. His charm earned him second and third glances from college girls. Socially, he didn't crave the spotlight but effortlessly engaged with everyone around him.

Beneath this polished exterior, Michael harbored a struggle. He wrestled with anxiety, and it was getting worse. This cast a long shadow over his achievements and social connections, unseen by friends who saw only the successful, charismatic guy with the talent, connections, and opportunities they desired. Most days, Michael managed to keep his anxiety at bay, using techniques and routines that offered him some semblance of control. But there were moments when the facade cracked, and the tide of worry and fear broke through his defenses. The contrast between his public persona and private turmoil was stark, a reminder to him of the layers of pain beneath the surface.

Michael's anxiety stemmed from a pressure to maintain his image of perfection and success. Constantly trying to excel in every arena of his life created an immense burden. His desire to meet the high standards he set for himself, along with the expectations he perceived others had of him, fueled his anxiety.

Michael managed to keep it all together until the moment he couldn't. One night, he fell apart, sobbing and shaking for hours. The following morning, he quit the team, moved out of the college dorm, and didn't look back.

I met him in a coffee shop where he now works as a barista. There's a calm about him, a serenity that suggests a hard-won peace. He looks at ease, and when he says he has found peace, you can tell he means it.

ANATOMY OF ANXIETY

Anxiety is a full-body emotion that many of us know far too well. When it floods our senses, it takes over, rendering us fumbling, mumbling shadows of ourselves. We experience sweaty palms, shortness of breath, racing heartbeat, chest pain, dizziness, nausea, flushes or chills, difficulty breathing and talking, tingling, numbness, tremors, racing thoughts, confusion, and feelings of disconnection from our bodies.

Anxiety is a broad term encompassing many distinct types, such as panic disorder, generalized anxiety disorder, specific phobias, obsessive-compulsive disorder, acute stress disorder, and post-traumatic stress disorder. Each of these forms highlights different aspects and triggers of anxiety, illustrating the condition's complexity.

Anxiety is one of the most significant mental-health challenges of our times, and it is difficult to resolve because it is intertwined with our humanity. Humans have always been anxious about *something*, following the fall, as we can see in the first conversation recorded between God and man.[1]

It is not surprising that researchers have called the USA "the most anxious nation on the planet" as they have observed an exponential rise in worry, fear, apprehension, depression, and other anxiety-related conditions over the past few decades. These statistics were already on the rise before the COVID-19 pandemic, but then the isolation and stress of the pandemic caused these numbers to escalate even further.

> ANXIETY IS ONE OF THE MOST SIGNIFICANT MENTAL-HEALTH CHALLENGES OF OUR TIMES, AND IT IS DIFFICULT TO RESOLVE BECAUSE IT IS INTERTWINED WITH OUR HUMANITY.

In 2018, a staggering 63 percent of college students in America reported experiencing severe anxiety, a situation that worsened with the onset of COVID-19.[2] Worldwide, depression rates surged by 28 percent compared with prepandemic figures. By 2022, anxiety had been diagnosed in more than 42.5 million American adults.[3] Despite these alarming numbers, only 36.9 percent of those struggling with anxiety disorders sought medical or professional help, leaving many without the support they desperately needed. Mental-health professionals warn that these elevated anxiety levels are likely to persist for some time.

The situation is even more dire for teenagers. According to

the National Institute of Mental Health (NIMH), teens experience more anxiety than adults. A 2021 survey revealed that anxiety disorders affected 19 percent of American adults and nearly 32 percent of teenagers. Among teen girls, the rate was even higher at 38 percent, compared with 26 percent for teen boys.[4] These figures are on the rise, with more than half of Generation Z expecting "the worst to happen."[5] Extensive studies involving thousands of young people show that today's average anxiety level among youth surpasses that of psychiatric inpatients from the 1950s.[6]

To complicate matters, there is a special kind of anxiety that Christians experience. Anxiety pulls us in diverse directions, causing us to fluctuate between highs and lows in our faith. We believe we are not supposed to feel anxious, so any hint of that emotion can cause guilt and shame. I was in a conference once where the speaker was preaching on the sin of worry, and somewhere in the middle of the message, I found myself feeling worried about being worried! Thankfully, I am mature enough to reject the idea that worry is a sin. It's a symptom.

If you suffer from any form of anxiety, let me assure you, you are not alone. You are not the first Christian to experience some form of anxiety, and you won't be the last. We all experience stress on a broad spectrum, with occasional worry at the low end and full-on panic disorder at the high end. And some people hit every note on that spectrum like a virtuoso pianist performing "Bohemian Rhapsody" on a grand piano.

While we interchange the terms *anxiety, fear,* and *worry,* it's essential to recognize the nuances that distinguish them, especially in the context of their biblical usage. Anxiety and fear, though related, are not identical; they're more like cousins than twins. Understanding the difference is key to grasping the deeper meanings of these emotions in biblical passages and our experiences, allowing us to address each with appropriate spiritual and practical responses.

Fear arises in the face of immediate danger, prompting a decisive fight-or-flight reaction to protect us. In contrast, anxiety extends beyond this instantaneous response, morphing into an ongoing, often disproportionate fixation on potential threats. Anxiety dwells in the realm of the unknown, exaggerating possible future scenarios without actual danger. This anticipation distorts our perception of what may never occur and traps us in a cycle of worry, projecting a shadow of doom over uncertain outcomes and robbing us of the ability to live fully in the present.

A cascade of what-ifs can be overwhelming, painting a future riddled with uncertainty and fear. Anxiety about job loss, financial hardship, relationship breakdowns, or health concerns can become a vortex, leaving us feeling powerless and petrified of the future.

PANIC AND SHAME

My journey with anxiety began in November 2010 when I had my first panic attack. My *first* panic attack. I kept it a carefully guarded secret for the first few years, telling no one except my wife. Amid the storm of anxiety and panic, the idea of sharing my struggle seemed unthinkable. My anxiety was compounded by the shame of feeling that I was somehow less spiritual because of what I was experiencing. Little by little, I've been able to open up and share the story with my kids, staff, church, and national conferences, offering hope to others battling anxiety and shame. I'll share some of that story with you as we journey through this chapter.

Your experience with anxiety might be much like my own, including the unexpected moment when the anxiety first makes its presence known. The initial reaction might be to keep this struggle private, shrouded in shame based on the mistaken belief that such feelings reflect a lapse in spirituality or strength. Yet as we gradually open up, sharing our experiences beyond our immediate circles, we join a community of voices offering solace and understanding to others traveling similar paths.

In moments when anxiety looms large, it can be comforting to remember that King David, a man celebrated for his courage, also carried trauma and anxiety with him. Despite being a formidable warrior, David contended with feelings of rejection and insecurity, which at times amplified his anxiety and fear. Pastoral theologians like Eugene Peterson have written extensively about David's struggle and how it serves as a potent reminder that our spiritual journey does not demand perfection. Peterson writes, "David provides a large chunk of the evidence that disabuses us of the idea that perfection is part of the job description of the men and women who follow Jesus. More narrative space is given in our Scriptures to the story of David than to any other single person,

> DAVID BEHAVED IMPERFECTLY, YET HE WAS PERFECTLY LOVED, JUST LIKE US.

and there are no perfectionist elements in it. The way of David is, from start to finish, a way of imperfection."[7]

David behaved imperfectly, yet he was perfectly loved, just like us.

King David's life resembles the long and winding path of a long-distance runner navigating unpredictable terrain. In his case, the terrain was his internal world, a world where the peaks of elation soared high and the valleys of despair sank deep. Through the fluctuations of his internal world, he anchored himself in the practice of worship.

Worship was his sanctuary in time.

FOOTSTEPS OF DAVID

David's life is well documented in the Bible. The books of Samuel, Chronicles, and 1 Kings read like a biography. Then, in the Psalms, we find David's personal reflections, which read more like a journal. Approximately half of the psalms are attributed to David. Many of them are again referenced in the New Testament, revealing that they were important to the earliest followers of Jesus. David did not sugarcoat or try to hide his fears, anxieties, sadnesses, and woes in the Psalms. Instead, he laid them out one by one, sometimes offering agonizing details about how troubled he was in his soul.

David means "beloved," but David's early years show that he was often treated more like a forgotten, ignored, and even despised member of his family. For example, when Samuel visited David's family to choose a future king, all his siblings were brought in as candidates before the prophet. David was left out in the field—no one thought to include him in this important moment.

We also know that David was a shepherd. Shepherding was hard, smelly work. He must not have felt beloved when he was alone with the sheep. While caring for the sheep, David faced dangerous predators, killing a lion and a bear. He was not pampered or protected like we imagine a beloved son would be.

One day, David was relieved of his shepherding duties to deliver food to his brothers, who were fighting in Saul's army. When his oldest brother, Eliab, saw David talking with other men in the army, he got angry and said, "Why have you come down here? And with whom did you leave those few sheep in the wilderness? I know how conceited you are and how wicked your heart is; you came down only to watch the battle."[8] David's response to Eliab underlines that this was not the first time he had been spoken to so harshly. "Now what have I done?" David said. "Can't I even speak?"[9] I am sure David did not feel loved at that moment.

These early experiences of being rejected, overlooked, underestimated, and mocked seem to have had a long-lasting impact on David's view of himself. Throughout his life, he seems to struggle with thinking that he is unworthy and insignificant. Despite his eventual success as a warrior and leader, David's writings reveal a man grappling with a wide range of emotions from anxiety to paranoia, often feeling misunderstood and fearing betrayal.

David's anxiety spiked when he was running from Saul. For thirteen years, David was pursued by the first king of Israel and his armies. To make matters worse, King Saul was once David's idol. It is nearly impossible to imagine how heartbreaking and stressful David's years on the run must have been. Psalm 142:4 records David's emotions at that time, revealing his desperate need and fainting soul: "I have no refuge; no one cares for my life."

Have you ever felt there is no refuge and no one cares for your life? If so, I want to assure you that there is refuge, and each line in this book is drawing you closer to it. Transformation is found on the journey, one step at a time, as we move closer into union with Jesus.

David's fears and worries outlined in the Psalms and on display throughout his life show a man dealing with anxiety. He writes, "I am faint" and "my bones are in agony."[10] He continues, "My soul is in deep anguish."[11] And he concludes, "I am worn out from my groaning. All night long I flood my bed with weeping."[12]

In his later psalms, David explicitly said that "anxiety was great within me."[13] Although it is impossible to diagnose a historical figure with a mental-health disorder, we can look at David's story and see the signs of what he was going through.

In the Psalms, David cried out about heartache, turmoil,

emotional pain, and anguish. He experienced heart palpitations and begged God for relief from his suffering. On one occasion, David said that his "soul was in deep anguish" within him, and on another, the "terrors of death" had fallen upon him.[14] He wrote that fear, trembling, and horror had overwhelmed him. David also frequently mentioned trouble sleeping, a common symptom of both anxiety and depression. He poetically described nights spent weeping, with his bed soaked in tears.[15]

Additionally, David felt weary and exhausted, further signs of anxiety and depression. These conditions are often diagnosed together, and the same medications are used to treat both. It's not surprising that David's psalms reveal signs of depression. He battled ongoing distress, a sense of despair, and a longing for relief. Regardless of whether his suffering was caused by his own actions or those of others, David experienced his emotions deeply—he was a *feeler*. And feelers are always more susceptible to anxiety and depression.[16]

DANCING WITH THE SCARS

I vividly recall experiencing some of those symptoms during my first panic attack in the winter of 2010. As I mentioned in an earlier chapter, during that period, Judith and I were navigating a particularly challenging phase at our church, marked by significant growth and expansion, and I was dealing with childhood trauma that had begun to surface at the most inopportune time.

During that crazy, stressful season, one of the NFL players in our church was chosen to be a contestant on *Dancing with the Stars*, and he invited us to attend a taping of the show. Quite honestly, I wasn't looking forward to it. I'm more of a Bass Pro guy than a *Dancing with the Stars* guy. The spandex and sequins freak me out. And I don't even know what I should appropriately focus on when watching people dance—clothes, shoes, fitness, moves, physiques? It's all too much for me, so I focus on analyzing my own shoes when I'm forced to attend performances that involve dancers.

The night before we flew to California, I woke up around 2:00 a.m. thinking I was having a heart attack. I struggled out of bed and made it a few feet, only to realize I was in significant physical distress. The world was spinning, my chest was exploding, and my mind was racing with unrestrained terror. I felt as if I were dissociated from my body—almost like having an out-of-body experience.

I woke Judith up and said, "Something is wrong with me. I mean really wrong." She dragged me to the car and drove me to the closest emergency room. When we arrived and I described my symptoms, they put me in a wheelchair and took me past every other person waiting and into an examination room.

Upon wheeling me into the room, the medical team acted swiftly, connecting me to heart monitors to track my cardiac activity; they administered an EKG to examine my heart's electrical activity and extracted several vials of blood for analysis. After an anxious hour-long wait, the doctor returned with a mix of news. The relief came first: I had not suffered a heart attack. But my concern quickly returned when he suggested an alternative cause for my symptoms: a panic attack.

What!

A panic attack?

There must be some mistake!

I don't have anxiety.

I'm just going through a stressful season.

Without hesitation, I rejected his diagnosis. My reasoning went like this: I'm not the anxious type. I don't live a timid and fearful life. I travel to dangerous places doing missions and humanitarian work. I enjoy hobbies like climbing mountains and chasing dangerous animals with a bow and arrow. I've even jumped out of airplanes without feeling anxious. *Okay, maybe that's a bit of an exaggeration.* But there was no way I had experienced a panic attack.

Then, a couple of months later, I had another.

And then another.

And another.

And another.

Over the next four years, I had somewhere around a dozen major panic attacks and countless minor ones. Each of them was terrifying. Since I couldn't distinguish between a panic attack and a heart attack, during each one I felt as if my life were in peril. I can't tell you how many trips I made to the hospital, thinking I was dying.

Anyone who has ever had just one panic attack knows that you never want to have another. It is not just the chest pain, the dizziness, the numbness in your arms, or the difficulty breathing. It is not just the feeling that you are being smothered to death. It is the inexplicable sense of terror—the sense of impending doom, the feeling that the universe is collapsing in on you and that you are dying.

There were times when Judith would drive me to the hospital in the middle of the night and we would sit in the parking lot for hours just to be close enough should I need help.

If the emergency room gave out frequent-flyer miles, I would have elite status for life!

Before that fateful night, *panic attack* was just a term to me, something I had read about but never truly understood. When the claws of panic clamped around my chest, it wasn't just the physical symptoms that overwhelmed me; it was the torrent of confusion, fear, and vulnerability that cascaded through my mind.

I remember lying there that night, the world spinning, my heartbeat thundering in my ears, feeling alienated from my body as if I were a spectator to my own distress. Each labored breath felt like a battle, each heartbeat a drum of war. But beyond the physical trauma was an internal dialogue, a voice that oscillated between reason and fear. *This can't be happening*, it whispered one moment, and in the next, *What if this is it?*

The helplessness wasn't just in the loss of bodily control but in the sudden, stark realization of my fragility and mortality. *You won't feel the sunshine on your face again. You won't be here for your wife and kids. You might not even make it into heaven.* In those dark, elongated minutes, my identity was challenged along with my deepest beliefs. I was no longer a pastor, a husband, a leader; I was a man grappling with the rawest form of human vulnerability.

Sharing this experience isn't just about recounting the event, it's about peeling back the layers of my emotional armor to reveal the tumult beneath. It's about showing that it's okay to acknowledge and express the chaos within. That night, I learned that embracing our vulnerabilities is not a sign of weakness but a pathway to strength.

It has now been eight years since my last major panic attack, and I write these words knowing there is no guarantee I will not experience another. What I am more confident in is the knowledge that the same God who was present to David in his crippling moments of anxiety walked with me through mine. He sat with me in hotel rooms, parking lots outside of emergency rooms, and in hospital examination rooms without judgment or condemnation. He held me during the moments I felt forsaken. He reassured me with his love, even though I felt like a failure as a pastor and spiritual leader. And by his grace, he began a work of healing that transcended my physical symptoms and resonated at the core of my being.

Even if I have another panic attack tomorrow, I have learned some keys to resting in him.

The struggle with anxiety is uniquely personal, and the path to overcoming it varies from one individual to another. Some find relief in medication, others in therapy, others in friendship, others in nature or in improving their diet, exercise, and medication. Some people try all the remedies and still carry the battle with anxiety throughout their lives despite living a productive and fulfilling life. Among them are names we recognize: Martin Luther, Abraham Lincoln, Winston Churchill, Charles Spurgeon, John Bunyan, and C. S. Lewis, to name but a few.[17]

> THE STRUGGLE WITH ANXIETY IS UNIQUELY PERSONAL, AND THE PATH TO OVERCOMING IT VARIES FROM ONE INDIVIDUAL TO ANOTHER.

But a common thread in these diverse experiences is that they require daily effort to manage the physical and emotional toll, whether through reading and quoting Scripture, mindfulness practices, therapies, medicine, or, as I discovered, the grounding power of worship. Inspired by David's example, worship became more than a weekly experience for me; it became a daily instrument in regulating my emotions, anchoring me during the worst of my emotional storms.

EMOTIONAL REGULATION

Before we discuss emotional regulation, let's take a quick look at thermoregulation. Understanding how our bodies balance their temperature will help us understand how to regulate our emotions.

Our survival hinges on our bodies' ability to maintain a stable core temperature. For our psychological systems to function normally, we must maintain an internal temperature of 97.5 to 99.5°F. We keep our temperature in that range through the process of thermoregulation. If we get too hot, our bodies sweat to cool us off. If we get too cold, we shiver to warm back up.

As every runner knows, this balance can be easily thrown off. That is why runners check the weather before a run and take plenty of water to keep them cool and hydrated. That is also why runners are wrapped in foil blankets at the end of marathons. Those blankets trap body heat so the runner doesn't cool down too rapidly and become hypothermic.

In the same way that marathon runners learn to regulate their temperature, we can learn to alter our emotional condition through diet and exercise, listening to classical music or comedy, reducing the amount of time spent watching screens, having conversations with friends, reframing accusations, stepping away from our desks every hour, and even driving home by a different route at the end of the day.

We don't know what techniques David employed, but we do know that music played an essential role in managing his internal state. His life, full of highs and lows, joys and sorrows, required spiritual thermoregulation. David experienced the intoxicating rush of God's blessing when Samuel anointed him. Then he had amazing victories, such as slaying Goliath and uniting the tribes of Israel. These were periods of intense emotional heat when energy, creativity, and confidence surged. But sometimes David's emotions burned too hot, causing impulsive decisions, moral failings, and familial strife.

David also experienced moments of bitter cold when he felt cut off from the warmth of God's presence. For many years, he lived on the run from Saul's jealousy. He was ridiculed by his wife and lost an infant child. Then he experienced the sacking of his beloved town, Ziklag. Later, one of David's sons, Absalom, murdered his half brother, Amnon. Then Absalom tried to over-throw David and become king. These terrible tragedies plunged David into the cold grip of depression.

In the Psalms, we discover David's response to these swings of his emotional thermometer. Sometimes his psalms reveal a victorious warrior, jubilant, excited, and energetic, shouting out words of gratitude in praise. Sometimes his psalms show a soul haunted by the shadows of things he had done, things done to him, and things said about him. In response, he poured out his stone-cold anger, heartbreak, anguish, and despair, seeking the warmth of divine comfort. Whether David's emotions were high or low, he looked to God to regulate them.

David used worship as his weapon against anxiety and depression. He understood that offering worship doesn't mean denying pain. Rather, it's one of the ways we process our pain.

When the heat of mania threatened to consume him, David worshiped God. Worship channeled his energy into songs of praise. Instead of allowing the flame of his mania to run wild, worship was like a hearth that contained and directed it, a sacred space where passion could be transformed into a force for good.

When the cold grip of depression took hold, David worshiped God. God's presence was a refuge, a place where the chill of isolation met the warmth of divine love. Worship provided the warmth of connection and the reassurance that even in the cold, David was not alone.

When the uncertainty of anxiety rushed upon him, David worshiped God. Worship calmed the winds of worry. In worship, David found a rhythm that soothed his racing mind, a beat that steadied his steps. Focusing on God made him lift his eyes to something greater than his fears, tempering the anxiety that threatened to overtake him.

David regulated his spiritual temperature through worship.

In this way, worship was more than an expression of faith; it was a vital practice for his mental and emotional health. It was David's spiritual breathing, his way of inhaling divine peace and exhaling human anxiety.

Even during his lifetime, David was known for his ability to soothe through worship. When an evil spirit tormented King Saul, the king asked his officials to find someone to play the lyre to soothe him. One of the officials summoned David, who was so effective in calming King Saul that Saul made him an armor-bearer to keep him nearby. "Whenever the spirit from God came on Saul, David would take up his lyre and play. Then relief would come to Saul; he would feel better, and the evil spirit would leave him."[18]

I wonder how many dark and lonely nights David strummed his lyre to calm the storms raging in his own soul. How many times did the gentle melodies carry his prayers and tears to God, providing a balm for his troubled mind?

DARK NIGHT OF THE SOUL

"The dark night of the soul" is a phrase coined by John of the Cross, a mystic and poet from sixteenth-century Spain.[19] This term, embedded in Christian mysticism, describes a pivotal juncture in the spiritual journey where the individual feels abandoned by God, plunged into a kind of existential despair. John of the Cross envisioned this dark night not as a divine forsaking but as a vital, albeit painful, phase of spiritual purification and growth. His writings, particularly in his poem "Dark Night of the Soul," detail this experience of spiritual desolation, in which all senses of comfort and the perceptible presence of God are stripped away, leaving the soul in a state of raw and barren yearning.

The essence of the dark night of the soul is a feeling of spiritual desolation, confusion, and disorientation. It signifies a period when one's previous understandings of God and faith are challenged, leading to a sense of abandonment and isolation. Yet according to John of the Cross, this harrowing experience is not punitive but transformative. It's a divine orchestration meant to strip away superficial attachments and deepen one's faith, cultivating a more authentic, unmediated union with the divine. This dark night serves as a crucible, dissolving illusions and ego attachments and ushering the soul into a purer, more mature relationship with God.

For people today, the dark night of the soul transcends its spiritual origin and resonates with anyone undergoing significant personal trials. It has come to symbolize those moments when one feels lost, without direction or solace, often following major upheaval, loss, or existential crisis. This concept offers a lens through which to view our darkest trials not as mere suffering but as opportunities for growth and self-discovery.

Some forms of anxiety, including the dark night of the soul, need to be addressed through counseling, therapy, and medicine and by engaging in a safe, loving, and affirming community. But other forms of anxiety can be addressed only by pouring out one's soul as an offering to God in worship and prayer.

HAVE YOU LEARNED TO WORSHIP IN THE NIGHT?

At the risk of oversimplification, I believe that we can sing some negative emotions out of our souls.

We can sing the sadness out.

We can sing the madness out.

We can pour out our sorrow and disappointment through worship.

In the past few years, I've had nights when the painful memory of losing what I'd spent decades building has overwhelmed me with grief. On those nights, I wept until my pillow was soaked, and I played worship music so loud that neighbors three doors down could distinguish every word. Clinging to Jesus like a drowning man to a life preserver, I made it through the night by singing my way into God's presence. Worship not only kept my soul from falling apart, it kept me alive through the night.

Have you learned to worship in the night?

I'm not talking about worshiping with the lights switched off, although that may be worth considering if you feel embarrassed about how you might appear. I'm talking about worshiping God in the dark night of the soul. Have you learned to worship when the lights have gone off in your world and you feel as if you are one more painful moment away from losing your grip on your sanity? Have you learned to worship when waves of terror wash over your soul? Have you learned to sing as if you are singing for your life, future, and sanity?

> TURNING OUR FOCUS FROM FEAR TO FAITH TRANSFORMS ANXIETY INTO DEEPER WORSHIP.

I've ministered in enough predominantly Black congregations to be familiar with the phrase "I am saved, sanctified, clothed, *and in my right mind*." This phrase reflects a deeply held belief that being in Jesus' presence produces a balm of healing that touches the mind.

Sometimes you have to sing the hell out of your soul.

Sometimes you have to sing heaven into your heart.

Sometimes you have to sing your way into your right mind.

Turning our focus from fear to faith transforms anxiety into deeper worship.

Worship goes beyond the conventional forms of singing and prayer. It is an act of laying bare our fears, anxieties, and uncertainties before God. It is an act of burying our faces in the carpet and pouring out our souls in tears, groanings that cannot be articulated, and songs sung loud enough to drown out the voices in our heads.[20] This may be putting my Pentecostal roots on full display, but there is something profound about singing your way through the dark night of your soul. It demonstrates trust in the one who holds your future in the palm of his hand.

Research shows that when we sing or listen to music, our brains release dopamine and endorphins, which make us feel happy and relaxed. It's a great way to escape our worries, which is probably why it's good for our mental health. Singing can also help loosen up tight muscles and lower the amount of a stress-related chemical called cortisol in our bodies, helping us feel more at ease.[21] But what I'm proposing is more than that: worship is a spiritual weapon against fear, anxiety, and depression.

> WORSHIP WILL SUSTAIN YOUR SOUL IN YOUR DARKEST HOUR.

Worship will sustain your soul in your darkest hour.

SINGING ON THE CROSS

It is possible that even Jesus sang psalms during the dark night of his soul while dying on the cross. We know from eyewitness accounts that he quoted lines from the Psalms, but no observant Jew, let alone a rabbi, would consider stiffly reciting the words without song and movement. The Psalms are a hymnbook, and Jesus would have grown up singing and dancing to them. Consider the words of Psalm 22, which he recited in his last moments on the cross: "My God, my God, why have you forsaken me? Why are you so far from saving me, so far from my cries of anguish? . . . Yet you are enthroned as the Holy One; you are the one Israel praises."

In the words of Leonard Sweet, "Whether Jesus sang only

Psalm 22 or sang different psalms that incorporated other features of his crucifixion, he was connecting the dots for his disciples and for anyone else with ears to hear and eyes to see. . . . the question is not whether Jesus sang this Psalm of Tribulation and Triumph from the cross, but rather, how much of the Psalm did Jesus sing? . . . On the cross, Jesus sang Psalm 22."[22] I wonder whether Jesus, like David, was using the power of song to inform and comfort his own soul.

Theologically, worship recognizes God's sovereignty and goodness, a stance that inherently challenges the narratives of fear and despair that underlie anxiety. By focusing on God's attributes—his omnipotence, love, and faithfulness—worship recalibrates our focus, shifting it from our anxieties to assurances of divine presence and provision. This shift is not merely cognitive but has emotional and spiritual implications, fostering a sense of security and peace amid life's tumult.

Therapeutically, worship engages and aligns both mind and body, which is an effective response to anxiety. It encourages the expression of emotions, the articulation of fears, and the physical release of stress through acts of worship that engage the entire being. This holistic engagement is vital in managing anxiety, because it addresses not just the mental but also the physical manifestations of the condition.

Furthermore, worship fosters a sense of community and belonging, offering a counternarrative to the disconnection that often accompanies anxiety. In the corporate aspect of worship, we find solidarity, reminding us that we are not alone in our struggles. This sense of community is effective in mitigating the feelings of loneliness and alienation that exacerbate anxiety.

As with David, our internal emotional states fluctuate and change, much like a runner's pace. There are moments when we try to outsprint anxiety, and others when each step feels weighted down with worry. Long-haul sprints and running with ankle weights are exhausting. But worship ushers us into God's calm presence and helps us find a restful rhythm, a sustainable pace of centeredness and peace.

COMING HOME

Create a sanctuary of sound that soothes your soul. Begin a personal playlist filled with worship songs that resonate deeply with your spirit, songs that remind you of God's sovereignty, love, and peace. Choose pieces that uplift you, that speak to the depth of your heart, and that help you reconnect with God's presence.

Set aside a specific time each day to immerse yourself in worship. Whether it's during your morning routine or a midday pause, or as you wind down in the evening, make this time your routine. Play your playlist and let the music wash over you, carrying your anxieties away on its waves. As you listen, breathe deeply, allowing the lyrics and melodies to minister to your soul.

Engage in worship with your whole being. Sing along, raise your hands, or simply sit in stillness—whatever helps you to enter God's presence. Complement the music with prayer or by reading psalms that speak of God's power and peace. As you do, shift your focus from your fears and anxieties to the unshakable truth of God's promises.

PRAYER

Heavenly Father, in moments of anxiety, remind me to turn my thoughts to worship. Let your praises be the calm in the storm, centering my heart and mind on your sovereignty. Replace my anxieties with your peace that surpasses all understanding, anchoring my soul in the assurance of your faithful presence. May my worship be a weapon against worry and a declaration of your power over every circumstance. In Jesus' name, amen.

CHAPTER 7

RUNNING WITH SCISSORS

From Bitterness to Forgiveness

Then David said to all his officials who were with him in Jerusalem, "Come! We must flee, or none of us will escape from Absalom. We must leave immediately, or he will move quickly to overtake us and bring ruin on us and put the city to the sword."

—2 SAMUEL 15:14

The scenario is all too familiar, depicted countless times on TV, in films, and, unfortunately, in many real lives: a bitter husband, a bitter wife, and two costly lawyers attempting to mediate the end of their marriage. The husband's face is etched with contempt, his anger simmering. The wife, with her arms crossed firmly over her chest, refuses to glance at the man she once vowed to spend her life with. Bitterness has extinguished their love, turning them into adversaries.

Maybe you know this all too well. Bitterness turns allies into adversaries and love into a battlefield.

We have all experienced bitterness, either directed toward us or emanating from within us. This common emotional response can arise from various personal setbacks, including romantic breakups, friendship disputes, job losses, family conflicts, and betrayals of trust.

But what exactly is bitterness, and how does it drive us to run? Just as running often starts with the desire to escape or release stress, bitterness can begin as an emotional response aimed at escaping hurt or injustice. And, insidiously, bitterness is dangerous both to others and to ourselves, like running with scissors.

Bitterness can originate from experiences where we feel we have been wronged, mistreated, or subjected to injustice. It can arise from various situations—from interpersonal conflicts and betrayals to unmet expectations and unfulfilled desires. The root of bitterness is usually a hurt that has not been adequately addressed or healed, a wound that remains open and becomes a breeding ground for resentment.

Bitterness creeps into the depths of our souls and is usually characterized by prolonged anger, resentment, and hostility. It is born of a complex interplay of experiences, emotions, and perceptions that we fail to address and resolve. Rarely does a single event or feeling lead to chronic bitterness; instead, it is the culmination of unresolved hurt, compounded disappointment, and persistent anger that shapes our disposition and outlook on life.

One of the primary sources of bitterness is unresolved emotional pain. When we experience betrayal, rejection, or loss, the wounds inflicted upon our hearts can fester, slowly progressing into bitterness. The longer these wounds remain unhealed, the more likely they are to morph into a bitterness that colors our interactions with others and taints our view of the world.

Furthermore, bitterness thrives in the presence of negative emotions like envy, jealousy, and pride. When we allow these toxic emotions to take root within us, we open the door to bitterness.

Comparison, covetousness, and a sense of entitlement can distort our perceptions, leading us to resent the success of others and magnify our grievances. Nurturing these emotions, we nurture bitterness within ourselves, poisoning our relationships and corroding our inner peace.

Another factor that contributes to bitterness is a sense of unfairness. When we feel that we have been wronged, it can be all too easy to harbor grudges and nurse a sense of victimhood. This can fuel bitterness as we fixate on grievances and allow them to overshadow our experiences. The more we dwell on these perceived injustices, the deeper the roots of bitterness burrow into our souls, entwining with our sense of self and identity.

As Dr. Gregory Popcak puts it, "Bitterness is unforgiveness fermented."[1] It takes time to become bitter. This warning also offers the hope that we can address unforgiveness in our souls early enough to prevent it from fermenting.

Bitterness has been a destructive force throughout history, wreaking havoc and tearing families and communities apart. From the earliest stories we've seen, such as Cain's bitterness toward Abel, which led to the world's first murder, to Sarai's resentment toward Hagar, fueling family strife, to Absalom's bitterness toward his father, David, sparking rebellion and tragedy, the tales are as old as time. These stories illustrate the destructive power of bitterness, showing how it can escalate conflicts, erode relationships, and lead to catastrophic outcomes. Bitterness not only contaminates the one it inhabits but also defiles everyone who gives place to it. Bitterness is easily transplanted into the lives of those around us and can continue in families and communities for generations.

Have you ever heard of the Hatfields and the McCoys? Their famous family feud lasted for twenty-eight years, affected three generations, and claimed more than a dozen members of the two families.

Forgiveness isn't about forgetting the past but is about freeing the future from its grip.

BITTER THOUGHTS

When bitterness dominates our thoughts, it casts a dark shadow over everything, prompting cynical interpretations such as:

- "They're only being nice to me because they want something from me."
- "I'm always the one making sacrifices, and what do I get in return?"
- "This apology feels hollow. They're just trying to ease their guilt."
- "Why should I forgive them? They probably haven't changed a bit."
- "They didn't include me because they don't value me. It has always been this way."

Such thoughts reflect how bitterness can warp perceptions, leading to a cycle in which negative expectations are set and every subsequent interaction is interpreted through a lens of suspicion and resentment.

Bitter people are exhausting to be around.

Bitterness has a pervasive and destructive impact, eroding the foundations of marriages, straining family bonds, and fostering conflict within communities. It also contributes significantly to the divisive and polarizing language prevalent in today's political discourse. Most distressing, bitterness has subtly spread within churches, transforming places meant for sanctuary and unity into arenas of discord and division.

The good news is that we don't have to follow the path of bitterness; we may choose something better.

BITTER OR BETTER

I've never considered myself a bitter person. Sure, I experience moments of anger and can be critical when I'm not tending to my soul as I should. Though I have harbored ungracious attitudes from time to time, bitterness has never been one of them. I've always been proactive in guarding my heart against this corrosive emotion, choosing to forgive others swiftly and generously.

THE GOOD NEWS IS THAT WE DON'T HAVE TO FOLLOW THE PATH OF BITTERNESS; WE MAY CHOOSE SOMETHING BETTER.

But I recently faced an unsettling revelation. Despite my vigilance against bitterness, it had made its way into my heart. This realization hit me after a pastor friend shared an Instagram reel of another young minister delivering a sermon at a significant church. This person had previously worked with us and, during a challenging period, spread falsehoods about us, fueled harmful gossip, and contributed to the division within our church as we transitioned away from the global movement we were once part of.

While discussing the video with my wife, I made a disparaging remark about the young minister, believing my criticism was warranted. I went to bed and tossed and turned all night, feeling miserable. By morning, the weight of conviction was too much. I repented to my wife for the uncharitable things I had said, and together we prayed for God to bless him.

Does this absolve him of his actions? *Certainly not.* But it does liberate my conscience, freeing me to move forward unburdened by bitterness and resentment.

According to Stephen A. Diamond, an acclaimed clinical and forensic psychologist, bitterness can be defined as "a chronic and pervasive state of smoldering resentment."[2] That description certainly fits what we see in Absalom's life.

FOOTSTEPS OF ABSALOM

In the last chapter, we focused on David, covering his highlight reel: killing Goliath, running from Saul, and becoming the beloved king of Israel. But we left one painful story out: David's sinful behavior with Bathsheba and his orchestration of her husband's death.[3]

After David's transgression with Bathsheba, David repented, and God extended forgiveness to him.[4] But forgiveness didn't erase the repercussions of his actions. The subsequent chapter of his life was riddled with interpersonal strife, a testament to the enduring consequences of his choices.

The consequences we face because of our sinful choices aren't our payment for sin; rather, the blood of Jesus serves as the payment for our transgressions. The outcomes we experience stem from the law of sowing and reaping. While forgiveness realigns us with God and establishes a right relationship, it does not shield us from the repercussions of our actions.

As difficult as it is to face, we reap what we sow, particularly as it relates to willful sin, a blatant disregard for righteousness.

The repercussions of King David's transgressions were profound and far reaching, with his son Absalom at the epicenter of the tragedy. Absalom was David's third son, the child of David's fourth wife. The Bible includes an interesting detail about

Absalom: he was extraordinarily handsome, and his long flowing hair was cut only once a year. It weighed five pounds![5] This detail seems more than a footnote; it symbolizes Absalom's preoccupation with his appearance and possibly his need for identity and recognition.

Given his position in the line of succession, Absalom was not the immediate choice to inherit King David's throne. But his ambition to rule was unmistakable, indicating that he would resort to force, if necessary, to seize power. The heir to the throne was Amnon, David's firstborn son. In a troubling turn of events, Amnon harbored lustful feelings toward Tamar, his half sister and Absalom's full sister, setting the stage for a tragic family conflict. One day, Amnon carried out an evil scheme to rape Tamar, somehow convincing himself that this vicious assault would lead to love and marriage. Then after raping her, he hated her even more strongly than he first loved her.

When Tamar told Absalom what had happened, he was blinded by fury. This was a terrible injustice, a heinous crime, a grievous sin. Amnon needed to be brought to justice, but instead of having him arrested or seeking justice through proper channels, Absalom plotted his revenge. He waited for just the right moment. Two years later, he invited Amnon on a family road trip, got him drunk, and had him murdered.[6]

Interestingly, David's first response to Tamar's rape was similar to Absalom's: he was furious over what Amnon had done.[7] Then something bizarre happened: David did nothing about it. According to the record, he didn't even mention it. Recent translations taken from the Dead Sea Scrolls insert the additional comment that David "did not punish his son Amnon, because he loved him, for he was his firstborn." This offers some explanation as to why Absalom's anger and bitterness did not dissipate after he murdered Amnon. Instead, Absalom simply transferred his anger and bitterness toward his father. Some biblical scholars argue that Absalom blamed David for Amnon's actions and was incensed that David did not punish Amnon appropriately.

Regardless of the reason, David's family was in shambles by this point. His daughter was devastated, his heir was dead, and Absalom was on the run.[8] Absalom and David remained estranged for three years until Joab, one of David's trusted generals, facilitated Absalom's return.[9] But David, wary of his son's intentions, did not allow him back into the royal palace.[10] Instead, he confined him to house arrest within his own home. Although they were physically close, father and son were far from reconciled.

During the two years that followed, Absalom's life continued outwardly: he married a beautiful woman, fathered three sons, and appeared to settle into his constrained freedom.[11] Yet he harbored growing bitterness toward his father. This unresolved bitterness eventually hardened, setting the stage for rebellion just as David was finally prepared to mend their relationship.[12]

Though father and son were beginning to rebuild their relationship, Absalom's bitterness could not be contained. He cunningly began undermining David's authority, ingratiating himself with the kingdom's citizens and subtly turning their loyalty toward him.

When people brought a case to the king for judgment, Absalom would ask where in Israel they were from, and they would tell him their tribe. Then Absalom would say, "You've really got a strong case here! It's too bad the king doesn't have anyone to hear it. I wish I were the judge. Then everyone could bring their cases to me for judgment, and I would give them justice!"[13]

When people tried to bow before him, Absalom wouldn't let them. Instead, he took them by the hand and kissed them. Absalom did this with everyone who came to the king for justice, "and so he stole the hearts of the people of Israel."[14]

Absalom's strategy to usurp the throne was not a rash decision; instead it was a carefully orchestrated plot that unfolded over four years, mirroring the gradual growth of his bitterness. Bitterness typically develops slowly. It often starts with simple frustration, evolves into deeper discontent, and gradually begins to manifest through increasingly frequent and subtle criticisms. Over time, these criticisms become more overt and pointed.

Just as bitterness had slowly taken root and spread within Absalom, so too did his treacherous plans. Each day, as his resentment festered, his actions became more calculated, setting the stage for his ultimate betrayal. When the moment was ripe, Absalom's pent-up ambition and rage exploded, fueling him to challenge his father for the throne. He usurped King David's leadership, declared himself to be king, slept openly with his father's concubines to humiliate him, and waged war against him.[15] This act of treason was the culmination of years of growing bitterness and meticulous plotting.[16]

The end of the story is tragic. Absalom went to war against David, and twenty thousand men of Israel were killed.[17] In the heat of the battle, with the tide turning against him, Absalom fled on a donkey, and in his mad dash through the forest, his long hair got caught in the branch of a tree.[18] As he hung there, Joab and ten of his men came upon Absalom and killed him. When David heard the news, he wept bitterly: "O my son Absalom! My son, my son Absalom! If only I had died instead of you—O Absalom, my son, my son!"[19]

> RELEASING BITTERNESS ENABLES US TO RECLAIM OUR PEACE AND RECOVER OUR JOY.

Bitterness take us to places of unimaginable pain and sorrow.

Releasing bitterness enables us to reclaim our peace and recover our joy.

ROOT AND FRUIT

Absalom's story is a cautionary tale. What began as a desire for justice for his sister spiraled into murder, treason, and, ultimately, his death. His story underscores the importance of addressing bitterness before it embeds itself in our hearts and drives us to destructive actions.

Bitter individuals display a range of negative behaviors—hostility, sharp criticism, anger, and a relentless tendency to find fault in others. Beneath this harsh exterior, they are like seething volcanoes of unresolved anger and hurt. The Scriptures caution us about allowing a "bitter root" to take hold in our lives.[20]

The term *bitter root* refers to the roots of a tree and serves as a stark warning: if bitterness is not confronted and uprooted through repentance and forgiveness, it will become embedded in our souls. This entrenched bitterness can harden our perceptions of those who have wronged us, making our judgments and resentments feel justified and immovable over time. The Greek word for bitterness (*pikria*) describes an inward sourness that corrodes both our inner peace and our outward demeanor.[21] Like acid, bitterness eats away at our emotional and spiritual health, often manifesting in unkindness, sarcasm, cynicism, and other harmful attitudes. As bitterness surfaces, it magnifies negativity, spreading its toxic effects to those around us. Over time, it results in a hardened, scornful disposition that isolates us and poisons our relationships and communities.

Bitterness is not merely a fleeting emotion but an issue that will take root and grow if left unchecked. Addressing it requires effort—acknowledging pain, seeking to extend or receive forgiveness, and allowing God's grace to heal and transform. Only then can we break free from the prison of bitterness and embrace a life filled with peace, joy, and healthy, loving relationships.

Consistently speaking negatively of someone who has offended us could be a sign that bitterness is trying to take root in our hearts. Recognizing this, it's crucial to confront these feelings through repentance and blessing the offender. Otherwise, the roots will grow deeper and we will find ourselves bearing the fruit of bitterness.

The adage "Bitterness is drinking poison and expecting the other person to die" aptly illustrates the self-destructive nature of bitterness. The irony is that the bitter person suffers the most, although they may also be the victim. If bitterness is the poison, the antidote is to bless the person who has offended them.

Some of the most challenging words to read when you are drowning in resentment are "Vengeance is mine, says the Lord." The New International Version renders it this way: "Do not take revenge, my dear friends, but leave room for God's wrath, for it is written: 'It is mine to avenge; I will repay,' says the Lord. On the contrary: 'If your enemy is hungry, feed him; if he is thirsty, give him something to drink. In doing this, you will heap burning coals on his head.'"[22]

Another way of looking at it is that bitterness reflects a reluctance to trust in God's plan. It shows resistance to surrendering our pains and wounds to God's ways of healing and his timing for justice.

INJUSTICE AND AUTHORITY

Both David and Absalom dealt with unjust authorities. David dealt with a king who was trying to kill him. Absalom dealt with a king who failed to protect his sister and punish her assailant. But their responses were completely different.

At one point, David had the opportunity to kill King Saul, who had been relentlessly pursuing him through the desert and making his life unbearable. Yet David refused to harm Saul, instead declaring, "May the LORD judge between you and me. And may the LORD avenge the wrongs you have done to me, but my hand will not touch you. As the old saying goes, 'From evildoers come evil deeds,' so my hand will not touch you." Despite the injustice he faced, David chose to trust God to bring justice rather than taking matters into his own hands. Although Saul acted unjustly, David responded with unwavering integrity.[23] Absalom ignored his father's example. When he faced an injustice, he took matters into his own hands, killing his brother and trying to overthrow the king. His actions show a lack of trust in God and a lack of respect for authority.

There is a right way to address injustice. Ignoring injustice with the flimsy excuse that "God will work it out" is not an option. As Christians, we are called to speak truth to power, be a voice for the voiceless, and work toward a more just society. God calls his people to be a prophetic light, standing in contrast to the world's darkness. But addressing injustice inappropriately can cause even more harm. While anger is often unhelpful and poorly justified, we can be angry without sinning. We can speak against injustice honorably, aiming for peacemaking and resolution. We can dismantle systemic injustices without burning everything down. As N. T. Wright says, "Almost any government is better than anarchy." Tyranny is bad, but anarchy is worse.

The Bible teaches us much about authority and submission, yet these concepts have often been misused to dominate and abuse people. They have been improperly used to justify slavery, perpetuate domestic abuse, control the vulnerable, and misuse power within churches. This misuse is far from what God intends, yet he risks the abuse because of the importance of this issue. Submission to authorities matters deeply to God.

Submission means voluntarily placing oneself under the

authority of another. It is a choice, an act of will. Submission is not to be offered reluctantly, like a defeated soldier submits to his conqueror, but willingly, as a student submits to a wise, kind, and compassionate teacher.

SUBMISSION WAS CENTRAL TO JESUS' LIFE AND IS A GUIDING PRINCIPLE FOR HIS FOLLOWERS.

Submission was central to Jesus' life and is a guiding principle for his followers. But applying this principle to our imperfect human relationships is challenging. Unlike Jesus, who submitted to a perfect Father, we navigate a landscape marred by flawed authority, making spiritual authority a complex issue.

In an age rife with spiritual abuse and church hurt, I offer the following section gently for your consideration.

SEVEN LEVELS OF AUTHORITY

In a broken world, implementing the principles of authority and submission can be challenging. But God provides a framework for authority that protects those who choose to follow the way of surrender. My friend Rick Godwin, senior pastor of Summit Christian Center, has spent more than forty years teaching on the seven levels of authority and how they interrelate. His framework is invaluable for accepting authority without enabling the abuse of power.

First, the highest and infallible level is sovereign authority, which is absolute and perfect. This level of authority is reserved for God alone and is shared between the Father, the Son, and the Holy Spirit. Sovereign authority is unchanging and encompasses all.

Second, one level beneath, we discover veracious authority—the authority of truth. Truth issues from God, is manifested in creation, and is recorded in the Bible. Jesus is the personification of truth, and we study the Scriptures because they testify of him. Although this authority is constant and transcends all cultural and temporal boundaries, it is considered secondary because of our limited understanding of truth.

Third, there is the authority of conscience, an internal guide given by God to each of us. Although fallible and susceptible to misinformation, this authority allows us to engage in behaviors not expressly forbidden in the Scriptures while allowing others to abstain. The New Testament example of eating meat sacrificed to idols falls under this authority.

Fourth, delegated authority refers to the authority entrusted to individuals within a community relative to their roles and positions. This is the first level of authority humans exercise in serving and leading others. Examples include spouses, parents, civic leaders, teachers, bosses, first responders, and church leadership. Delegated authority can change in different seasons of life, such as parental authority diminishing as children grow into adulthood.

Fifth, stipulative authority, otherwise known as legal and contractual authority, is upheld in societal laws and agreements and must also be respected because it is considered ordained by God. Paul said that this authority is constituted by God and proceeds from him. If you enter a legal agreement, you are bound to the authority of that agreement.

Sixth, in interactions with different cultures, we should respect the authority of local customs and traditions as long as they don't contradict the rule of conscience, truth, and God. Paul appealed to the authority of customs in his guidance to the church at Corinth.

Seventh, functional authority comes into play when individuals have the necessary skills or experience for specific tasks, allowing them to lead even in the absence of formal authority. For example, if you arrive on the scene of a deadly crash and you are the only person who knows CPR, you have the authority to act even though you may not be wearing a uniform.

Understanding these nuanced levels of authority helps prevent misuse and promotes respectful engagement with the concept of authority. Other than sovereign and veracious authority, every other level is an entrustment, not an entitlement. No one has the right to assert dominance over you, abuse you, or violate your conscience. Any claim that you are "not under authority" should be considered in light of the specific level of engagement.

The seven-levels-of-authority framework provides a robust structure to safeguard against the abuse of power by delineating boundaries and roles. Establishing sovereign and veracious authority as divine ensures that no human authority is absolute, preventing the idolization of leaders.

The authority of conscience empowers us to evaluate external directives against our internal convictions. Delegated and stipulative authorities emphasize operating within legal and ethical limits, ensuring accountability. Functional authority acknowledges situational leadership based on competence, protecting against decisions by unqualified figures. Collectively, these levels promote a balanced power dynamic, ensuring authority is exercised responsibly and ethically, protecting against potential abuses.

This framework is not meant to be absolute authority (see what I did there?) but rather a helpful way of thinking through how authority works. Regardless of how we may stratify it, authority and submission are essential companions on the journey of following Jesus.

We see so much unnecessary confusion and destruction in Absalom's life because he tried to usurp God's sovereign authority in punishing Amnon, and again when he tried to usurp his father's authority as king. He ignored the delegated authorities in the kingdom, customs, and traditions, and it's safe to assume he ignored the authority of his conscience.

Most likely you've seen and felt the pain caused by abuses of authority, and I'm sorry you have had to experience that. I want to extend my deepest repentance on behalf of any church leader who has misused their authority and hurt you, whether intentionally or unintentionally. In my pastoral life, I, too, have hurt people. Often I've had the right motives but have used imperfect means to lead others. And there have been times when my motives have not been pure. Please forgive me. Please forgive us as leaders in God's holy and precious church.

> JESUS INVITES US TO EMBRACE HIS EASY YOKE, OFFERING THE PEACE AND REST THAT COME FROM ALIGNING OUR WILLS WITH HIS.

Jesus invites us to embrace his easy yoke, offering the peace and rest that come from aligning our wills with his. This invitation is grounded in the understanding that God's authority surpasses all others and that his power, perfect and benevolent, is always oriented toward our ultimate good. When we fully acknowledge this, we gain the strength and courage to release our bitterness and stop our fruitless struggles. Accepting his sovereign rule allows us to live under his gracious authority, leading to a life marked by peace and liberation from our burdens.

BITTERNESS AND FORGIVENESS

In preparation for a recent sermon on forgiveness, I asked my social-media followers, "What is the most painful thing you've had to forgive someone for?" The responses were heartbreaking.

- "One of my relatives murdering another. Still tough after thirty years."
- "Someone taking advantage of my immigration status to take everything from me."
- "My ex-husband taking my only child from me."
- "Betrayal."
- "My dad trying to kill me."
- "Trying to forgive myself for what I did to my parents."

Life is painful, and not just in the world of social media.

In four decades of pastoring, I've heard stories that make me wonder how forgiveness is even possible if not for Jesus.

With full respect to the idea that spiritual formation is a journey and not a series of simple steps, I want to offer practical pastoral advice on overcoming bitterness. Overcoming bitterness requires a commitment to honesty and a willingness to look within, face difficult truths, seek understanding, and embrace the grace to change. Sometimes the roots of bitterness are deep and complex, especially when they stem from trauma or long-standing issues. In such cases, you may need to seek the guidance of a pastor, counselor, or mental-health professional to find the support and strategies needed to address and overcome your recurring feelings.

The first step in overcoming bitterness is recognizing and acknowledging that you feel bitter. This is often the most challenging part because it requires admitting that these negative feelings are affecting your well-being and possibly even your relationships. Notice that you are running with scissors and are in danger of stabbing yourself or those you are bitter toward. It means looking inward and asking why certain events continue to trigger such strong reactions. Admitting to these feelings does not equate to weakness; rather, it marks the beginning of wisdom and the path to healing. It requires courage to acknowledge that your heart harbors bitterness, especially when it feels justified.

Understanding the source of your bitterness involves revisiting painful memories and examining them honestly. It's about connecting the dots between past experiences and your emotional state. This process isn't about assigning blame but about understanding the impact these experiences have had on you.

Once you've recognized these bitter feelings, it is important to understand their origin. They may stem from unresolved conflicts, betrayals, or disappointments that have not been adequately addressed. Reflecting on the events and experiences that led to these feelings can provide important insights and clarify what needs healing.

Finding healthy ways to express feelings associated with bitterness can be cathartic and prevent these emotions from being internalized or manifested in harmful ways. This could involve talking to a trusted counselor, writing in a journal, or, most important, pouring your heart out to God in prayer.

The next step involves choosing to release the bitterness. Forgiveness is a powerful antidote to bitterness, but it's often misunderstood. Forgiveness doesn't mean forgetting the past or excusing others' wrongs. Instead it's about releasing the grip of resentment and anger for one's well-being. It's a commitment to healing and moving forward.

Addressing the bitterness in one's soul is about seeking freedom from the past. It's about making peace with one's memories, not being enslaved by them. This process fosters resilience and opens the heart to more joy, peace, and meaningful connections with others.

To guard against the return of bitterness, we must cultivate a spirit of gratitude. Gratitude plays a vital role in combating bitterness by shifting our focus from what we lack to what we have been given. When we cultivate a spirit of gratitude, we train our minds to see the beauty and abundance surrounding us, even amid hardship and loss.

MARIA'S JOURNEY

Maria carried the weight of bitterness for years after her business partner betrayed her, stealing a lucrative client and leaving their joint venture in ruins. The betrayal cost Maria not only her business but also her trust in close relationships, fueling resentment that tainted her interactions with others. It wasn't until Maria attended a workshop on forgiveness that she saw the possibility of shedding her bitterness. Inspired by stories of others who had overcome similar pain, she started a journey of introspection and healing. Maria reached out to a counselor who specialized in business disputes and personal betrayal, and worked through her feelings and slowly started to forgive—not for her partner's sake but for her own peace and future.

Through months of counseling and effort, Maria learned to reframe her narrative from one of victimhood to one of survival and growth. She recognized that her bitterness was holding her back from opportunities and joy in other areas of her life. With time, Maria forgave her former partner and even reached out to mend their relationship. They didn't restart their business, but she achieved closure and regained her peace of mind. Maria's story became a testimony in her community, inspiring others to confront their bitterness. She often shares her experience, emphasizing the power of letting go of the past and embracing personal renewal.

Jesus' sacrifice on the cross stands as the ultimate model of forgiveness. His words, "Father, forgive them, for they do not know what they are doing," resonate through the ages, reminding us of his unfailing mercy.[24] By embracing his grace, we are empowered to forgive, not through our strength but through his power and love. Forgiveness liberates us from the chains of bitterness, releasing us to live in freedom.

My experience in extending forgiveness has been easier than expected for one simple reason: I am mindful of how undeserving I am of forgiveness for my own sins. The grace and mercy extended to me by Jesus, who pardoned my transgressions, washed away my guilt and shame, and granted me hope and a future, inspire me to be generous in extending forgiveness. Reflecting on the extravagance of his sacrifice, I find it impossible to harbor bitterness within my heart.

> JESUS' SACRIFICE ON THE CROSS STANDS AS THE ULTIMATE MODEL OF FORGIVENESS.

This commitment does not diminish my resolve to hold others accountable or prevent me from setting appropriate boundaries. What it does is establish justification for why I must extend forgiveness. Each act of forgiveness releases me from torment and from those who have tormented me, and it brings me closer to refuge and rest. Forgiveness is a release of the past. It is a chance to put down the scissors and to take a bold step into an unburdened future where freedom and joy await.

COMING HOME

Begin the morning by examining your heart for any traces of bitterness that might have taken root the previous day. Before the day begins in earnest, take a moment to sit with God in the quiet stillness of the morning. Ask him to reveal any lingering resentment or hurt and to help you uproot it before it takes hold.

Pray for the person or situation contributing to that feeling. Even if it's difficult, lift them up to God, asking for his blessing and guidance. As you do, invite God to soften your heart, replacing bitterness with his peace and love.

Reflect on moments of mercy from the previous day. Whether they were extended to you or by you, let these memories fill your heart as you prepare for the day ahead. Allow these moments of grace to shape your attitude and interactions, reinforcing a mindset attuned to forgiveness and mercy.

By starting your day with this focus, you cultivate a mindset that is more resistant to bitterness and more open to the transformative power of God's grace. Each morning becomes an opportunity to reset and renew, ensuring that you move through your day with a heart attuned to the presence and work of God in your life.

PRAYER

Lord of Mercy, I thank you for your unending grace that covers all my faults. Help me to release my guilt and embrace the grace you freely offer. Let your spirit of forgiveness permeate my heart, teaching me to forgive myself as you have forgiven me. Remind me daily of your love, which does not keep a record of wrongs but renews and restores. Let this knowledge mold me into an instrument of your grace, extending mercy to others. In Jesus' name, amen.

CHAPTER 8

RUNNING RAMPANT

From Indulgence to Temperance

King Solomon, however, loved many foreign women besides Pharaoh's daughter—Moabites, Ammonites, Edomites, Sidonians and Hittites. They were from nations about which the LORD had told the Israelites, "You must not intermarry with them, because they will surely turn your hearts after their gods." Nevertheless, Solomon held fast to them in love. He had seven hundred wives of royal birth and three hundred concubines, and his wives led him astray.

—1 KINGS 11:1–3

I encountered the phrase *running buck wild* in my midteens and it made a definite impression. It was more than just a local saying; it epitomized a full-on Southern experience, summoning me to live dangerously. As a teenager eager to escape the confines of my religious upbringing, those three words felt like a thrilling invitation.

There was just one problem.

I wanted to follow Jesus *and* run buck wild.

For some reason, those two approaches seemed to mix like oil and water, creating a conflict within my young soul, a conflict familiar to every teenager instructed to "run from anything that stimulates youthful lusts."[1] At the time, I did not realize that the desires awakened in my adolescence would not simply be quieted by living with reckless abandon or by fleeing from lust; they would need to be confronted and addressed repeatedly throughout my lifetime.

This journey stretched across the horizon of my adult years, and I knew it would be long and grueling. There were periods when my stride was effortless, buoyed by an effervescent grace. Yet there were also times when I ran with the determination of one pursued by the relentless hounds of youthful desires.

Throughout this journey, I learned to appreciate the gift of pleasure in its proper context without allowing it to consume me. Indulgence promises satisfaction but often leaves us emptier than before; it makes us restless, always on the move, like a shark searching for its next meal.

Perhaps you've paused at that last paragraph, questioning my word choice.

Did he actually mean "pleasure"?

Is pleasure a gift?

For what purpose?

It's common for some Christians to conflate pleasure with sin, mistakenly believing the two to be synonymous. This perspective is both incorrect and harmful to our spiritual formation, because it compels us to reject things we recognize as good and pleasurable. By requiring ourselves to shun beauty, wonder, and pleasurable sensations, we risk severing our connection with the essence of God's creation, which is permeated with joy and beauty meant for our enjoyment and well-being. Such misalignment can lead to spiritual dysfunction, where we become incapable of appreciating or acknowledging the goodness in life that God intends for us. This impairment hinders our ability to live fully and love freely, diminishing our spiritual and emotional health.

But the truth is that pleasure, when experienced within the boundaries God has set, can be a divine gift that enriches our lives. This understanding challenges us to rethink and perhaps even redefine our relationship with pleasure, recognizing its rightful place as part of God's good creation.

Everything within our hearts is programmed to enjoy the pleasures God has provided for us, and we resonate with him when we see, hear, taste, touch, or feel them. Whether

> PLEASURE, WHEN EXPERIENCED WITHIN THE BOUNDARIES GOD HAS SET, CAN BE A DIVINE GIFT THAT ENRICHES OUR LIVES.

it's a beautiful piece of art, a breathtaking sunset, or the explosion of flavor on our tastebuds when we bite into a juicy mango, the world is filled with good pleasures created for nothing more than our enjoyment.[2]

We don't need thousands of tastebuds, the ability to enjoy music, or the capacity to see the color spectrum for survival; these exist for our pleasure. Likewise, the world doesn't need more than ten thousand bird species and four hundred thousand types of flora except for our enjoyment.

One serene afternoon beside the Luangwa River in Zambia, my wife and I observed 104 bird species, each adorned in a stunning array of colors. Among our sightings were birds with zebra-striped bodies and vivid, fuchsia-colored heads, others with wings that shimmered iridescently like mother-of-pearl, and some that seemed like fluttering rainbows. The God who delights in all that is good and pleasurable isn't content with drab gray birds.

In the beginning, a good God created a good world and placed a good man and woman in it to enjoy its goodness.[3] God intended for us to find pleasure in all he has provided and to steward it for his glory.

REDEEMING PLEASURE

In his book *Redeeming Pleasure*, Jeremy Jernigan frames the issue this way: "When discussing pleasure, we must look at it from a balanced view, careful to explore its nuanced pros and cons. Our culture has turned *pleasure* into a highly charged word. For some, it's sexual, bringing up the ideas of sensuality and debauchery. That's often combined with a healthy dose of shame and guilt. For others, it's unattainable, no matter how badly you want it. These people conclude that life wasn't designed for us to enjoy it. For others, it's misleading and never materializes when you expect it."[4]

I think Jeremy is right, and I would add that some people also limit their pleasure to what they consider to be sacred practices, such as worship, prayer, fellowship, and Bible study—perhaps even extending to activities such as gardening. This conditioning leads them to find joy exclusively in these areas and often to viewing the enjoyment of more secular pleasures as inappropriate. This restrictive view limits the full experience of all that God created for our pleasure, which can also be embraced within a healthy, spiritual life. If gardening can be pleasurable, so can food sourcing, culinary preparation, coffee drinking, and wine tasting. These gastronomic delights offer us the chance to savor God's provisions in their myriad forms. If we accept these pleasures, then it is a small step to embrace other sensory enrichments such as decorating our dining spaces and enjoying music during meals. These activities enhance not only our enjoyment of the food but also the overall experience, making each meal a celebratory act of gratitude.

The biblical perspective makes clear that God created all people with the capacity to enjoy life and its many pleasures. He does not oppose pleasure; rather, his concern is with pursuits of pleasure that lead to sin. This distinction is necessary for understanding the role of pleasure in a faithful life: it is the pursuit of pleasure at the expense of our spiritual lives that is discouraged, not the experience of pleasure itself. So pleasure, when enjoyed within the boundaries of a moral, ethical, and spiritual framework, aligns with God's intentions for human fulfillment and joy.

As Solomon once put it, "Go, eat your food with gladness, and drink your wine with a joyful heart, for God has already approved what you do."[5]

No biblical character exemplifies the paradox of pursuing God while running buck wild like Solomon does. Although the Bible does not specify his age, context clues suggest that King Solomon was likely in his mid- to late teens when he ascended the throne, which meant his hormones were primed to surge through his body at any given moment. Despite his commitment to God's ways, Solomon was also driven by needs and desires. These desires, including his sensual cravings, became more pronounced as he matured, shaping his reign and his legacy.

FOOTSTEPS OF SOLOMON

Solomon's run is unlike that of the other biblical characters we've explored thus far. Unlike those who ran from threats or adversaries, Solomon was not seeking to escape anything. Rather, he passionately pursued everything he desired: wealth, wisdom, pleasure, satisfaction, adventure, knowledge, and power.

Shortly after ascending to the throne, Solomon had a pivotal dream in which God offered him anything he desired.[6] Reflecting on the immense responsibilities of his new role, Solomon requested a "discerning heart to govern [God's] people and to distinguish between right and wrong" rather than asking for wealth or long life.[7] Pleased with Solomon's selfless choice, God not only granted him the wisdom he sought but also bestowed upon him wealth and honor far beyond that of any other king of his time. This early decision highlighted Solomon's initial commitment to wise and just leadership, setting the stage for the golden age in Israel.

Despite a promising start, Solomon's early reign, marked by wisdom, wealth, and honor, gradually gave way to less noble pursuits. Initially committed to leading with discernment and devotion, Solomon shifted his focus as his quest for knowledge, excitement, and worldly pleasures overshadowed his pursuit of wisdom. The Scriptures detail his plunge into indulgence, portraying his wealth with metaphors as abundant as stones in Jerusalem. This descent is exemplified by his monumental projects, such as building his palace, which took thirteen years to complete—significantly longer than the seven years spent building the temple—reflecting a shift from spiritual devotion to personal glory.

Furthermore, Solomon's extensive marriages, totaling seven hundred wives and three hundred concubines, initially served as political alliances but ultimately entangled him with numerous foreign deities, leading him astray from his monotheistic roots. This indulgence, and the construction of altars for these deities, illustrates his journey from a wise king to one consumed by worldly desires, culminating in a spiritual crisis. His story serves as a reminder of the perils of losing sight of one's foundational beliefs amid the pursuit of earthly pleasures.

SOLOMON'S IDOLS

Idolatry, in both its literal and metaphorical forms, was central to Solomon's spiritual decline, and it continues to be a stumbling block for many spiritual leaders today. As I write this chapter, news of another prominent pastor stepping down amid allegations of sexual misconduct has just broken. This pattern seems persistent and, regrettably, I anticipate that similar incidents will continue to emerge. This recurring issue disturbs me, reflecting a crisis within the pastoral community. Repeated moral failures undermine the integrity of church leadership and cast a long shadow over the affected families and congregations.

While Solomon's idolatry was tied up in foreign wives, wooden gods, and unholy temples, spiritual leaders today often succumb to a different kind of idolatry—the idolatry of ministry, the idolatry of success, the idolatry of their personas and ambitions. We worship the constructs of achievements and recognition.

We make our idols, and then our idols break us.

Solomon's story of indulgence and spiritual decline offers a cautionary tale. This warning is not just for spiritual leaders. For the business professional, it serves as a reminder that success, when it becomes an idol, can lead one away from ethical practices and personal integrity. For the young parent, it warns against idolizing our children above the worship of God. Similarly, a student should see in Solomon's story a warning about the perils of prioritizing achievements or social standing over learning and character development.

> WE MAKE OUR IDOLS, AND THEN OUR IDOLS BREAK US.

The risk is the same in each case: whether in academia, business, relationships, or any other field, sacrificing our core values for fleeting gains can lead to serious personal and professional consequences.

The decline starts when we permit small indulgences into our lives, those seemingly minor things we know aren't healthy, yet we justify them by thinking, "I work hard and deserve a reward for the sacrifices I've made." This rationalization can lead us down a slippery slope, gradually eroding our souls and leading us away from our values.

The metaphor Solomon uses in his later years—"Catch for us the foxes, the little foxes that ruin the vineyards"—encapsulates this concept.[8] In the Scriptures, the vineyard is a metaphor for provision, a metaphor for a flourishing life, and the "little foxes" are the minor allowances, the small indiscretions, the hidden indulgences that can compromise one's spiritual life and leadership. Don't deceive yourself into thinking the little foxes are not a big deal; they are. This metaphor serves as a warning to guard against small transgressions that erode the foundation of one's character and, by extension, one's influence and legacy.

How many little issues are you ignoring because they seem like minor indiscretions, not major infractions?

Little foxes destroy big vineyards.

HALT

Another adage relevant to Solomon and to us is "Heavy is the head that wears the crown."[9] Leadership involves making major decisions that can be both exhausting and isolating. This is evident in Solomon's life; despite his numerous wives and concubines, he seems to lack fulfilling relationships.

Solomon's story prompts us to consider whether any leader, regardless of their power or following, ever feels truly understood or known on a personal level. This is particularly relevant for pastors, who, despite being in the public eye and surrounded by congregants, often experience painful loneliness, their struggles invisible to the communities they lead.

Beyond idolatry, indulgence, and isolation, many spiritual leaders fall because of their woundedness. Being wounded is part of the human experience, but handling these wounds is critical, especially for leaders. Neglecting them can allow them to worsen, negatively affecting life and leadership.

The recovery community uses the acronym HALT (hungry, angry, lonely, tired) to identify states that increase vulnerability to temptation. This concept encourages pausing to assess feelings and address the root of cravings. The principle is valuable for pastors and spiritual leaders who face significant temptations and challenges. By applying the HALT checklist, they can identify and manage these vulnerable states before they lead to severe issues such as idolatry, indulgence, isolation, and emotional wounds.

The wordplay between our susceptibility to sin when we ignore the HALT danger zone and the way that sin halts our lives when we succumb is obvious. When leaders sin, the fallout spreads to their congregations and families, leading to broader church disillusionment and decline. Solomon's decisions impacted all of Israel; his lavish lifestyle and policies, such as heavy taxes and forced labor, led to national discontent and division, illustrating how personal actions can drastically affect community well-being.[10]

CHASING THE WIND

If we had only historical accounts of King Solomon's reign, his fame might not reach the heights it does today. Thankfully, like his father, Solomon also recorded his thoughts and prayers.

His writings in Proverbs and Ecclesiastes give us insights into Solomon's heart, and perhaps our own as well.

Solomon had unparalleled wealth and resources. He led a life of indulgence beyond anything most of us can imagine. His existence was marked by a relentless pursuit of everything the world had to offer. From wealth and wisdom to pleasure and power, Solomon chased after these things with a fervor that suggests he was trying to outrun something deeper within himself. This was Solomon running from his inner pain, trying to fill the void with external achievements. And yet even Solomon grew weary. His pursuit of pleasure failed to satisfy and led to a discouraging soul-exhaustion.

In the book of Ecclesiastes, Solomon's reflections reveal the futility of his pursuits. "'Meaningless! Meaningless!' says the Teacher. 'Utterly meaningless! Everything is meaningless.'"[11] Despite achieving more than any king before or after him, Solomon concluded that his pursuit of fulfillment through pleasure was empty and unfulfilling. "So I came to hate life because everything done here under the sun is so troubling. Everything is meaningless—like chasing the wind."[12]

Solomon's story serves as a reminder that running from our pain through indulgence leads only to emptiness. Like Solomon, we must turn toward God to find the refuge and rest our souls seek.

THE PURSUIT OF PLEASURE

This tension between enjoying earthly pleasures and pursuing God isn't unique to Solomon; it is a timeless challenge, especially for those raised in a legalistic religious environment. Growing up in such conditions forces us to navigate the conflicting paths of desire and guilt, striving to reconcile our natural human inclinations with God's expectations and constantly feeling like we are falling short.

One of the best books on ordering our desires is by my friend and former professor A. J. Swoboda. In *The Gift of Thorns*, he writes,

> There are times when it's good to hope, with the psalmist, that God will give us the desires of our heart (Ps. 37:4). But there are also times when the desires of our heart are distorted and untrustworthy and deathly to their end. The Christian way isn't the uncritical pursuit of our desires *du jour*. No, the Christian call is to follow the one who made us out of his desire and gave us our own.
>
> Unresolved questions tumble around inside many of us. Which desires do we obey? What longings should be crucified? Which are good? Or bad? What about those deep, cavernous, hidden, sometimes unspoken, churning, burning, unquenchable, and all-too-often unwanted cravings that we spend much of our lives forced to live alongside? We must open ourselves up to this kind of interrogation because, in the end, our relationship to desire shapes everything in the temporal and everlasting.[13]

Managing this tension effectively involves understanding that Christianity does not require us to forsake all earthly pleasures; instead, it encourages us to enjoy these pleasures in ways that align with our spiritual values. As we reflect on this truth, the apostle Paul's statement to the Romans is pertinent: "Blessed is the one who does not condemn himself by what he approves." This perspective helps us seek pleasures that enhance rather than detract from our spiritual lives, guiding us to make choices that promote both personal satisfaction and spiritual growth. By adhering to this principle, we can enjoy life's pleasures in moderation, trusting that they will contribute to our spiritual formation.

The pursuit of happiness holds a significant place in American cultural identity, yet the church has approached the pursuit of pleasure with caution, contention, and even apprehension. Historically, Christian thought has wrestled with the notion of pleasure, influenced by philosophical doctrines like Platonic dualism, which viewed the body and its desires with skepticism. This philosophy posited that the body and spirit are distinct, promoting the denial or even mortification of the body to achieve spiritual ascendance. These ideas influenced early Christian perspectives, portraying pleasure as a realm to be carefully managed or avoided rather than embraced.

Then in the fourth century, Augustine of Hippo brought a new understanding of pleasure to the church. His autobiographical work *Confessions* traces his story from a hedonistic young man indulging in the pleasures of the flesh to one totally devoted to God. He honestly recorded how he struggled between earthly and spiritual desires in his prayer, "Give me chastity and continence, but not yet."[14] Ultimately, Augustine realized that fulfillment and joy are found only in a deep, abiding relationship with God. This epiphany is at the heart of his famous statement, "You have made us for yourself, O Lord, and our heart is restless until it rests in you."[15]

The medieval period saw Christianity adopting a more ascetic stance, with figures such as Thomas Aquinas offering nuanced views on pleasure. Aquinas acknowledged that pleasure is a natural part of human experience but must be aligned with divine law. He wrote, "No man can live without joy. That is why a man deprived of spiritual joy goes over to carnal pleasures."[16] This perspective brings balance, showing us that while pleasure is not inherently evil, it must be tempered by moderation.

The Reformation introduced new dimensions to the Christian understanding of pleasure. Martin Luther, breaking away from the asceticism of monastic life, advocated for the enjoyment of life's pleasures as gifts from God. He famously asserted, "God does not want knuckleheads to be in his kingdom; this is why he took away reason from them. For God likes seeing us enjoy what he has created."[17] Luther's perspective reflects a shift toward seeing earthly pleasures as part of God's blessings, provided they are enjoyed within the bounds of Christian moderation and thankfulness.

The relationship between Christianity and the pursuit of pleasure continues to evolve in the modern era, influenced by diverse cultural, social, and theological currents. C. S. Lewis articulated a view of pleasure that integrates joy with a Christian vision of the good life. He suggested that pleasures are not to be embraced or shunned uncritically but understood as signposts to the divine: "Pleasures are shafts of the glory as it strikes our sensibility. But they are not the thing itself; they are only the scent of a flower we have not found."[18] Lewis's metaphor captures the contemporary Christian endeavor to reconcile pleasure with a deeper pursuit of spiritual fulfillment.

Lewis sums it up when he says, "God cannot give us happiness and peace [and pleasure] apart from himself because it is not there. There is no such thing."[19] This perspective is closely aligned with that of Charles Simeon, who emphasized the dual lessons for Christians: "to enjoy God in everything and to enjoy everything in God." Both thinkers embrace a theology that intertwines enjoyment with spirituality, suggesting that true happiness and fulfillment derive from an appreciation and reverence for God's provision and presence in all aspects of life.

We can enjoy the pleasures of life without being corrupted by them—or fearing corruption from them. Pleasure is not our adversary, it's our ally in celebrating the divine gifts of everyday life.

CHRISTIAN HEDONISM

More recently, the concept of "Christian hedonism," proposed by John Piper, has gained considerable traction within various Christian circles. When I first encountered the term *Christian hedonism*, I must admit I was a little alarmed. *Okay, a lot alarmed!* The idea of aligning hedonism, a philosophy traditionally linked to the unchecked pursuit of pleasure, with Christianity was startling. In my view, *hedonism* was closely associated with lust, and to be clear, there is no redemptive value in lust whatsoever.

Lust is voracious, all consuming, satiated only in fleeting moments and never truly satisfied. It objectifies the image of God and cannot be justified under any conditions. It must be crucified and replaced with something far more satisfying. When I was a teenager wrestling with the allure of running buck wild, I thought my only option was to white-knuckle it through moments of lustful temptation. As a youth, I spent countless hours fasting and praying that God would make me dead to temptation. Somewhere along my journey, I learned a better way; instead of feeding my lust and giving in to its demands or living dead to my passions, I ran to the only one who could satisfy my inner longings. Ultimately, I learned to find pleasure in God and in what he provides for my enjoyment.

Fear is often used as a deterrent to prevent sin, particularly when addressing the consequences of infidelity. Warnings focus on the devastating impact of betrayal—broken families, damaged reputations, and the emotional pain inflicted on loved ones. While these cautionary tales may momentarily dissuade someone, fear alone rarely sustains moral integrity. For instance, the

Ashley Madison scandal, in which a website dedicated to facilitating affairs was hacked and its users exposed, revealed that
even the fear of discovery wasn't enough to stop people from
pursuing harmful choices. True change requires more than fear;
it demands a transformation of the heart. There is a better way.
Instead of battling sin with sheer willpower, imagine a life filled
with joy and meaningful connections where the allure of sin pales
in comparison. Cultivate satisfying personal relationships where
passion runs deep. Picture a marriage so fulfilling that betrayal
seems impossible, with a connection to your spouse that brings
joy and happiness.

Devote yourself to loving and serving your children, viewing
them as heavenly gifts. Embrace your vocation with such dedica-
tion that the temptation to cut corners disappears. This approach
isn't just about resisting temptation, it's about creating a life so
rewarding that wrongful desires lose their appeal.

Here lies a choice: will you build a life grounded in lasting
satisfaction that naturally repels evil, or will you spend your life
fighting against desires that secretly captivate you?

This brings me back to the concept of Christian hedonism.
Piper first presented this idea in his book *Desiring God: Meditations
of a Christian Hedonist*. Though the term may be provocative, it is
rooted in the notion that "God is most glorified in us when we are
most satisfied in him."[20] Piper argues that seeking pleasure in God
is not just acceptable but essential to Christian living, aligning
the pursuit of divine joy with the highest purpose of human existence. According to Piper, a Christian hedonist flees the lusts of
the flesh and finds lasting, abundant joy and satisfaction in God.

This pursuit of pleasure in God has a twofold effect: it brings
joy to us and glory to God. God desires our complete love and
yearning because this glorifies him, much like a chef derives
pleasure and recognition from the enjoyment people find in his

meals, an artist from the admiration of his paintings, or a musician from the appreciation of his music. In the same manner, God receives pleasure and glory when we find our greatest pleasure in him, when we find and enjoy him in every aspect of his creation.

We are given a choice: to seek pleasure apart from God or to seek pleasure in and through God. When we chase after pleasure according to our desires, we find it fleeting and diminished. But when we pursue pleasure according to God's design, our experience of it is not only preserved but amplified, offering a richer, more fulfilling engagement with the divine. This enriched pursuit emphasizes that contentment and joy are found not in the superficial but in a meaningful relationship with God.

> WE ARE GIVEN A CHOICE: TO SEEK PLEASURE APART FROM GOD OR TO SEEK PLEASURE IN AND THROUGH GOD.

The challenge we face in understanding Christian hedonism lies in the word *hedonism* itself, which typically connotes a selfish, indulgent pursuit of pleasure. But Christian hedonism redirects this pursuit toward something infinitely more fulfilling. By redefining pleasure as something achieved through spiritual fulfillment rather than worldly satisfaction, Piper's framework invites believers to a higher, more divine form of joy. This is not about rejecting pleasure but about recalibrating our understanding of where true pleasure comes from, directing our desires toward God, who is the source of all that is good and joyful.

This recalibration requires a shift in how we live. It calls for a focus on cultivating a relationship with God, seeing every moment and every interaction as an opportunity to experience and reflect God's love. This could mean finding God in the mundane, seeking him in the challenges, and acknowledging him in moments of joy. It is about recognizing that every good gift comes from above and seeing God's hand in every part of our existence.

I should sense the pleasure of heaven when I savor a slice of pizza, share my table with friends, laugh with family, tease my grandkids, bask in the sunshine, breathe in fresh mountain air, watch a sunset, stroll through the park with my wife, climb a mountain peak, stalk a dangerous animal with my bow and arrows, watch football, enjoy a concert, rest deeply, drink fine wine, and eat lemon squares. Likewise, you should experience the pleasure of heaven when you enjoy whatever it is that makes you smile.

A proper theology of pleasure challenges us to seek pleasure in God and to contribute to the joy and well-being of others. By deriving our pleasure from God, we are filled with an overflowing love that compels us to serve, give to, and care for others. This is not a burdensome duty but a natural overflow of the joy we experience in God. In this way, a theology of pleasure serves the believer and has the potential to impact the wider community, spreading joy and love in ever-widening circles.

PLEASURE SUBORDINATED

Enjoying pleasure is indeed a gift, yet, like all gifts, it must be cherished with moderation. Pleasure that demands too much from us ceases to be a gift and can become a distraction or a destructive force on our spiritual path. It can be a gentle servant or a harsh and demanding master. This is where the virtue of moderation becomes essential—not as a limit to joy but as a means to enhance and sustain it. Moderation helps us balance our indulgences, ensuring that our enjoyment contributes to rather than detracts from our spiritual and personal growth. It teaches us to savor each moment and each pleasure with a heart full of gratitude, recognizing them as God-given gifts to be enjoyed in harmony with his design for our lives.

When the pursuit of pleasure becomes our principal aim, we risk being led astray, diverting our focus from more significant pursuits like deepening our relationship with God and serving others. The proper perspective is not to chase pleasure for its own sake but to integrate it into a deeper commitment to God. In this pursuit, pleasure emerges as a byproduct of our devotion, not the primary goal. This shift in focus moves us from seeking transient delights to cultivating a lasting and fulfilling connection with God, enriching our lives with authentic joy.

Moderation is not about denying ourselves pleasure but about engaging with it wisely and purposefully. By managing how we experience pleasure, we ensure it remains a healthy part of our lives, enhancing our ability to live fully in God's grace.

> TEMPERANCE IS NOT ABOUT DEPRIVATION BUT ABOUT FINDING TRUE FULFILLMENT BEYOND EXCESS.

Temperance is not about deprivation but about finding true fulfillment beyond excess.

This shift in focus keeps pleasure in its rightful place as something to be experienced naturally through our engagement with God's love and grace. As we align our lives more closely with God's will, we experience the fullness of joy that comes from that alignment rather than the fleeting satisfaction of worldly pleasures. This deeper joy is more sustaining and fulfilling, enriching our lives and enabling us to be vessels of God's love and pleasure to others.

An honest reading of the Bible reveals that God has joy at the center of his plan for our lives. That joy is never at the expense of obedience, humility, and sacrificial living but rather the result of it. As King David proclaimed, "You will show me the path of life; / In Your presence is fullness of joy; / At Your right hand are pleasures forevermore."[21]

HOLINESS AND PLEASURE

In redefining our relationship with pleasure, it's crucial to recognize that its pursuit is not at odds with our spiritual growth. Rather, it complements and even enhances it. Leonard Sweet eloquently captures this concept in his reflections on holiness in *Designer Jesus*, viewing holiness not as a burden of strict adherence to commandments but as an expression of joy found in divine connection.

Sweet writes,

> Holiness is the ultimate pleasure zone. Holiness is not about getting better at doing what God commands us to do. Holiness is about getting better at enjoying God and pleasing God. True holiness is rapture, not restriction; wholehearted devotion, not dutiful obedience. True holiness seeks not to perfect performance for a divine audience, but to deepen intimacy with the divine presence. Pleasing God arises not from grimly following the rules, but from freely lavishing love upon Love itself. Holiness is thus the ecstasy of full presence—of being so engulfed in worship that analysis ceases. Like a kiss too pressing for thought, it is consummation beyond critique. In these timeless moments of rhapsodic reverence, we are fully known and adored by the Source who adores all creation. We rest in the romance of reciprocity. The false divide between sacred and sensual collapses. Holiness becomes celebrating the divine in the beauty of being.[22]

Sweet invites us to embrace a more joyful and vibrant spirituality where the pursuit of holiness involves engaging with the pleasures God has placed in our lives. He suggests that our spiritual practices should not merely fulfill obligations but be acts of love and enjoyment that draw us closer to Jesus. When we engage with our faith in this manner, every act of worship becomes an opportunity to experience the pleasure of being in God's presence.

Who wouldn't run to a holiness defined by pleasure?

Who wouldn't run from a holiness defined by displeasure?

King Solomon's life, rich with wisdom and folly, illustrates the critical need for moderation in this pursuit. His journey shows that without moderation, even the pursuit of holiness can lead to excesses that distract and detract from our spiritual objectives. Solomon's excesses eventually overshadowed his desire for wisdom and led him away from the pleasures that were meant to enrich his connection to God. His story is a reminder of the balance required to enjoy the gifts of life and spirit in a way that honors God and fulfills our deepest needs. As we learn to incorporate moderation into our pursuit of pleasure, we not only avoid the pitfalls of excess but also cultivate a more fulfilling relationship with God.

> WHO WOULDN'T RUN TO A HOLINESS DEFINED BY PLEASURE?

COMING HOME

Use the Sabbath as a sacred time to reflect on the pleasures that shape your life. As you enter this day of rest, ask yourself: Do the things that bring me pleasure draw me closer to God, or do they distract me from him? Are my sources of joy aligned with my spiritual values, or do they pull me away from the path God has set before me?

Choose one day each week to fast from a particular indulgence. This could be anything that consumes a significant amount of your time and attention—whether it's food, technology, social media, or another form of entertainment. Let this fast become an act of surrender, a way to loosen the grip that worldly pleasures might have on your heart.

Redirect the time you would usually spend on these activities. Instead of indulging, dedicate those moments to prayer, meditation, or reading Scripture. Allow the absence of these pleasures to create space for God's presence to fill. Engage in spiritual disciplines that deepen your connection with him, letting these practices strengthen your spirit and resolve.

Let the Sabbath be a time of spiritual realignment. As you fast, reflect on the role that pleasure plays in your life. Does it drive you, or does it invite you into a deeper relationship with God? Fasting teaches restraint, helping you gain control over your desires, and redirects your focus to the one who satisfies every need.

PRAYER

Father, help me to exercise restraint in the face of temptation and indulgence. Strengthen my resolve to pursue moderation and self-control rooted in your wisdom. May your Spirit guide my choices, helping me to live a balanced life that honors you in body, mind, and spirit. Teach me the discipline of self-restraint, not as a burden but as a liberating aspect of my spiritual journey. Enable me to find satisfaction and fulfillment in you rather than in the fleeting pleasures of this world. In Jesus' name, amen.

CHAPTER 9

RUNNING AGAINST THE CLOCK

From Fear to Urgency

"Go, gather together all the Jews who are in Susa, and fast for me. Do not eat or drink for three days, night or day. I and my attendants will fast as you do. When this is done, I will go to the king, even though it is against the law. And if I perish, I perish."

—ESTHER 4:16

From the moment I first experienced the Broadway musical *Hamilton*, I was captivated. The melodies, performances, and story line lingered with me long after the curtain fell. While I've watched it many times on streaming platforms, nothing compares to the electrifying thrill of experiencing it live on a big stage.

Last year, my wife and I were in London celebrating our fortieth anniversary when I saw a flyer on the street advertising *Hamilton*. We hadn't planned to see it again, but we couldn't resist. Although Lin-Manuel Miranda had hung up his boots years ago, the production was spectacular, and experiencing it in the company of a British audience brought out subtleties in the story line I had completely overlooked. Certain lines elicited roars of laughter from the Brits, reactions that were markedly different from mine, highlighting the diverse perspectives we hold on our shared history.

There is one scene in the musical that universally enthralls the audience: it's the song "Non-Stop." It resonates every time I've seen it, whether in New York, London, or right here at home in Arizona. There is a moment when the tempo picks up and the refrain urgently probes, "Why do you write like you're running out of time? Write day and night like you're running out of time. Every day you fight, like you're running out of time." When those questions start coming hard and fast, they are punctuated by sniffles throughout the audience and tissues are spontaneously produced to dry the tears.

> WHY DO WE DO EVERYTHING AS IF WE ARE RUNNING OUT OF TIME?

It's a valid question: why do we do everything as if we are running out of time?

I have met many fellow sojourners who feel they don't have enough time to go the distance.

Consider Ben, who, in a drug-fueled frenzy, threatened a family member with a weapon, engaged in a shootout with the police when they came to investigate, and went to prison, where he collided with the grace of God and surrendered his life to Jesus. After serving twelve years as a model citizen, he was released and eventually found his way to our church. He's starting over, but there are moments when he feels like he is running out of time because of the years he spent paying his debt to society.

Then there's Michael, who built a successful career based on co-sharing workspaces until the pandemic abruptly interrupted his industry and shut his company down. Overnight, his net worth plummeted and he was saddled with significant corporate debt. Now, in his late fifties, as he works to rebuild his financial life, he feels he is running out of time every single day.

Sherry is a neighbor who has spent her entire professional life in the banking industry, consistently pulling sixty-hour weeks as she climbed the corporate ladder. Along the way, she had two children she adores, but because of the demands of her work, she missed birthdays and family dinners and even left one vacation early because of a crisis in the office. Now that her kids are teen-agers, she feels she is running out of time to be the mom that she always longed to be.

From the opening to the final curtain, this urgency drives Alexander Hamilton just as it drives us. He was a man consumed by grand ambitions and an unending list of goals. His life was a whirlwind of constant motion—he never ceased moving, talking, or striving. Despite having no foreknowledge of his premature death at forty-seven, Hamilton lived as if every second counted, as if he were truly racing against time itself. The fear of running out of time compels us to accelerate our pace, as if by moving faster, we can slow the hands of the clock.

Fear and urgency often intertwine, creating a relentless drive that can lead us to feel like we are constantly racing against the clock. This frantic pace leaves us overwhelmed, exhausted, and disconnected from our purpose. In these moments, it's crucial to pause and reflect on where this sense of urgency stems from. Are we driven by a fear of failure, a desire to meet others' expecta-tions, or an internal pressure to achieve? Understanding the root of our urgency allows us to address it more effectively and find healthier ways to manage our time and energy.

I first read Virginia Brasier's poem "Time of the Mad Atom" in my early thirties and have carried these lines with me since:

This is the age of the half-read page.
And the quick hash and the mad dash.
The bright night with nerves tight.
The plane hops and briefly stops.
The lamp tan in a short span.
The Big Shot in a good spot.
And the brain strain and the heart pain.
And the cat naps until the spring snaps—
And the fun's done![1]

How many books have you read only halfway through?
Hopefully this isn't one of them!

How many projects have you abandoned because you under-estimated the amount of time it would take to accomplish them?

Remember back in 2020? When the COVID pandemic shut down the world, many of us entered quarantine thinking we would master a new skill, learn a new language, take up a new hobby, or write a book. Few of us did anything but binge-watch every available streaming service for months. *Present company included.* And when we were released from quarantine, we started running again.

The theme of running out of time strikes a haunting chord within us all, whether or not we actually have chronophobia. It's a universal dread, rooted in our souls, reminding us that our days are limited and urging us to chase our dreams before it's too late. It plays like a record stuck on a scratch, repeating the same line over and over.

Do I have enough time?

Do I have enough time to follow my dreams or is it too late?
Do I have enough time to get married, have babies, and
    watch them grow up?

Do I have enough time to build a second career and achieve some milestones?

Do I have enough time to fit in that last trip before the kids leave home and start their own families?

Do I have enough time to see my grandkids grow up and enter the world?

Time anxiety manifests in a number of ways, from feeling as if we are always running late, to feeling uncertain about whether we have what it takes to reach our dreams, to our discomfort with aging, to living with regret because of opportunities that have passed us by.

I know that feeling.

The first line of this book is "I was born running." From my earliest moments, I have lived with the sense that one life is not long enough to accommodate every dream, visit every destination, experience every adventure, reach everyone with the gospel, build something that impacts the world, raise a family, and leave a legacy.

I graduated from high school at seventeen and went to college.

I met my college sweetheart, and we got married less than a year later.

Did I mention that we "ran away" and got married? ·

Yes, we eloped. The full story is one for another time, but here's the summary: I went through the motions of asking for Judith's father's blessing, which he graciously extended. We posed for wedding photos and ordered invitations, but then some family tension developed over our choice of the officiant. When our families seemed hopelessly deadlocked, we eloped and got married at the justice of the peace. It was 10:00 on a Monday morning! We had no one to bear witness, so the justice's assistant went to the bar next door and pulled out two guys who signed our marriage license. *Yes, they were in a bar on Monday morning!*

I ran through my twenties, planting two churches and starting a family. I ran through my thirties, preaching the gospel in fifty countries. I ran through my forties and fifties building churches, growing and expanding them, traveling to fifteen more countries, and trying to be present to my wife and kids.

At this stage of life, as I write this sentence on the cusp of turning sixty, I feel that same internal drive, although it kicks in later in the morning and ends earlier in the day! I am running to rebuild our church after the events of the pandemic,

> LET FAITH, NOT FEAR, SET YOUR PACE IN THE RACE AGAINST TIME.

the unresolved racial dynamics in our community, the political divisions in our nation, and our withdrawal from a global church (which I've written about elsewhere[2]). And yet, despite the urgency I live with daily, I feel something else, something comforting and reassuring.

For the first time in my life, I truly believe I have enough time to do everything God has planned for me to do.

And so do you.

Let faith, not fear, set your pace in the race against time.

FOOTSTEPS OF ESTHER

The book of Esther begins with King Xerxes throwing a lavish party for all his nobles, officials, and military leaders. The lead-up to this party is intense: For a full 180 days he displays the vast wealth of his kingdom and the splendor and glory of his majesty. Then the king holds a seven-day-long banquet where the wine flows freely as he revels in his riches and power.[3]

After a week of festivities, King Xerxes seeks to flaunt yet another of his prized possessions—his beautiful wife, Queen Vashti.[4] But Vashti defies his orders, refusing to be paraded as a trophy before his inebriated guests.[5] Humiliated and feeling disrespected, Xerxes sees his authority undermined. Having spent the previous six months showcasing his wealth and power, he finds himself unable to command obedience from his own wife. In a fit of anger and desperation to reclaim his prestige, Xerxes makes a drastic decision. He banishes Vashti, strips her of her royal title, and effectively ends their marriage, asserting his dominance in a public display of authority.[6]

Once Xerxes' fury subsides, he decides it is time to acquire a new queen.[7] He sends commissioners out to every province of his realm to find the most beautiful women in the land and bring them to his palace. There they undergo twelve months of beauty treatments until they are considered attractive enough to be paraded in front of the king. They have to do what Queen Vashti had refused to do—come at the king's command and be ogled and judged on their appearance alone.

We tend to romanticize these events as though this were a massive Miss America pageant or an extreme version of *America's Next Top Model*, where the prize was marrying a king. But this was essentially human trafficking. Jewish tradition holds that Esther hid from the king's commissioners for four years because she did not want to be queen. Of course, she was eventually caught and brought to the king's courts and forced to be the queen, but it is important to remember that Esther had no agency and was not a willing participant in her marriage. The king was more attracted to her than the other women in his harem, and so she was elevated to the role of queen.[8]

We know very little about Esther's background before she entered the king's court. All that Scripture tells us is that she had neither father nor mother and she was raised by her cousin Mordecai.[9] Throughout the book of Esther, Mordecai features multiple times, advising and guiding Esther. The first time this happens is when he tells Esther to conceal her Jewish identity from the king.[10] She follows his advice until she can't hold the secret in any longer.

Though the book of Esther spans only ten chapters, it brims with tense, action-packed moments akin to those in a dramatic TV series. After the banishment of Vashti, the plot thickens as Mordecai uncovers an assassination plot against the king.[11] He relays this to Esther, who informs the king, leading to the conspirators' execution.

In the next episode—excuse me, chapter—the narrative escalates as the king elevates Haman to a position of great power, commanding all to kneel and honor him. Mordecai's refusal to bow enrages Haman.[12] Unlike Xerxes, who merely banished Vashti, Haman plots a far more sinister revenge. His fury drives him to seek the annihilation of all Jews, vowing not to rest until Mordecai's people are wiped out.[13]

As part of his evil plot, Haman convinces King Xerxes to issue a decree that on a set date, everyone in his kingdom should kill the Jews and plunder their goods.[14] When Mordecai hears this decree, he responds by fasting, putting on sackcloth and ashes, and wailing.[15] Then he sends a message to the palace instructing Esther to beg the king to spare the lives of her people, even though approaching him without being summoned is punishable by death.[16]

Esther found herself in a position to make a difference, a position she had not sought, desired, or prayed for. Yet God had placed her there. Her role as queen was an unwanted grace. Perhaps, like Paul, she had prayed multiple times for her thorny circumstances to be removed.[17] But God did not take away her discomfort. Instead, he provided her with the grace to navigate her unwanted circumstances. There was a bigger plan in place; God had positioned Esther in a place of power "for such a time as this."[18]

When our fears drive us, we lose sight of God's perfect timing.

We can learn a lot from Esther's reaction to the clock. Despite the urgency of the situation, Esther does not let fear dictate her response. Instead of acting rashly, she pauses for three days to fast and pray, and asks others to pray for her. Esther knows she needs God's courage and wisdom to save her people, and she knows that she cannot face the situation alone.

God hears their prayers and intervenes in numerous ways. First, he gives Esther insight into how to approach the king. Second, he makes King Xerxes favorably disposed toward Esther. Then he gives the king a touch of insomnia.

> WHEN OUR FEARS DRIVE US, WE LOSE SIGHT OF GOD'S PERFECT TIMING.

The night before Esther's banquet, King Xerxes can't sleep, so he starts reading the history of his reign. This royal bedtime story includes the incident of Mordecai's uncovering the assassination plot. Upon realizing that Mordecai has never been rewarded for his actions, King Xerxes decides to do something special for him. The very next day, Xerxes gives Mordecai a royal robe, puts him on a royal horse, and parades him around the city. After a day of honoring a Jewish man, King Xerxes is in a good frame of mind to hear a request to save all the Jews.

At Esther's banquet, King Xerxes says, "Queen Esther, what is your petition? It will be given you. What is your request? Even up to half the kingdom, it will be granted."[19] Then Esther reveals her Jewish heritage and asks King Xerxes to spare her and her people. He immediately agrees, and in the last few chapters, every wrong is swiftly righted: the Jews are saved, Haman is executed, and Mordecai becomes second in command over the kingdom.

Though Esther had every reason to panic and react in fear, she refused to let the idea that she was running out of time dictate her behavior. Instead, she leaned into the wisdom of the previous generation and cooperated with God's timing.

TIME SCARCITY

The concept of time scarcity describes the feeling of being perpetually rushed or running out of time. This psychological perception stems from the belief that there isn't enough time to meet personal or professional demands, leading to heightened anxiety, stress, and a persistent sense of urgency. These feelings can significantly influence decision-making and negatively impact our well-being.[20]

The repercussions of time scarcity are far reaching, affecting economic decisions and social behavior. People who experience time scarcity might opt for high-cost loans or postpone necessary health checkups in their preoccupation with immediate pressures. High school graduates might elect not to attend college, fearing they won't have enough years to accomplish their dreams. This mindset can also lessen empathy and impair our ability to respond effectively to others' needs.[21]

I want to encourage you to face time scarcity with five simple words of reassurance. May these words calm the anxiety raging in your heart.

Time is on your side.

Those words may not be easy to accept if you are desperately running from disappointments toward your hopes, dreams, and longings. Yet they are true. Time is on your side because God has set a time for every purpose under heaven.[22]

This is an essential reminder, especially when we're young, bursting with dreams, and it feels like the future is an eternity away. Conversely, in the later stages of life, it may seem like all our opportunities are behind us. But whether you are twenty or seventy, I want you to embrace the truth that God has allocated exactly the time you need to achieve everything he has laid out for you to do. You do not need to live in fear or frustration, worried that time is running out. You do not have to spend every day striving to *achieve* what he intends for you to *receive* in his divine timing. Time is on your side because time is held in the hands of a loving and faithful God who also holds your life with tenderness and care.

For most of us, the ticking clock is an illusion, a figment of our imagination. We don't know how much time we actually have left—there's no looming disease or impending disaster dictating our days. This sense of urgency is purely psychological and, more often than not, unjustified. The psalmist teaches us to "number our days, that we may gain a heart of wisdom,"[23] not so that we will live in fear and frustration.

We find rest when we release our fears, surrender our striving, and trust the exquisiteness of God's timing.

GENERATIONAL LIFE CYCLES

The relationship between Esther and Mordecai is described in Scripture as that of cousins, yet interpretations vary. Some Jewish scholars suggest Esther was Mordecai's wife, while the first-century historian Josephus posits that Mordecai was her uncle. What remains clear, though, is that Mordecai was older than Esther and served as a trusted advisor whom she relied on for guidance.

Regardless of the exact nature of their relationship, the story of Mordecai and Esther vividly illustrates two generations working against time to save their people. Esther, young and thrust into challenging circumstances, and Mordecai, experienced and driven by a desire to safeguard his heritage, together navigated these tumultuous events.

Today we see a similar generational shift. Generation X is stepping into roles of authority, grappling with doubts about their capabilities, while baby boomers are driven by a sense of urgency to leave a positive legacy for future generations. When both of these generations are at their best, they partner with each other to bring about the greater good.

It's common to celebrate Esther as the pivotal figure in her story, but Mordecai's role was equally necessary. His encouragement, insistence, and investment were essential for Esther to take the bold steps she did. Their intergenerational bond and cooperation were crucial in averting disaster for their people.

So many younger people today need to hear Mordecai's message to Esther: "You are at the right place at the right time. This is hard, but you can do it. I know you don't want to be in this position and it will cost you something, but you are doing the right thing."

Mordecai invested in Esther. He gave her his time and attention and shared his wisdom and insight. Each younger generation craves and deserves that from the older generation. At the same time, Esther listened to Mordecai and followed his advice. This is how healthy generational partnerships are formed.

INTERGENERATIONAL RUNNING CLUBS

In the heart of Minneapolis, a unique running club called Stride Together exemplifies the power of intergenerational connection through sport. This club meets weekly at a community park, attracting a diverse group of runners ranging from enthusiastic toddlers and teens to spirited seniors in their seventies and beyond. Each session begins with stretching led by a retired physiotherapist who shares insights into maintaining joint health, followed by a run around the scenic park lake, with different tracks for various fitness levels.

Stride Together isn't just about running, it's about building relationships. After their runs, members gather for coffee and storytelling. Younger members are paired with older ones in a mentorship program called Pace Partners. Here the wisdom of experience meets the vibrancy of youth as stories from the older generation inspire the younger, and youthful energy motivates the elders. For instance, eighty-year-old George, a former marathon runner, shares tales of races run in distant lands, while fifteen-year-old Mia teaches him about the latest running apps and gadgets.

The club also organizes monthly community events, such as the Generations Relay. Each team comprises members from at least three different age groups, emphasizing cooperation across generations. These events are a highlight for the community and attract local media attention, showcasing the benefits of intergenerational activities.

Through these interactions, Stride Together illustrates the power of generational harmony, showing how sports can bridge ages and foster a community spirit that uplifts every member. It serves as a model for other cities, demonstrating that when generations run together, they move forward together, not just on the track but in every aspect of community life.

The church should be the largest, healthiest, and most enthusiastic running club on the planet. This concept isn't just about promoting physical health, it's about fostering a spiritual endurance that perseveres through life's challenges. By integrating the principles of intergenerational support found in running clubs like Stride Together, the church can create a dynamic environment where the wisdom of the elderly empowers the energy of the youth, and vice versa, cultivating a spiritually nurturing space for all generations.

In this spiritual running club, every member, regardless of age, contributes to the pace and direction of the church. The older generation brings wisdom, patience, and resilience learned through years of faith under trial, while the younger generation injects energy, innovation, and a connectedness to the ever-evolving world. Just as in a relay race runners pass the baton between them, a church that embraces this model passes down faith and values from one generation to another, ensuring that spiritual passion and community bonds remain strong. This encourages an active, not passive, faith that is constantly growing and progressing. This approach doesn't just build healthier individuals, it fosters a healthier, more vibrant community united by shared beliefs and the collective journey of faith.

THE FEAST OF PURIM

Once while in Israel, I drove toward Jerusalem as the sun set, bathing the city with warm, rich red-and-orange tones. It was the first night of the Feast of Purim, and the city was bursting with life and energy. The streets bustled with revelers, faces hidden behind masks, joyfully reenacting the story of Esther. Some among the crowd carried effigies of Haman, which were soon to be hung from trees and, in some extreme cases, set ablaze.

Caught in the festive spirit, a young girl dressed in a purple gown fit for royalty and topped with a tiny crown clutched her father's hand. He, in a flowing blue robe and a striking red hat, seemed to share her excitement. I watched them for two blocks as the slow pace of our car, in bumper-to-bumper traffic, matched their stride. Their body language, warm and genuine, spoke of a bond rooted in the rich soil of tradition and gratitude. Together, they demonstrated a picture of the enduring passage of faith from one generation to another.

In the story of Esther, there is another generational linkage that is often overlooked today but would have been evident to an ancient Jewish audience. The text introduces Mordecai as a member of the tribe of Benjamin and a descendant of Kish. This lineage is significant because King Saul also came from the tribe of Benjamin and was the son of Kish.[24] This connection implies that Mordecai, and therefore Esther, was not just a random figure in the Persian Empire but was linked to Saul.[25] This genealogical detail enriches the story, providing depth and a sense of historical continuity that might have resonated strongly with Jewish readers, reminding them of their heritage and God's enduring provision for his people.

Then when Haman enters the story, he is referred to as "the Agagite."[26] The word *Agagite* is used five times in the book of Esther but not seen anywhere else in the entire Bible. It means "the descendant of Agag." Agag was an Amalekite king who fought against King Saul. God told Saul to wipe out all of the Amalekites, including their livestock.[27]

But when God delivered the Amalekites into his hands, Saul disobeyed both commands. Saul killed almost all of the Amalekites but spared King Agag's life.[28] Also he killed only the weak or injured livestock and took the best of the sheep and cattle for himself.

This act of disobedience led God to reject Saul as king and paved the way for David to assume the throne. But the consequences of Saul's disobedience didn't end there. Five hundred years later, there was still hatred between the descendants of Agag and the descendants of Saul.

Now it makes sense why Haman's anger toward Mordecai sparked in him a desire to kill all the Jewish people. It was his chance to avenge his family. As if to make this extra obvious, Haman's plan included killing all the Jews and plundering their goods, just like Saul did to the Amalekites.[29]

Another part of Esther's story that we tend to gloss over is how King Xerxes reversed his decree. He could not simply repeal the command for everyone to attack the Jews on a certain day because an official edict could not be overturned. Instead, King Xerxes gave the Jewish people "the right to assemble and protect themselves; to destroy, kill and annihilate the armed men of any nationality or province who might attack them and their women and children, and to plunder the property of their enemies."[30]

So the Jewish people rose up to defend themselves and killed eight hundred men, including the ten sons of Haman, who were impaled on poles. Three times in the book of Esther we read that the Jewish people did not lay their hands on the plunder. Even though it took five hundred years, the Jewish people finally fulfilled the command God gave to Saul to kill the Amalekites and not touch the plunder.

Just as God gave the Jewish people five hundred years to fulfill his command, he also gives us countless opportunities to turn from our sinful ways and follow him. God reaches out to us in love, offering grace and forgiveness no matter how many times we mess up. As the saying goes, we never fail God's tests, we just keep taking them over and over until we get them right.

Esther and Mordecai's story is celebrated every year by the Jewish people on the Feast of Purim.

GOD AT WORK

Esther is the only book of the Bible that does not mention God. This has led some people to discredit it as a secular book or even to wonder why it's in the Bible. But God is at work throughout the story, overcoming darkness with light and overthrowing evil plots with divine providence.

Yes, sometimes we have to look a little closer to discover God within the story, but isn't that how our stories often feel?

As biblical scholar Michael V. Fox writes, "When we scrutinize the text of Esther for traces of God's activity, we are doing what the author has made us do. The author would have us probe the events we witness in our lives in the same way. He is teaching a theology of possibility. The willingness to face history with an openness to the possibility of divine providence, even when history seems to weigh against its likelihood, as it did in the dark days after Haman's decree. In this way, the book offers a stance of profound faith."[31]

WE DON'T HAVE TO FEAR RUNNING OUT OF TIME BECAUSE GOD IS IN CONTROL OF ALL OUR DAYS.

God is always at work even when we cannot see him, feel him, or understand his ways. The book of Esther reminds us of this truth and invites us to trust how God is working out all things for good, even in our darkest days. We can trust that God is with us even when everything is messy and nothing makes sense.

God is overcoming evil.

God is redeeming the world.

Our lives are the canvas on which God paints his masterpieces, subtly but surely.

No matter how urgent the situation, there is no need to fear, for God is with us always.

We don't have to fear running out of time because God is in control of all our days.

We don't have to run from our mistakes or unfulfilled longings because God has numbered our days aright.

COMING HOME

At the start of each week, perform a spiritual time audit. Track how you spend your hours each day, paying special attention to moments of unnecessary haste or unproductive anxiety about deadlines and commitments. Notice where your time is consumed by the pressures of urgency rather than the peace of God's presence.

Use this audit to reorganize your schedule. Reflect on the patterns that emerge and identify areas where you can create more space for rest and reflection. Reprioritize your tasks in a way that aligns with God's guidance, allowing his wisdom to direct your daily activities.

In prayer, invite God into your schedule. Ask him to help you prioritize your tasks, to remove the fear of missing out, and to instill a sense of peace and purpose in your routine. Let this prayer be an invitation for God to take the lead in your life's rhythm, aligning your pace with his timing.

This practice is about more than just managing time; it's about living in God's time. By regularly auditing your week, you mitigate the pressure of urgency and cultivate a life that is paced by grace rather than driven by stress. Let your schedule be a reflection of a heart that rests in the assurance of God's perfect timing.

PRAYER

Creator of Time, slow my hurried steps and quiet my racing heart. Teach me to trust in your timing rather than succumb to the urgency imposed by fear. Help me prioritize my days according to your guidance, finding peace in the knowledge that you are in control of all things, including time itself. Grant me the serenity to work diligently while also resting confidently in your perfect plan for my life. May my days reflect a balance of productivity and peace, knowing that you are the author of both. In Jesus' name, amen.

CHAPTER 10

RUNNING THE GAUNTLET
From Defiance to Delight

> But Jonah ran away from the LORD and headed for
> Tarshish. He went down to Joppa, where he found a
> ship bound for that port. After paying the fare, he went
> aboard and sailed for Tarshish to flee from the LORD.

—JONAH 1:3

I f I close my eyes, I can still see the flannelgraph that my Sunday
school teacher used to tell us the story of Jonah and the whale.
For those who missed that extraordinary moment in church history back in the seventies, some innovative person decided the
most compelling way to teach kids Bible stories was to use cutout
felt images of Bible characters that stuck like magic to a flannel
background. It was riveting technology for a kid raised in a home
without a television!

A generation later, when my own children were young,
their primary understanding of Jonah was shaped by *Jonah: A
VeggieTales Movie*, featuring characters like Bob the Tomato and

Dad Asparagus. This whimsical retelling introduced them to the biblical story through catchy songs and colorful, animated vegetables, making the ancient tale accessible and entertaining. As a result, they could recount Jonah's adventures with a mix of reverence and humor, which may not be unlike the original telling. Many theologians see Jonah as more of a divine comedy than a moody piece of biblical literature in the Minor Prophets.

As fun as those depictions are, neither could possibly reflect the drama in Jonah's story. I'm not sure Phil Vischer, James Cameron, or even Christopher Nolan could capture it on film. The tale's emotional currents and the existential dilemmas Jonah faces—his flight from God's presence and his grappling with God's kindness and mercy—are aspects that demand serious consideration of this little book containing a big message.

Thomas John Carlisle, the famed poet and Presbyterian minister, wrote, "I was so obsessed with what was going on inside the whale that I missed seeing the drama inside Jonah."[1] Many of us make that same mistake. There is a lot of compelling dramatic action in Jonah's story as he runs from God, gets caught in a storm at sea, is thrown overboard, and is swallowed by the great fish.[2] But the deeper issue is what was happening in Jonah's soul to disengage him from God's calling on his life.

THERE IS NOTHING THAT CAN SEPARATE US FROM GOD'S LOVE.

If we can understand why Jonah fled, we might also learn how to address what drives us to run from God's presence.

Even though none of us are called to ancient Nineveh, we are all called to something, to someone, to somewhere. God's plan for each of our lives involves making a difference in the world around us—ministering to the hurting, standing for justice among the oppressed, and sharing the love of Jesus with people far from him. Embracing this calling requires recognizing where God is leading us and summoning the courage to step forward, overcoming the fears that often hold us back, just as Jonah eventually did.

There is nothing we can do to escape God's love.

There is nothing we need to do to earn God's love.

There is nothing that can separate us from God's love.

Depending on the path we choose, that could be good news or bad news.

Just ask Jonah.

RUNNING FROM GOD

Have you ever run from God?

Have you ever tried to escape what you considered to be the narrow and uncomfortable confines of his will? Perhaps it was anger or fear that fueled your flight, or maybe it was the deafening silence from the heavens during times of turmoil that drove you away. Maybe life became too busy and overwhelming to fit your relationship with him into your packed schedule.

How far did you run into the shadows? There may have been fleeting moments, lost weekends, or years devoted to evading the sound of God's voice. You may have run long enough that you convinced yourself God had given up and wanted distance from you too.

In those times of fleeing, did you ever consider what it might take to step back into the light of God's presence? You may have thought that only through sweeping gestures of repentance, acts of penance, or dramatic declarations could you bridge the gulf. Perhaps you considered grand overtures—pledging church attendance every Sunday, reading Scripture from cover to cover, vowing never to run again. Or maybe the magnitude of such undertakings seemed too Herculean, and so you just kept running.

Here's a beautiful and simple truth: no matter how far or fast you've tried to run from God, he has been with you every step of the way. He has never left your side. Even if you feel distant from him now, God is closer than you could ever imagine—closer than the very breath you draw. He desires for you to find and know refuge and rest in him.

> HERE'S A BEAUTIFUL AND SIMPLE TRUTH: NO MATTER HOW FAR OR FAST YOU'VE TRIED TO RUN FROM GOD, HE HAS BEEN WITH YOU EVERY STEP OF THE WAY.

Driven by the unconditional love of a perfect parent, God relentlessly pursues us. Whether we are as lost as a prodigal or as resentful as an elder sibling, God never ceases to advocate for the return of his children. Continuously beckoning us to reconnect and commune with him, he remains steadfast in his pursuit of reconciliation.

Jonah is often called the runaway prophet. He wanted nothing to do with God's message and had no interest in being God's messenger, so he ran for his life. Yet God pursued him relentlessly. We all know how the story ended.

FOOTSTEPS OF JONAH

The book of Jonah is four chapters long, containing forty-eight verses and about thirteen hundred words. It takes only fifteen minutes to read, yet it tells us everything we need to know about God. Jonah's story opens a window into God's heart and reveals glorious truths about God's deep and abiding love for us.

The name *Jonah* translates to "dove" in Hebrew, a symbol

rich with significance in both the Old and New Testaments.[3] In the story of the flooding and renovation of the world, a dove plays an essential prophetic role.[4] Noah, whose name also means "dove," released the bird periodically to assess the postflood conditions; its failure to return signaled that it was safe to leave the ark. The dove, thus, served as a witness of the earth's recovery. One commentator says this is an image of the Spirit—that the Spirit could not find rest in the old world, but only in the new creation. Throughout history, the dove has been a witness of and an agent in the recreation of the world.

Jonah is the birdman, although he behaves more hawkish than dovish in his response to Ninevah.

In the early days of his prophetic ministry, Jonah had a successful track record of his prophecies coming to pass. He had prophesied that the king would greatly expand the borders of his kingdom.[5] When this occurred, it brought economic prosperity to the entire country and made Jonah quite the respected leader. He was popular and appreciated and, in the words of the kids, living his best life.

Everything changed when God called Jonah to Nineveh—a city he dreaded—to deliver a message he resisted. Abruptly, Jonah was shifted from spreading a message of prosperity among his beloved people to proclaiming judgment upon a people he despised. His response was to flee as far from his new assignment as possible.

Nineveh was the capital of Assyria, the most powerful empire in the world, located 550 miles northeast of Jonah's home. It was a magnificent and terrifying city situated along the banks of the Tigris River in what is modern-day Iraq. In recent years, archaeologists have uncovered the ruins of ancient Nineveh near the contemporary city of Mosul in Iraq.

The Assyrians had an unrivaled reputation for cruelty and

have been considered "as a terrorist state."[6] When their armies captured a city, they committed unspeakable atrocities and then commemorated them on inscriptions for future generations to see. These horrific crimes against humanity included such torture as skinning people alive, decapitation, mutilation, and piercing the chins of prisoners with ropes and forcing them to live in kennels like dogs.[7] Ancient records from Assyria boast of this kind of cruelty as a badge of courage and power.

Jews understandably harbored intense animosity toward the Assyrians. They despised their brutality, idolatry, and arrogance. Traditionally, prophets in Israel were sent only to the Jewish people. Although prophets like Isaiah, Jeremiah, and Amos occasionally issued prophecies concerning pagan nations, none were assigned to actually go to them. So for Jonah, a Jewish prophet, being sent to preach in gentile Nineveh was abhorrent, a lowly and degrading assignment.

Though Nineveh was a cruel and brutal city, it was inhabited by people whom God deeply loved.

Instead of going northeast to Nineveh, Jonah decided to run west to Tarshish, which is in modern-day Spain. *It seems like a good choice to me—the Spanish Riviera over an Assyrian torture camp!*

To complicate matters even more, the ancient Israelites were not seafarers, they were people of the land. According to Old Testament scholar Chad Bird, "Almost every OT reference to ships and sailing entails Gentiles in some way."[8] The exception is found with Solomon's ships of Tarshish, which were a source of his great wealth.[9] The sea was a place of chaos and danger, and it contained God-defying monsters such as Leviathan.[10]

God said, "Go east." Jonah said, "I'm going west."[11] There was a 2,500-mile gap between God's call and Jonah's desire. In many ways, Tarshish was the opposite of Nineveh. One was a big city full of enemies, while the other was a beautiful, exotic seaside town. As Eugene Peterson observes, Tarshish was a "far-off and sometimes idealized port."[12] It was "Shangri-la."[13]

Ironically, "Jonah uses the command of the Lord to avoid the presence of the Lord."[14]

To get to Tarshish, Jonah first had to go down to the port of Joppa to catch a ship. This is the first occurrence of the phrase "going down" in the book of Jonah, and it becomes a pattern in Jonah's life. He went down to Joppa,[15] down to the hold of the ship,[16] down into the sea,[17] and finally down into the belly of the great fish.[18] He kept descending into a dark place.

That is not merely wordplay. It is a description of what happens when we run from God's plan for our lives. Anything less than living in surrendered obedience is a step down from God's highest and best use for our lives. Now, that might not always be obvious to everyone around us, because we can live in luxury and still be living beneath God's plan for our lives. Conversely, we can live in poverty and still be living our best life. The quality of our lives is less about our circumstances and more about our interior state. Is our interior world aligned with God's will and ways?

Jonah sought to flee 2,500 miles from where God had directed him, yet the greater distance lay between his desires and God's will. Aware of both what he wanted and what God required, he faced the daunting task of aligning his will with God's. This required introspection and a surrender to God's plan, a process that could lead not just to acceptance but to delight in God's will. Instead of engaging in this inner work, Jonah chose to run, stubbornly clinging to his desires.

As Jonah watched the shoreline of Joppa fade into the distance, he may have leaned back with a sigh of relief, convinced he was escaping God's demanding call. But his temporary security was just an illusion. He was squandering his resources on a journey he would never complete.

How could he have not remembered the haunting and comforting words of King David:

> Where can I go from your Spirit?
>> Where can I flee from your presence?
> If I go up to the heavens, you are there;
>> if I make my bed in the depths, you are there.
> If I rise on the wings of the dawn,
>> if I settle on the far side of the sea,
> even there your hand will guide me,
>> your right hand will hold me fast.[19]

Is it truly possible to flee from God?

Where can we find refuge from the one who is our Refuge?

Why would we seek sanctuary from the one who is our Sanctuary?

Before long, the gentle rocking of the waves lulled Jonah into a deep sleep in the lower hold of the ship. As he rested peacefully, "Then the LORD sent a great wind on the sea, and such a violent storm arose that the ship threatened to break up."[20]

The terrified sailors began praying to their pagan gods, but when no response came, they resorted to casting lots to identify who was responsible for invoking this divine wrath. When the lot fell to Jonah, he confessed everything.[21] He then urged the sailors to throw him overboard to quell the storm. Initially reluctant, the sailors made every effort to navigate through the tempest, but as the storm intensified, they finally conceded.[22]

As soon as Jonah was thrown down into the sea, it stopped raging.[23] The sky went from stormy to sunny in an instant. While the sailors made vows to this powerful new God, "the LORD provided a huge fish to swallow Jonah."[24] We don't know how painful and terrifying that must have been for Jonah, but one thing is clear: his life had just gone from bad to worse. When Jonah decided to flee from God's calling, he probably thought that nothing could be more terrible than going to Nineveh. Jonah learned the hard way that it always costs more to resist the will of God than it does to submit to the will of God.

Tim Keller, in his book *The Prodigal Prophet*, explores "two ways of running from God" by contrasting the story of Jonah and the teachings of Paul to the Romans.[25] Keller points out that Jonah's story shows us "two different strategies for escaping from God." According to Paul in Romans, some people outright reject God and revel in sin.[26] Others stick closely to religious rules, thinking that they're doing what's right by knowing and following the law.[27] Yet Paul concludes that both those who blatantly sin and those who pride themselves on their piety are running away from God.[28]

Keller ties this concept to the parable of the two sons in Luke 15:11–32, where one son tries to break free by rejecting his father's values and squandering his inheritance, while the other son obeys every rule, but with a heart full of resentment. Keller explains that both sons are essentially doing the same thing: they're using different methods to keep control and keep God at a distance. This behavior reflects a deeper issue: a lack of trust in God's good intentions for us, leading to a relationship with him that's more about bartering than connection. Jonah embodies this struggle in the narrative, sometimes rebelling, sometimes obeying, but always wrestling with his understanding of God's will and his place in it.

Jonah was fully aware that he was defying God, and he recognized that his time in the fish's belly was a punishment for his disobedience. Yet, remarkably, he endured three days in the grim confines of the whale's digestive system before he finally called out to God for deliverance. This delay speaks volumes about Jonah's reluctance to submit to God's will and highlights the profound stubbornness of the human heart. His ordeal illustrates the extreme lengths to which we might go to resist divine direction, even when this resistance leads us into dire situations.

Jonah finally reached a point where he could offer the sincerest prayer possible: "Lord, help me!" This plea embodies true humility, devoid of negotiation or bargaining. It is an acknowledgment of powerlessness, a desperate cry from one who has reached his limits, and it is the kind of prayer that compels God to act.

> DESPERATION CAN BE A BLESSING IF IT TURNS OUR HEARTS TOWARD THE LORD.

Desperation can be a blessing if it turns our hearts toward the Lord.

In his brilliant examination of Jonah's prayer, Robert Solomon highlights the elegantly crafted poetry that Jonah uttered from the belly of the fish, despite his extreme distress. Solomon notes that the poetic nature of Jonah's prayer is enriched by its inclusion of lines from the Psalms, Israel's sacred songbook.[29] As Peterson notes, "Not a word in the prayer is original. Jonah got every word—lock, stock, and barrel—out of his Psalms book."[30]

In his state of anxiety, Jonah borrowed lines from David's lament, showing us two things: Jonah's heart was anchored in God's Word, and even in the depths of despair he had not succeeded in finding a place where God was not present.

When Jonah stopped running, the Lord delivered him from his distress.[31]

Covered in slime, he surrendered to the Lord's plan for his life.

Can the same be said of us?

After arriving back on the seashore, Jonah received God's

command to go to Nineveh a second time. Though still hesitant, he yielded to God's will.[32] Though he was initially defiant, Jonah's compliance in his darkest moment marked a turning point in his faith, but it was not enough. God wanted more than Jonah's reluctant obedience; he sought Jonah's heart, yearning for a deep relational connection with his stubborn prophet. Therefore, Jonah's story does not conclude there.

When Jonah proclaimed God's call to repentance in Nineveh, the Ninevites responded with humility, and God, in his mercy, forgave them.[33] Although Jonah's mission succeeded, he struggled with feelings of failure. He was angered by the kindness shown to the Ninevites, whom he viewed as undeserving and a continuous threat to Israel.[34] Even more, Jonah felt his prophetic reputation was compromised by what he perceived as God's excessive grace and reluctance to punish.

Having personally benefited from God's kindness, Jonah paradoxically resented its extension to the Ninevites.

How could you, God!

I wonder how many battles with God throughout history have begun with "How could you?"

How could you allow this?
How could you require this?
How could you expect this?
How could you demand this?

The story of Jonah concludes abruptly, leaving many questions unresolved. This contrasts sharply with the book of Esther, where God's presence is felt despite his name never being mentioned. In Jonah's case, the story ends with a powerful scene of God imparting wisdom to an obstinate prophet, underscoring the relentless nature of grace and mercy.

In conclusion, God made a plant grow over Jonah, and the shade brought him comfort. Then God sent a worm to attack the plant and make it wither. As Jonah mourned the loss of the plant, God sent a scorching wind and made the sun blaze down on his head. From his pain and anger, Jonah dramatically declared that he wished he were dead. Then God said, "You pity the plant, for which you did not labor, nor did you make it grow. . . . And should not I pity Nineveh, that great city, in which there are more than 120,000 persons who do not know their right hand from their left, and also much cattle?"[35]

In the final verse of the final chapter, God's heart shines through once again. He is revealed as gracious and merciful, slow to anger, and abounding in steadfast love. His compassion for the Ninevites, who live in what he calls that "great city," is on full display.[36] And as Chad Bird puts it, "Jonah is the patron saint of all those scandalized by the audacious mercy of a God who says, 'I forgive you,' when the world screams, 'Punish.'"[37]

God poured out his grace upon Jonah and Nineveh, just as he has abundantly lavished his grace upon us. We don't have to run from sin or judgment.

UNWANTED GRACE

Somebody once said, "Inside a fish isn't a great place to live, but it is a great place to learn."

Within the belly of the fish, Jonah spent three days in contemplation, slowly recognizing that he was not so much trapped by God's judgment as enveloped in his grace.

Judgment carries a sense of finality and abandonment, while grace represents God's persistent pursuit. Grace reaches out to our stubborn and rebellious hearts, offering another chance to surrender.

Jonah struggled with this. The grace he received was uninvited and unwanted, disrupting his life and steering it in an unwelcome direction, which left him resentful. Despite his being a prophet, his grasp of grace was incomplete. Grace is not about getting what we want, it's about being equipped for what God intends for us. It prepares us to thrive, even when it manifests through challenging and unwelcome circumstances. Sometimes the grace we resist most is what we need the most.

Unwanted grace is the call to be single when you want to be married, and the call to be married when you want to be single.

Unwanted grace is the call to care for a sick family member or to endure physical sickness yourself, while believing and waiting for a miracle to come through.

Unwanted grace is the challenge of serving in a place where you are not recognized for who you are while still maintaining love and compassion for those you serve.

Unwanted grace enables you to respond with a yes to God even when your flesh may scream no at him.

Unwanted grace is God's unwavering invitation for us to embrace risks greater than we ever envisioned, confront challenges bigger than we ever anticipated, and engage in battles more formidable than we ever could have imagined.

> ULTIMATELY, UNWANTED GRACE PRESSES US TO MAKE A CHOICE: DO I WANT TO BE LIKE JONAH OR JESUS?

Unwanted grace is the opportunity to become more than we ever dreamed we could become by becoming less than we ever wanted to be.

Ultimately, unwanted grace presses us to make a choice: do I want to be like Jonah or Jesus?

GREATER THAN JONAH

Having grown up in church, I can recall hearing more than one traveling evangelist tell the story of his conversion and calling into ministry using the Jonah metaphor: "I ran from God until he chased me down, broke me down, and called me to do something great for him." As interesting as those stories were, something in me questioned the virtue of running from God. I had no desire to run from him. As I mentioned earlier in this book, I ran from a long list of things that hurt, but Jesus wasn't on that list. He was my refuge, not my tormentor.

I was the kid at the front of the class holding his hand high saying, "Pick me, Jesus! Pick me! I'll serve! I'll go! Send me!"

Jesus was my role model, not Jonah. The one who said, "Father, I delight to do your will," not the reluctant prophet with a hardened heart, was the pattern for my life.[38]

Anyone can be a Jonah.

Anyone can run from a difficult marriage.
Anyone can run from an unfulfilling career.
Anyone can run from their responsibilities.
Anyone can run from someone else's need.
Anyone can run from a dying church in need of revival.

There's nothing hard about running away from what God wants from us. It doesn't take talent, discipline, sacrifice, or faith to flee. Running is the easiest thing to do. Seeking refuge in the security of God's will and ways is the harder work. But that's where lasting peace is found.

The safest place to be is *not* in the center of God's will.

Yes, I said it.

Yes, I mean it.

The will of God can be a dangerous place to be.

Just ask the prophets.

Just ask the martyrs.

Just ask Jonah.

Just ask Jesus.

The will of God is not the safest place to be, it is the *only* place to be.

Have you ever noticed the connection that Jesus has with Jonah? Jesus loved Jonah and referenced his story on more than one occasion. When Jesus refers to "the sign of Jonah" and describes himself as "greater than Jonah," he is drawing a parallel between Jonah's experience and his own mission of redemption.[39] Jonah, though inadvertently, became a sacrifice to calm the storm for the sailors, mirroring how Jesus would one day willingly give his life to save humanity. But there are significant differences between them. Unlike Jonah, who was thrown into the sea because of his disobedience, Jesus was sinless.[40] Jonah's ordeal brought him close to death underwater, whereas Jesus truly died and bore the weight of humanity's sins.

Just as Jonah spent three days and nights in the belly of the fish before emerging back to life, Jesus similarly lay in the tomb for three days and nights before his resurrection.[41] Following his deliverance, Jonah spent forty days preaching to the Ninevites, mirroring the forty days Jesus spent ministering to his followers between his resurrection and ascension.

The distinction between Jesus and Jonah lies in their responses to God's will. Jonah initially fled from God, resisting his command, before reluctantly obeying. Compliance, while better than defiance, is not God's desire for his children. God desires not just obedience but for his children to find joy in his will, as Jesus exemplified perfectly.

Jesus embraced his unwanted grace. He surrendered his will

to God. He willingly prayed, "Not my will but yours!" Jesus did not defy God's call, and he did not merely comply with it. Jesus delighted in doing the will of the Father.

We often think of Jonah's story as the story of a man swallowed by a great fish, when really it is a story of a man being swallowed by God's grace. This is unwanted grace summoning a man to do what he doesn't want to do. But that is the reality of grace.

Grace is invasive.

Grace is intrusive.

Grace makes demands upon us.

Grace empowers us to do great things.

And when everything is said and done, God's grace is always sufficient.[42] It is more than enough to strengthen us, to empower us, to enable us, to sustain us, and to delight us.

BACK-ROW BELIEVER

Tyler found his spot in the back row each Sunday, watching the congregation from a distance. He liked it there—close enough to hear every word, yet far enough to retreat into his thoughts. His love for Jesus was genuine, but unassuming, marked more by a quiet consistency than fiery zeal. Basketball was his real passion, and throughout high school, he dreamed of turning his varsity achievements into a college scholarship.

As graduation neared, Tyler's hopes for a basketball scholarship faded, but two academic scholarships came in, offering him options he hadn't considered. One was to the University of Arizona, two hours south, a fresh start far from everything familiar. The other was to Arizona State, just minutes from home. Tyler chose distance, eager for independence, but a persistent, quiet tug on his heart prompted him to reconsider before the school year began. It wasn't a dramatic revelation but a growing sense that perhaps there was more to his journey than escaping the familiar. Ultimately, he chose the scholarship closer to home, deciding to live at home for his first year of college.

That year, something shifted. The casual faith of a back-row observer began to deepen as he engaged more in his family's discussions about faith and purpose. And it didn't hurt that he met a beautiful young lady at church who loved Jesus and enjoyed sitting on the front row! Tyler's newfound engagement with his faith led him to transfer to a private Christian college for his sophomore year, where he not only played basketball but also completed a degree in business with a minor in biblical studies.

Today, Tyler is no longer the kid on the back. He stands at the front, leading our congregation as a pastor. His journey from casual believer to dedicated servant was marked not by a single, monumental event but by many small, faithful steps toward embracing God's call. I've had the privilege of witnessing first-hand how the quiet kid from the back row grew into a man who now pastors others, imparting the lessons he has learned from running to Jesus and not from him. I know his story well because Tyler is my youngest son.

JUST LIKE JONAH

Standing on the dock of the Jaffa fishing harbor near where Jonah may have embarked on his ill-fated journey to Tarshish, I recently felt a strange connection to his story. Before this moment, I had never been able to emotionally identify with Jonah because I had never seen myself as a reluctant recruit when it came to ministry. But standing on the dock under a full moon in that ancient seaport, the rolling waves before me inviting escape, I felt a moment of connection with what must have driven Jonah's heart as he sought to flee from his calling.

There are many reasons we run from God's will. Some of them are spelled out in Jonah's story, others I have seen in my years of pastoral counseling, and some I have experienced within my own heart.

Most Christians recognize the call to follow God and surrender to his will, yet living this out daily proves challenging. These are hard and difficult strides for many, even under the best of circumstances, and our day is far from ordinary. The path of self-denial often is marked not by a single sacrifice but by a thousand small surrenders along the journey. We might need to forsake our comfort and relinquish our desire for control. We might need to face our fears and tread unfamiliar paths. We might need to resist carnal temptations and address trauma that predisposes us to sin.

At the heart of every struggle to embrace God's will lies a struggle to understand God's character. Jonah saw God as too merciful. Many today perceive him as too vengeful, judgmental, strict. Yet the only one who ever followed God's will perfectly—Jesus—related to God as his loving Father. Jesus lived with the knowledge that he was God's beloved son, that God was pleased with him, and that he could trust in God's goodness and love. This confidence in God's character greatly facilitated Jesus' ability to align with God's will.

Reflecting on Jonah's journey underscores a vital lesson: our understanding of God shapes our response to his call. If Jonah had cultivated a more intimate relationship with God, recognizing him as compassionate and just, perhaps his story would have unfolded differently. This insight beckons us to deepen our own relationships with God, moving beyond seeing him merely as a distant authority to embracing him as a loving Father whose plans, though challenging, are rooted in his perfect desire for our welfare.

Jonah's story challenges us to reflect on how we view God's character. It asks us to consider whether we are resisting his guidance out of fear or misunderstanding. By aligning our perception of God with his loving nature, we can change our approach to his calling—from reluctance to eager acceptance, from fear to trust.

Responding to God's call on our lives may seem perilous, and the outcomes may be uncertain. Yet like Jonah, we are called not just to obey but to trust in God's great mercy and love. The more we grasp God's goodness, the less we will be inclined to run from God's call. We will be content to rest in his ever-loving arms, no matter where they carry us. Remarkably, we will find joy not in the absence of difficulty but in the presence of God, who walks with us every step of the way.

COMING HOME

Set aside a contemplative moment to explore your perceptions of God. Take a piece of paper or open a journal and draw a line down the middle to create two columns.

In the first column, write down your past perceptions of God. Reflect on how you've understood his nature and character throughout your life. Perhaps at times you've viewed God as demanding, distant, or punitive. Be honest with yourself—this is a space for uncovering the subconscious beliefs that may have shaped your relationship with him.

In the second column, contrast these views with how God is portrayed in this chapter. Note the aspects of grace, pursuit, and invitation that reveal God's loving and relational approach. Highlight how these characteristics differ from your earlier perceptions, focusing on the warmth and intimacy of God's true nature.

After completing this list, take time to meditate on each point of contrast. Consider the instances in your life when you may have resisted God's will out of fear or misunderstanding. As you meditate, allow the truths of God's character to reshape your heart and mind, moving you closer to an authentic relationship with him.

This practice is about rediscovering who God is. Let it be a step toward healing any misconceptions you've held and embracing the God who relentlessly loves and pursues you. By reflecting on these contrasts, you open yourself to a deeper, more genuine connection with the one who calls you by name.

PRAYER

Joyful Father, infuse my spirit with the delight found only in your presence. As I navigate life's challenges, help me to see the joy and blessings you place along my path. Turn my heart toward thanksgiving and celebration, and help me let go of defiance to embrace the abundant life you offer. Fill me with a spirit of joy that overflows to others, making my life a testament to the goodness and beauty of your grace. In Jesus' name, amen.

CHAPTER 11

RUNNING TO JESUS

From Disappointment to Hope

> *Early on the first day of the week, while it was still dark, Mary*
> *Magdalene went to the tomb and saw that the stone had been removed*
> *from the entrance. So she came running to Simon Peter and the other*
> *disciple, the one Jesus loved, and said, "They have taken the Lord*
> *out of the tomb, and we don't know where they have put him!"*
>
> —JOHN 20:1–2

I don't know whether you've ever noticed this, but on the greatest morning in human history—the morning when Jesus was raised from death to life, the morning when time divided and history split in two, the morning his disciples should have been gathered in a joyful celebration—everyone was running!

Mary was running.[1]

Peter was running.[2]

John was running, apparently faster than Peter, and he wanted us to know![3]

The disciples were running.[4]

The first Easter Sunday opened with an acute sense of disappointment. When the women disciples arrived at the tomb early that morning, they expected to find Jesus' body, to anoint him again, and to continue their mourning. Instead, they encountered the empty tomb, a bewildering outcome that contradicted their grim expectations and left them grappling with shock and disbelief. The absence of Jesus' body not only confounded them but also deepened their sorrow, as it seemed to rob them of closure. This unexpected turn of events stirred confusion and chaos among them as they struggled to understand what had happened. Their disappointment was not just about unmet expectations but about the unsettling reality that their understanding of death and promise was being challenged.

Yet it is in these moments of acute disappointment that Jesus' resurrection brings unparalleled hope. His triumph over death fulfills the promises of God and redefines our understanding of life and eternity. Through his resurrection, we are given a living hope, as Peter writes: "Praise be to the God and Father of our Lord Jesus Christ! In his great mercy he has given us new birth into a living hope through the resurrection of Jesus Christ from the dead."[5] This hope assures us that even in our darkest moments, God's redemptive power is at work, bringing new life and renewed purpose.

> DISAPPOINTMENT IS OFTEN THE PRELUDE TO GOD'S GREATEST REVELATIONS OF HOPE.

Disappointment is often the prelude to God's greatest revelations of hope.

I'm not one to lean on dictionary definitions in my writing or speaking—it feels a bit elementary, and if you've read this far, I'm confident you've made it through the third grade. That said, I do have a particular fascination with words prefixed by *dis*. This interest isn't just rooted in my college days, when "dissing" someone was the ultimate power move. I believe that words like *discouragement*, *disappointment*, *displacement*, *discontentment*, and *disillusionment* reveal insights through the emotions they stir within us.

I invite you to read that last sentence aloud.

It's hard to say those words without the air going out of your lungs.

The prefix *dis* robs those words of what they offer; it sucks the life out of courage, appointment, placement, contentment, and the illusion that things are going to turn out well.

Mary knew all the *dis* words too. Her life was marked by disappointment before she met Jesus, and after a couple of joyful years of following him, serving him, resourcing his ministry, and being spiritually formed by his teaching, she felt its familiar sting again. Disappointment served as the bookends of her relationship with Jesus.

Can you relate?

Has your story turned out as you had hoped?

Often when our stories don't turn out as we had hoped, we find ourselves reacting much like the disciples on the morning of the resurrection. We run, not necessarily from something but toward the hope of finding something to quell the disquiet within us. This response is driven by the human need to resolve uncertainty and make sense of events that defy our expectations and disrupt our plans.

Just as the disciples raced toward the tomb, we, too, use running to search out answers. *How can this be? Something must have gone wrong!* We exhaust ourselves with the demand to understand, driven by the circumstances that challenge our vision of how things should be.

This movement is often fueled by shock—a feeling all too familiar to us, whether in minor setbacks or life-altering events.

Disappointment can catch us off guard, confronting us with a reality that falls short of our expectations. It pushes us into motion, sometimes without direction, as we try to escape the discomfort of unmet expectations. Like the disciples, who were bewildered to find the tomb empty, we may discover that life's pivotal moments do not always go as planned, challenging our faith and expectations.

For many, disappointment isn't just a fleeting shadow, it becomes a relentless cycle. People find themselves caught in a loop where high hopes crash into harsh realities, leading to even deeper dissatisfaction. This emotional flywheel—cycling from hope to frustration and from dreams to disillusionment—defines their lives. Escaping this sequence is difficult as each disappointment reinforces the pattern, making it harder to imagine a different outcome.

Around and around, running the gauntlet of expectation and disappointment is exhausting. Despite our efforts to break free, the pattern repeats over and over again. After a while, we realize that our disappointment has taken on a life of its own, no longer responding to our usual ministrations. The Bible stories that once filled us with hope now feel boring and dry. The prayers that used to turn us toward God now seem pointless. The church that used to embrace us now seems overeager to fix us, reinforcing how lost and alone we feel.

Disappointment drives us into desperate actions as we strive to escape its grip. It can lead us into despair, convincing us that nothing will ever change, and keeps us constantly running. We might chase after what we hope will be a final, fulfilling achievement, not realizing that no accomplishment can satisfy. Alternatively, we might flee from the pain of unmet expectations and limitations, too frightened to confront our emotions.

Each cycle of expectation, limitation, and letdown draws

us further inward, blinding us to anything but our accumulating failures amid the ruins of our dreams. We may still speak of hope, like that promised by the resurrection, but without seeing its evidence in our lives, we risk losing the capacity to envision or strive for it.

On the very first Easter weekend, the disciples faced the worst disappointment imaginable. They had expected big things from Jesus. They expected big things *for* Jesus. In their minds, he was going to overthrow the Romans and usher the Jewish people into a golden age of power and prestige. He was going to vindicate their suffering. Their expectations reached a crescendo on Palm Sunday as Jesus rode into Jerusalem surrounded by shouts of "Hosannah! Blessed is he who comes in the name of the Lord!"[6] Finally, their king was going to assume his throne.

Those dreams crumbled when Jesus was arrested. Confusion and disbelief set in: *Why doesn't he resist? Why doesn't God intervene? Can this really be the end?* Hours later, their visions of power and influence shattered as Pilate washed his hands of the matter, sealing Jesus' fate on the cross.

Unable to face the depth of their disappointment, most of the disciples ran away, blinded by grief and lost in confusion. They could not bring themselves to watch Jesus begin the slow trek to his tortuous death. Their king had been conquered. With their entire world and all of their plans crashing down around them, the disciples were drowning in despair and disappointment.

Maybe you know these feelings well.

Our discomfort with the events of Good Friday cause many Christians to run as fast as possible from the crucifixion to Easter Sunday. We cannot bear the pain of Holy Saturday, so we run from it, trying to evade the helplessness of feeling in limbo. Something lurks in the shadows of the tomb that we are terrified to acknowledge, something that might brush up against our disappointment and uncover our well-hidden questions and doubts. It's even hard for most of us pastors to conclude a Good Friday service with anything less than, "It's Friday, but Sunday's coming!"

As Christians, we *are* called to keep our eyes focused on the resurrected Christ. We know the outcome of the story, and it is one of complete and total victory. This hope in the resurrection is at the heart of everything we believe, but not at the expense of learning to walk through the Silent Saturdays of life.

There was one disciple who didn't run on Holy Saturday, one follower of Jesus who watched them crucify her Lord, one woman who visited Jesus' tomb on Easter morning. While the rest of the disciples were too shrouded in their own sorrow to move toward Jesus, Mary Magdalene went to the tomb. She did not go singing, "Hallelujah!" She went led by a holy longing to anoint Jesus' body with spices and perfumes in an effort to delay decomposition.[7]

There in the garden, weeping by the tomb, Mary heard the Gardener call her name.[8]

In our moments of deepest sorrow, Jesus meets us with unshakable hope and resurrection power.

The last Adam reclaimed in the garden tomb what the first Adam had lost in the garden of Eden. In that moment, the despair of Holy Saturday gave way to the dawn of a new creation. God was remaking the world through Jesus. The brokenness of the past was met with the hope of new life, and Mary was the first to bear witness to his triumph over the grave.

FOOTSTEPS OF MARY

Mary Magdalene is one of Jesus' closest and most faithful followers, and she is mentioned more than a dozen times in the

New Testament. Yet despite her being a central figure in the Gospels, there is a lot we don't know about her. We know she was liberated by Jesus from seven demons, but that takes place before she makes her first appearance in the story.[9] In gratitude, she dedicated herself to following Jesus, supporting his ministry financially as he traveled and preached.[10] Mary stood by the cross as Jesus was crucified,[11] observed where he was buried,[12] and was the first to visit his tomb on the morning of the resurrection.[13] Notably, she was also the first to witness the risen Christ. This encounter, which we will discuss later in this chapter, culminates with Jesus "commissioning" her to share the good news with his other disciples.[14]

Jesus loved Mary as much as he loved his other disciples, and she plays a key role in his ministry despite her lack of visibility in the text. So why is the story of Mary Magdalene shrouded in mystery? Why do some people call her the apostle to the apostles, while others claim she was a prostitute? Why have some even mistakenly identified her as Jesus' wife? From popular fiction to renowned religious research, there are plenty of different opinions about Mary Magdalene. She is one of the most controversial figures in the Bible.

There is something about Mary that leaves us all wondering.

The controversy surrounding Mary Magdalene starts with the fact that, because she was a woman in the first century, we are given far less biographical information about her than her male contemporaries. Her name, Mary, was a common one, derived from the Semitic name Miriam. This popularity is reflected in the New Testament, which mentions the name Mary fifty-four times. It is used for several different figures, including Mary, the mother of Jesus; Mary of Bethany; Mary, the mother of James and John; Mary, wife of Cleophas; Mary, the mother of Mark; and even "the other" Mary.

Further, her descriptor, "the Magdalene," tells us very little about her. Most assume *Magdalene* refers to her hometown, in much the same way that Jesus is called "Jesus the Nazarene." Those two names share a connection in Greek and Aramaic, just as they share a common ring in English, and would have implied a connection between the two.[15]

The name Magdala is derived from *migdal*, which was a low stone tower used for holding fish, something common in fishing villages. To complicate matters, *migdol* is the Hebrew word for tower, while *magdala* is the Aramaic form of tower.

Identifying Mary's community is complicated by the existence of at least two ancient villages in Israel named after *migdal* or *magdal*, both of which no longer exist. Some scholars suggest she was from Taricheae, also known as Magdala Nûnîya, corresponding to the modern-day community of Migdal—a place I particularly enjoy visiting in Israel.[16]

Modern-day Migdal is the site of the Magdala Center, which houses one of the most important archaeological finds in the past fifty years, one of only seven first-century synagogues in Israel. Jesus might well have preached in this synagogue, and Mary may have attended there as well.

Another interpretation suggests that *Magdalene* refers to Mary's profession or her hairstyle, specifically indicating that she was a hairdresser—a profession inferred from the word *magdala*, which implies someone who braids hair.[17] This was considered one of the few socially acceptable jobs for Jewish women at the time. Unfortunately, cultural associations at times linked braided hair with prostitution, a stigma that has been erroneously applied to Mary Magdalene since early in church history, as we will explore further.[18]

The third explanation suggests that *Magdalene* was simply a nickname. Jesus was known for giving meaningful nicknames to those around him, and kind, insightful ones. He dubbed Peter "the Rock" and James and John "the Sons of Thunder."[19] Similarly, "the Tower" could have been an apt moniker for Mary, symbolizing her formidable strength and resilience. She was indeed a tower—a tower of hope, leadership, and commitment, steadfastly rising above her station, history, and disappointment in life.

Mary was a strong supporter of Jesus, generously giving of her resources. When Matthew, Mark, and Luke listed the group of women who traveled with Jesus and financed his ministry, they listed Mary Magdalene first.[20] This nickname could have reflected her high standing among Jesus' followers. It also served a practical purpose, differentiating her from the many other Marys in the Bible.

If Mary Magdalene was such a pivotal figure in Jesus' inner circle, the first to witness his resurrection and the first entrusted with proclaiming the good news, why isn't she more revered in the church today? Some may hastily claim it's because she was a prostitute. But it's important to clarify two points: First, even if this were true, a troubled past does not disqualify anyone from God's kingdom. More important, let's set the record straight: *nowhere* in the Bible is Mary described as a prostitute. History has repeatedly borne false witness against the Magdalene.

Why, then, has the rumor about Mary's virtue persisted for so long? What purpose does it serve to tarnish her reputation and cast a shadow of shame over her legacy?

COMPOSITE MAGDALENE

On September 14, 591, Pope Gregory I delivered a sermon that erroneously identified Mary Magdalene as the unnamed sinful woman in Luke 7 who anoints Jesus' feet.[21] Although the Bible does not specify the sinful woman's identity or her sin, Pope

Gregory asserted that she was a prostitute and that the seven demons Jesus had liberated Mary from represented the seven deadly sins (or vices), commonly known as lust, greed, sloth, wrath, envy, pride, and gluttony. In this single sermonic train wreck, Pope Gregory created what scholars have called the "composite Magdalene." Richard Hooper provocatively sums up the pope's confusion with this equation: "Jesus' feet + ointment + hair + Mary of Magdalene + Mary of Bethany + sinful woman = Mary the whore."[22]

In 1969, the Catholic Church formally dissociated Mary from the identity of the sinful woman who anointed Jesus' feet, thereby exonerating her. Despite this clarification, the misconception that had persisted for more than four hundred years proved deeply embedded in cultural and religious narratives, and the label stuck.

They always do.

Why was this fiction sanctified as fact? Pope Gregory's authority, compounded by the general illiteracy of the populace prior to the advent of the printing press, meant few people could question his assertions or verify the scriptural accuracy of his claims. And those who could have spoken up remained silent.

The motive behind Pope Gregory's conflation of the stories and characters is unclear. It may have been as simple as a theological blunder. We all make them. Some of us have even made them in the pulpit only to realize it later. Sometimes years later! It is also possible that Pope Gregory I, like many before and after him, was influenced by the pervasive challenge posed by strong female figures in religious narratives and opted to marginalize their roles.

Peter the Rock.

Mary the Tower.

Imagine how much healthier our ecclesiastical structures

would be today if Mary were valued for her contribution to the establishment of the church.

FROM DISAPPOINTMENT TO HOPE

After Jesus cast seven demons out of Mary Magdalene, she became one of his most faithful followers.[23] She supported him financially and followed him closely. While most of the disciples betrayed, denied, or abandoned Jesus when he went to the cross, Mary stood by him. During Jesus' darkest moment, Mary Magdalene was there. She did not allow fear to shake her faith.

But that is not to say she did not struggle with despair and disappointment after he died; she was only human, after all. Along with every one of the other disciples, she must have been overwhelmingly sad and confused when her Savior died. She had centered her whole life around him and likely had no idea that their time together would end so abruptly.

Not only was she grieving the death of her friend but also she was grieving the future she had imagined with him. She had given of her time and money, investing her whole life in following Jesus. Surely all of the disciples had had high expectations that their sacrifices would be worth it when he came into power. Those expectations had likely been growing for years, like a graph trending ever upward, inflating with each miracle, strengthening with each sermon, heightening with each interaction.

Now those expectations had crashed violently into the most unexpected, unimaginably horrible limitation: Jesus was dead. The disciples entered the cycle we know so well: expectations and limitations leading to disappointment. But Mary didn't stay there for long. She resolved her running quickly. She didn't let disappointment drive her to flee from her faith.

Life is full of disappointments, both relational and spiritual.

We've all experienced them: the shattering of a dream, the end of a friendship, the loss of a job, the betrayal of trust, the erosion of innocence. Each loss brings a wave of emotional pain. It's one thing to be disappointed with your husband, wife, kids, friends, boss, pastor, and the car dealer who sold you a lemon, but it's completely different when a kind, loving, faithful, compassionate, and just God seems to let you down.

Can we talk about this for a moment?

This is the painful secret we often keep hidden: there is no disappointment like the disappointment we feel when Jesus doesn't come through in our time of need.

Lord, where were you?

Where were you when my marriage fell apart?
Where were you when my child got sick?
Where were you when my dreams evaporated into thin air?
Where were you when we went through that existential
    crisis as a church?

Those are the questions we all ask when God doesn't come through as we had hoped, and they're rooted in our belief that we not only know God's promises but also know God's timing and the processes by which he works. But the truth is, we have only one of those things locked down: we have a book full of the promises of a God who is faithful.

What does that leave us with? The option to give up the one thing we do have and walk away, or to cling desperately to his promises while trusting his timing and his way of bringing them to pass.

We can trust God's heart even when we can't track his hand.

We can trust God's will even when we don't understand his ways.

We can trust God's Word even when it doesn't appear to be working.

It's worth making the journey to the tomb, even if it's only to mourn. We might approach with a heart full of sorrow, expecting only loneliness and loss. But in that sacred, quiet place, we may find more than we ever imagined. The tomb, which once symbolized the end, may reveal itself as the very place where new life begins.

As we stand in the shadow of what feels like death, we shouldn't be surprised if we find resurrection blooming right before our eyes. The grave, which seemed so final, may transform into a garden—a place where beauty springs from brokenness and where hope rises from the ashes of despair. It's there, in the place of our deepest sorrow, that we may realize the power of Christ's triumph over death and the boundless possibilities of new beginnings.

WHEN DREAMS DIE

In March 2022, a dream I had nurtured for twenty years came to an abrupt end. I've referenced it publicly in sermons and writings, but it's impossible to reference disappointment without revisiting it here. For almost two decades, I leaned into a global church for relationships and resources, building two thriving congregations by following their leadership playbook. Over time, my friendship with the senior pastors grew stronger, eventually leading us to join the movement.

Those were extraordinary days marked by joy and fruitfulness. Our church exploded with new growth and our services were packed with young adults at a time when most churches weren't connecting well with that demographic. My adult children were enthusiastically involved and passionate about our global mission, and my grandkids had a spiritual home for the next generation.

And then it all suddenly imploded. The reasons were complex, as they often are. What began as a flourishing local church led by humble, sincere, and godly leaders gradually became a global movement. As the movement grew, power dynamics crept in, institutional rigidity set in, and a subtle but pervasive sense of elitism began to surface, eroding the simplicity and purity that had once defined the church. Our passion for Jesus and his church was increasingly overshadowed by a preoccupation with influence and success. It would be far too easy to place blame on one or two individuals, but the reality was much deeper and broader than that. The culture itself had become problematic.

With time and reflection, I've come to see what I was once blind to—my own complicity in fostering an unhealthy culture. But let's be honest: understanding *how* something disappointing happened and grappling with *why* it happened are two very different things. The *whys* touch both our rational and emotional parts. The heart struggles to reconcile what the mind can so easily rationalize. Most of our disappointment in life is emotional rather than rational. We feel injustice deep in our souls, and it triggers questions that aren't easily satisfied.

Our congregation's response to the bitter disappointment of what transpired was to sit in a season of lament.

Do you know how hard that is when everything in you wants to either slide into deep, dark despair or run far, far away?

Each summer, we study a book of the Bible section by section, verse by verse. Because the summers in Phoenix are scorching and our air conditioners struggle to keep our large auditoriums sufficiently cooled with thousands of warm bodies in the room, we tend to keep the studies as positive and encouraging as possible. In one of our planning sessions immediately after the crisis, our executive pastor tentatively proposed that we study the book of Lamentations.

Lamentations?

We've spent three months crying ourselves to sleep each night and you want us to spend the entire summer lamenting?

He was right.

It wasn't easy for some members of our community; hundreds left, including one worship leader who said her kid didn't want to be part of a sad church any longer. That was hard to hear, but many people within our community leaned in hard and lamented in hope. The healthiest kind of lamentation is the hopeful kind, the kind that reminds the soul of God's goodness and faithfulness.

> I remember my affliction and my wandering,
>> the bitterness and the gall.
> I well remember them,
>> and my soul is downcast within me.
> Yet this I call to mind
>> and therefore I have hope:
>
> Because of the LORD's great love we are not
>> consumed,
>> for his compassions never fail.
> They are new every morning;
>> great is your faithfulness.
> I say to myself, "The LORD is my portion;
>> therefore I will wait for him."[24]

Lamenting gave birth to hope, and this hope sparked joy within our community, opening a door of promise and possibility.

FREQUENCY OF THE SOUL

Sometimes the only solace for a broken heart is to lament. A crushed spirit often finds its only voice in a sigh, a groan, or a heartfelt plea: "Help me, God." These expressions not only are appropriate but also resonate with God himself, who understands our lament as the soul's true frequency. The psalmist's words "deep calls to deep" capture this communion.[25]

Lamentation is a passionate expression of grief, an honest outcry from a heart in pain, grappling with the paradox between suffering and the assurance of God's goodness. It allows us to inhabit the tension in which we confess, "Lord, I believe, yet I am in pain. I believe, yet I am full of questions. I believe; help my unbelief."

Lament is not just a reaction but an act of faith in the face of disappointment. In some circles, there is pressure to quickly overcome disappointment or slap a smile on a sad situation. Instead of sitting with people in their grief, many Christians rush in with trite solutions, unhelpful prescriptions, or impatient responses. They are uncomfortable with other people's pain and disturbed by their questions. In these moments, questioning God's will, goodness, or plan may even be labeled mistakenly as a lack of faith.

As singer-songwriter Michael Card once said, "Churches are embarrassed, almost panicky, that there are situations to which they have no answer. We want to present Jesus as the answer man, and we don't want Jesus to look bad. And if that's your theology, Jesus can look very bad at funerals."

Especially his own.

Despite her overwhelming grief after witnessing Jesus' crucifixion, Mary still went to the tomb to anoint his body. Her actions remind us that the timing of God's miraculous interventions often remains unknown to us, compelling us to keep showing up—through doubt, despair, and disillusionment. We must continue to show up, even when we feel like giving up, when our sorrow is so intense we could throw up, when the impulse to flee is overwhelming, when our circumstances scream that God is untrustworthy, and when our words of praise are choked in our throats like lumps of coal.

Disappointment is the enemy's strategy for causing us to lose heart. It always moves us from our God-given appointment. In the worst of disappointments, God offers us the greatest opportunities to make our marks, to win our battles, to be transformed into what he is making us, and to serve the world.

The journey from disappointment to reappointment is navigated not by running away from the pain but by running toward the empty tomb and the risen Savior. It is in this sacred place that we find the strength to transform our laments into songs of hope, remembering that our faith is not in vain, and our cries are heard. Here, at the entrance to the empty tomb, we realize that our deepest laments are met with triumphant love, a love that turns mourning into dancing and brings life from death.

Run, Mary, run.

Running to Jesus transforms our disappointments into divine appointments.

When I think about overcoming disappointment, I'm reminded of the legendary track-and-field athlete Jim Thorpe, the first Native American to win a gold medal in the Olympics. His story is one of remarkable resilience. On the morning of his competition at the 1912 Olympics, Jim faced an unexpected setback: his shoes were stolen. But instead of letting this loss derail his dreams, he found two mismatched replacements in a garbage can. One shoe was

> RUNNING TO JESUS TRANSFORMS OUR DISAPPOINTMENTS INTO DIVINE APPOINTMENTS.

so large that he had to wear two socks to keep it on his foot. Yet despite this challenge, Jim went on to win not just one but two Olympic gold medals that day.

This story speaks volumes about the power of perseverance. Just as Jim Thorpe refused to be defeated by his circumstances, we, too, must push forward with unwavering determination. But our race is not simply about physical endurance, it's about running toward the empty tomb and the risen Jesus, where ultimate victory is found. As you run, listen for his voice calling your name just as he called Mary's. And when you hear it, let it draw you into the garden of resurrection hope, a place where every disappointment is redeemed, where every setback is a setup for something greater, and where your soul finds the rest it has been longing for.

COMING HOME

Begin each morning by inviting hope into your day. Start with a few quiet moments of meditation, focusing on Scriptures that speak of hope and God's faithfulness. Let these verses settle deep within your heart and serve as the lens through which you view the day ahead.

Carry this sense of hope with you as you move through your day. Seek out the signs of God's promises being fulfilled, whether in the gentle kindness of a friend, the beauty of creation, or the unfolding of a long-awaited answer to prayer. Look for God's hand at work in both the small, everyday moments and the significant, life-changing events.

Turn your attention to God's goodness. By expecting and searching for his goodness, you'll see your disappointments transformed into divine appointments. When you encounter challenges, let this practice of hope remind you that God is always moving, always faithful, and always working for your good.

PRAYER

Lord Jesus, in my disappointments, be my hope. When outcomes fall short of my expectations, remind me that your plans are higher and your ways are better. Strengthen my faith to see beyond setbacks, finding hope in your eternal promises. May your steadfast love be the anchor for my soul, reassuring me in every season of life, turning my disappointments into divine appointments that reveal your greater purpose. In Jesus' name, amen.

CHAPTER 12

FINDING SANCTUARY
From Restlessness to Refuge

Then the LORD said to Joshua: "Tell the Israelites to designate the cities of refuge, as I instructed you through Moses, so that anyone who kills a person accidentally and unintentionally may flee there and find protection from the avenger of blood."

—JOSHUA 20:1–3

Have you ever had a dangerous experience that sticks in your memory for years or even decades? I have one from when I was about eight years old, and it remains as vivid as if it happened yesterday. Our newspaper boy was a kid named Mitch. To say he had a bad attitude is an understatement; he probably had the worst attitude ever possessed by any twelve-year-old in the history of bad attitudes. He may have even been possessed!

Mitch had a full-grown beard by the seventh grade.

He had biceps that could rival a bodybuilder's arms.

He chewed tobacco and spat wherever he pleased.

He took orders from no one.

Despite numerous requests from my dad, Mitch would hurl the newspaper at our front door like a ninety-mile-an-hour fastball every day as he rode by on his bike. Inside the house, I would see my dad flinch, the muscle in his jaw clenching. I knew a showdown was inevitable. And honestly, I was fine with that because, for some reason, I didn't like Mitch, mainly because he scared me. I mean he really scared me.

One day as Mitch came barreling down our block on his bike, launching newspapers at doors, I reached my breaking point. Psychologists might call it a break with reality. I dashed onto the sidewalk and started hurling names at him.

Initially, it was just innocent rhyming with his name.

But within moments, I blurted out a word that rhymed with Mitch. I didn't even know what it meant, but Mitch sure did!

He dropped his bike and charged at me. It was the dead of winter in Sturgis, South Dakota, and by some stroke of luck, I was holding a snowball. Without a second thought, I threw it in self-defense, and to this day, I can't say whether God guided the snowball or the devil did, but it struck Mitch right on the forehead.

Unfortunately, he didn't topple like Goliath.

Even worse, throwing the snowball at him just made him angrier.

With a howl, he sprinted after me. What followed is still a bit of a blur, even fifty years later. But I do recall running as fast as I could down the sidewalk, up the front steps, and through our house, darting into the kitchen with Mitch hot on my heels, presumably ready to kill me. I'll never forget the sight of my father stepping out of his bedroom, taking one look at the scene as Mitch was about to catch me, and then shouting with a thunderous voice, "Mitch, what are you doing in my house? Leave my son alone!"

That was the day I understood the power of a safe refuge.

KIBBUTZ BE'ERI

During my visits to Israel, particularly within kibbutzim or k'far communities, I'm always drawn to the buildings marked by the word *miklat*. These are bomb shelters designed to shield the residents from incoming rocket fire.

I visited Israel last year as a guest of the Jewish National Fund just seven weeks after the Hamas attack that left twelve hundred dead, hundreds more wounded, and an entire nation traumatized.[1] The attack was the deadliest terrorist attack against Israel since the state's establishment in 1948, and the death toll was unprecedented. It will go down as one of the worst terrorist attacks in history.[2] I went to bear witness to the atrocities, to stand in solidarity with my friends, and to hear the stories of victims who had family members taken hostage back into Gaza.

The sights and sounds will stay with me for a lifetime: bullet-riddled homes, bloodstained floors, hastily abandoned toys, and the response of the Iron Dome to the relentless mortar bombardment.

> EVEN PLACES DESIGNED WITH SAFETY AS THE HIGHEST PRIORITY ARE VULNERABLE.

In Kibbutz Be'eri, each residence is equipped with a safe room, and every smartphone features a government app alerting residents to incoming rockets and mortar rounds, along with the time available to reach the shelter before impact. Given Be'eri's proximity to Gaza, the residents had a mere fifteen seconds to seek safety when under attack. But despite their intended purpose for protection against rocket attacks, many of the safe rooms lacked locks, making them vulnerable to penetration by small weapons fire. The Hamas terrorists swept into the kibbutz in an avalanche of violence, and ninety-six members of the community were killed, twenty-six taken hostage, and a thousand others forever traumatized.

Even places designed with safety as the highest priority are vulnerable.

We need a refuge that is abiding and eternal. Our safety lies in God, who offers a protection that surpasses all human measures. In him we find a shelter that no force can breach, a steadfast refuge in times of trouble. God alone is our ultimate place of safety, our unwavering stronghold amid life's greatest dangers.

THE RUNNER'S FOOTSTEPS

The concept of safe refuge in the book of Joshua is considerably more complex than was my escape from the newspaper boy. Joshua describes a tale of two cities. One type of city that God commanded the Israelites to establish in the promised land is known as the "cities of the Levites."[3] Forty-eight such cities were scattered throughout the land, serving as the priestly hubs of the nation. These cities were strategically placed along the nation's perimeter.

The cities of the Levites were intended to be a "saturation presence" within the land, dedicated to worship, biblical teaching, and spiritual nurture, and acting as a witness of God's kingdom to the neighboring nations.[4] They existed to infuse the land with the knowledge of God. It's entirely possible that when the prophets spoke of "the glory of the Lord covering the earth," they were envisioning these cities, where God's glory was vividly demonstrated through people who faithfully lived out his word in their daily interactions.

Of these forty-eight cities, six were designated "cities of refuge" to serve as safe havens for those seeking sanctuary from their adversaries. Joshua established three of these communities on each side of the Jordan River: Kedesh, Shechem, and Hebron to the west, and Bezer, Ramoth, and Golan to the east.[5]

The Mosaic law prescribed capital punishment for murderers, yet it also provided refuge in designated cities for those who unintentionally caused death.[6] These cities of refuge served as those safe places. In a society where retribution was often swift and severe, these communities provided a vital alternative to the "eye for an eye" justice prevalent in the ancient Near East. Known as the "avenger of blood," the closest relative of the deceased held the authority to exact vengeance, leaving little room for legal process or consideration of intent. There was no "innocent until proven guilty" or trial by a jury of peers. Your fate was firmly in the hands of the one who had the most reason to hate you and the least reason to assess motive or intent.

Rather than simply decreeing mercy, God established places of refuge, underscoring the importance of both mercy and justice. Those seeking asylum in these cities were not absolved of responsibility; upon arrival, they faced a judicial inquiry before the city's leaders. If their case was deemed accidental, they were granted sanctuary until the death of the high priest, ensuring their protection from vengeance, but also imposing on them a period of exile. However, if they left the sanctuary before the high priest's death, they would become vulnerable to the avenger's pursuit and potential death.[7]

The establishment of these sanctuaries within the Levitical cities likely stemmed from the belief that the Levites, as impartial judges, could temper the avenger's vengeful impulses. Their role as mediators between the Israelites and God, owing to their consecration as priests, positioned them to mediate peacefully between the assailant and the victim's kin, preventing further bloodshed.

According to the Sefer Hachinuch, a medieval commentary, the cities of refuge had three purposes: the perpetrator's repentance, their physical safety, and the emotional security of the victim's loved ones, who wouldn't have to see the perpetrator anymore.[8] In this balance of mercy and justice, the cities of refuge stood as reminders of God's compassion and the necessity of fair adjudication, offering an expression of his heart within the fabric of ancient Israelite society.

To ensure easy access to the cities of refuge, the equivalent of superhighways were built leading to them. It was the duty of the Sanhedrin to keep those roads in the best possible condition so that fugitives could reach their destinations. Every hill was leveled, every river was bridged, and the road had to be at least thirty-two cubits (fifty-two feet) wide, which is twice as wide as normal roads of the time.[9] Along those wide, open roads were guideposts bearing the word *Miklat* ("Refuge").[10] There also were two students of the law appointed to accompany the fleeing person and to pacify, if possible, anyone chasing the fugitive.

Another unique aspect of these cities is that they were always open. Unlike most other cities, whose gates could be shut with iron bars, the gates of the six cities of refuge always remained unbarred. The last thing God wanted was for someone to run for their lives only to reach the place of safety and find it locked. Everyone was welcomed: citizens and immigrants, Israelites and refugees, rich and poor, men and women, young and old. No one was to be turned away from the refuge of God's provision because of their age, ethnicity, or economic status. Everyone was allowed access to the grace of God.

These sanctuary cities were established directly by God, without any political agenda, unlike the contemporary concept of sanctuary cities. They weren't mere geographical locations; they symbolized the opportunity for a fresh start, graciously bestowed by God's unfailing grace. In the cities of refuge, we witness God's mercy and grace in action. There is a wideness to his provision. Not only did God provide these beautiful refuges for those who might need them but he organized and ordered things in such a way that nothing would hinder the desperate from accessing his provision.

Think back to the last time you made a momentous mistake, a failure, a sin.

Think of the moment when everything seemed to freeze and the weight of realization settled heavily on your shoulders. Perhaps it was a simple misstep, a slip of the tongue, or something more profound, with consequences echoing far beyond the immediate. Regardless of its magnitude, the aftermath was likely painful—a rush of embarrassment, a knot of regret tightening in your stomach, the familiar sense of failure and condemnation.

How many times have you beaten yourself up over what you have done? Have you gone over and over it trying to figure out how you could have stopped it, wishing you could rewrite the ending? It's a relentless cycle, a futile attempt to undo what has been done.

But what if there was a way out of this maze of guilt and shame?

What if there was a refuge from the unending barrage of self-critique and remorse, a sanctuary where the echoes of mistakes fade into the background, replaced by peace and acceptance? Would you want it? Would you enter it?

The cities of refuge offer a vivid illustration of safety and symbolically point to Jesus, who provides the ultimate sanctuary for our souls. In Jesus, we discover what we've been running for all along: provision for our unmet needs, healing for our open wounds, and the fulfillment of our holy longings. In Jesus, we find forgiveness of our sins, a fresh start, and cleansing from guilt and shame. He shields us from our adversaries, offers a haven for our restless hearts, and promises a hope and a future.[11]

In Jesus, we find everything we need. He is our protector, our safe house, our unshakable fortress, and our strong refuge. Anchoring our lives in him ensures the deepest peace and security, making him the most reliable foundation upon which we can build our lives.

Home is not just a place, it's the state of being truly known and loved by God.

When we come to Jesus, we can stop running. We can settle in and put down roots. We can live without looking over our shoulders, and without fearing that the enemies of our souls and of our peace, happiness, and joy will overtake us. We don't have to live in fear of being overcome by the things that seek to destroy us.

These cities vividly portray the refuge we find in Jesus and exemplify the kind of community God envisions for his church. We are called not just to attend church but to build a sanctuary in a troubled world—a city of refuge. The church isn't merely a building, it's a living organism within society, a beacon of hope and safety.

> HOME IS NOT JUST A PLACE, IT'S THE STATE OF BEING TRULY KNOWN AND LOVED BY GOD.

In his masterpiece *A Place for You*, Paul Tournier beautifully describes the church not just as a physical edifice but as a living, breathing sanctuary where restless souls driven by unmet needs, unhealed wounds, and holy longings can find refuge and rest in the arms of Jesus. Tournier envisions the church as a place of encouragement and nurture, where the echoes of divine compassion reverberate through the community it succors. It's a place where individuals are welcomed with open arms, where their struggles are met with understanding and their vulnerabilities are embraced without judgment. This dynamic community serves as a manifestation of God's love, offering a space where personal relationships cultivate healing and foster a sense of belonging.

The church that embodies the person of Jesus is our city of refuge.

Tournier also explores the innate human desire to localize God, a reflection of our need to meet God in specific times and places. Yet he gently reminds us that while our intentions might lean toward confining God to these spaces, the place we seek is found in God himself.

As we finally cease our running and step into the serene embrace of God's presence, we discover the peace and acceptance that mark our true place in the divine story. This place is not defined by physical boundaries but is a spiritual state in which the soul finds its ultimate connection with the Creator. In this sacred space, the discord of our lives—our fears, doubts, and conflicts—is transformed into a harmonious symphony of faith and trust. Here, embraced by God's unconditional love, we experience reconciliation with the parts of ourselves we once struggled to accept.

Envision our churches as modern-day cities of refuge, places where anyone, regardless of their past or present, can find a sanctuary of unconditional love. The path to building such a community is not without its challenges. It's messy, it's uncomfortable, and it often requires us to confront our own shortcomings. But this is what we're called to do. Each person who steps through our doors carries a unique story, one marked by both pain and hope, and they are all deserving of our deepest love and grace. By wholeheartedly embracing our call to be a safe and loving community, our churches can become beacons of hope and healing, reflections of the boundless love of God to all who enter.

But to truly transform our churches into cities of refuge, we need to look beyond mere cosmetic changes—beyond the buildings, the worship services, and the programs. What's required is a transformation from the inside out, a shift in the very heartbeat of our congregations. Mercy, grace, and safety must be not just ideals we aspire to but the very essence of who we are. It means cultivating an environment where every soul seeking refuge finds not just a warm welcome but a sense of belonging. This vision demands more than open doors; it demands open hearts—hearts that embrace all without hesitation, without reservation, and without exception.

When the love of Christ overflows from within us, our churches naturally become sanctuaries of light, drawing in those who are weary and burdened. We are called to be more than just a welcoming committee; we are to be companions on the journey, guiding others toward the peace and solace that only Jesus can provide. With every door we open and every hand we extend, we invite the weary to experience the profound rest and renewal that come from encountering the living Christ. In this sacred space, they hear the gentle call, "Come to me, all you who are weary and burdened, and I will give you rest. Take my yoke upon you and learn from me, for I am gentle and humble in heart, and you will find rest for your souls."[12]

Imagine if every church fulfilled its calling as a city of refuge. Picture a community where the doors are always open, where mercy, grace, and unconditional love are more than just sermons, they are the lifeblood of the community. Reflect on the sanctuaries in your experience where you've found peace, acceptance, and renewal. Now consider how you might be a part of creating such places and spaces for others.

How can your church more faithfully embody a sanctuary on earth?

How can your home become a beacon of hope in a dark and weary world?

How can your daily conversations with others become sacred spaces that provide refuge and rest?

EARTHLY REFUGES

Eugene Peterson's insight that "all theology is rooted in geography" resonates with me deeply. It underscores how our spiritual experiences are intricately connected to the physical spaces we occupy. Just as the land influences our journeys, the places we encounter shape our understanding of the divine.[13]

Throughout my journey, I have discovered sanctuaries—temporary though they may be—that have embraced me with the soothing whispers of comfort and familiarity. These are the places where my soul finds peace, where the relentless pursuit of purpose momentarily subsides, allowing me simply to exist. In these tranquil refuges, my heart feels truly at home, as close to heaven as one might find on earth. These sacred spaces remind me that our theological insights are often mirrored and molded by the geographies we traverse.

For me, this includes my first childhood home in Sturgis, South Dakota. *Yes, the one where Mitch tried to exact vengeance!* The first home my parents owned was simple and unassuming, a tiny house on Lazelle Street, and it remains a comforting memory. It was here, in the innocence of youth, that I first experienced a sense of space and place and the comforting embrace of a place called home.

Years later, I found it again in the first house my wife and I stretched our limited budget to purchase. Nestled on the hill behind St. Francis Hospital in Tulsa, this home was where our family put down roots and experienced the satisfactions of home ownership.

Across continents, my soul found a safe place in the Andros Guest House in Cape Town, South Africa. Before its transformation into a sophisticated boutique hotel, it was a little guest home where I experienced an inexplicable sense of rest over the years. I remember the first time I walked into this sanctuary after thirty hours of nonstop travel; it was as if I had stumbled into a cottage in the garden of Eden.

In recent years, I've found a sense of place at Seven Canyons in Sedona, Arizona. This little community is my favorite place on the planet, where the wind-shaped red rocks conspire with lush green fairways to present a rare and beautiful contrast. When Judith and I visit there, conversations, prayers, and words on paper all seem to flow effortlessly.

Last, I feel a sense of being home in the Heron Cove at The Salish on Orcas Island. Commissioned by Dr. Sweet and designed and built by the visionary James Hubbell, Heron Cove is more than a cottage, it is a living, breathing embodiment of a dream to live in harmony with the natural world. For more than two years, Hubbell labored to transform natural materials into a sanctuary that not only provides rest but inspires those fortunate enough to spend a night or two within its embrace.

In sharing my safe spaces, I invite you to consider your own.

Can you recall those precious moments when you felt a sense of safety, a connection to a place that seemed to embrace your very essence? Such memories are not mere coordinates on a map, they are sanctuaries for our souls, temporal places in our eternal quest for refuge and rest.

Where have you felt truly connected?

Where are you fully at home in this vast universe?

Where have you felt welcomed and accepted?

Where are you able to be yourself, free from striving and pretending?

We all crave sanctuaries, safe havens where we can unwind and rejuvenate. Whether grand or humble, lavish or modest, these spaces are essential for our well-being—mentally, emotionally, and physically. They are vital refuges, offering respite from life's relentless demands.

In a world that never slows down, everyone yearns for a place where their hearts can find solace, where the ceaseless chase comes to an end. These sanctuaries are sacred spaces where weary souls can finally exhale, where burdens are laid down, and where the frantic pace of life slows to a halt.

Amid the chaos and noise of modern living, these havens ground us in tranquility and provide a much needed pause in the whirlwind of daily existence. They are sanctuaries of peace, where the outside world recedes and inner calm takes precedence.

Whether it's cozy corners in our homes, serene natural landscapes, or quiet retreats within the bustling city, these spaces hold immeasurable value. They offer a sanctuary for reflection, restoration, and renewal, a sanctuary where we can simply be, unburdened and free.

> NONE OF OUR EARTHLY REFUGES CAN COMPARE TO THE SANCTUARY WE DISCOVER IN JESUS.

Yet none of our earthly refuges can compare to the sanctuary we discover in Jesus.

He alone is the ultimate rest we long for, the safe haven that satisfies our deepest yearnings.

While earthly sanctuaries offer comfort and are essential, their relief is temporary. They provide a brief respite from life's pressures and chaos but cannot address the root of our restlessness. In contrast, Jesus offers a refuge that reaches the core of our being. His presence brings a peace that surpasses all understanding and provides a security unshaken by life's storms. In him we find rest that goes beyond cessation of activity; we find rest that is about being made whole and complete.

In Jesus our souls find peace and security—a refuge that transcends all others. He invites us to cast all our anxieties on him because he cares for us, promising that his yoke is easy and his burden is light.[14] This divine sanctuary is not confined to a physical location; it is a state of being where we are known and loved. In his presence, we encounter transformation, healing our wounds and meeting our deepest needs. The sanctuary Jesus provides is eternal, enduring beyond the fleeting comforts of this world. It is a place where our identities are affirmed, our purposes clarified, and our spirits renewed. Here we can lay down the burdens we were never meant to carry and find rest for our weary souls.

In the parable of the prodigal son, Jesus tells the story of a young man who, driven by a desire for independence and fulfillment, demands his inheritance and leaves his father's house.[15] He runs far away, seeking pleasure and satisfaction in a distant country. But his pursuits lead to disappointment and despair, and he soon finds himself destitute and alone.

In his lowest moment, the prodigal son remembers the safety and provision of his father's house. He decides to return home, not expecting to be welcomed back as a son but hoping to be received as a servant. To his surprise, his father *runs* to meet him, embracing him with open arms and celebrating his return. The father's unconditional love and forgiveness transform the son's life, offering him the sanctuary and rest he longs for. This parable reminds us that no matter how far we've run or how lost we feel, God's love is always ready to welcome us home. When we stop running and turn around to face him, to our surprise we discover that he is running toward us. He has planned for our quest for sanctuary to end in his embrace.

The journey home is rarely straightforward, and even when we're on the right path, we often carry a sense of yearning that's hard to articulate. Carol Lakey Hess describes this as the "strangeness and restlessness of the homeless spirit that yearns for God." She writes, "Even if we are centered in God, we groan at the brokenness of creation and yearn for redemption. That is why we see everywhere the use of the metaphors of pilgrimage and sojourn to describe human life."[16]

This language of pilgrimage resonates strongly. Even when we've found our way back to God, we're still walking through a world that's not yet fully redeemed. The groaning we feel isn't a sign of failure but a mark of faith—an awareness that our true home is still to come. Every step of this journey is significant, even the ones that feel heavy or uncertain, because they're drawing us closer to the one who calls us home.

As we draw this book to a close, we circle back to where we began: the timeless pursuit of refuge and rest that shapes our human experience. Here in this eternal sanctuary, our unmet needs, hidden wounds, and holy longings no longer dictate our path. In the words of T. S. Eliot, "We shall not cease from exploration / And the end of all our exploring / Will be to arrive where we started / And know the place for the first time."[17]

Now that you understand the reasons for your flight.

Now that you know why you are exhausted.

Now that you have released the weight of your burdens.

Now that you have discovered a sanctuary for your soul.

You can come to him.

You can rest in him.

You can stop running.

You can stop running because the home you've been searching for isn't somewhere far away, it's in the presence of God. James C. Wilhoit captures this beautifully: "We are all born homesick, longing for a land and a way of life we have never directly experienced, but which we know is somewhere, or at least ought to exist."[18]

This homesickness is a gift, a divine pull toward the life we were created for. It's why nothing else truly satisfies—not success, not relationships, not even the good things we've built. Our longing points us back to the one who created us, who invites us into his rest. It's an invitation to stop striving, stop searching, and simply rest in the knowledge that we are loved, held, and finally home.

COMING HOME

Dedicate a special space in your home as your personal sanctuary. Choose a spot that naturally draws you in, where you feel at ease and unhurried. This could be a cozy prayer corner, a serene garden bench, or a comfortable chair by a window—anywhere that invites you to slow down and connect with God. Let this be a place that speaks to your soul, where the atmosphere itself encourages quiet reflection and intimacy with God.

Transform this space into a spiritual haven. Consider the elements that bring you peace and help you focus your thoughts on God. Decorate this space with items that enhance peace and reflection, such as candles to symbolize Christ's light, a Bible to keep God's Word at the center, inspirational books that uplift your spirit, soothing artwork that brings calm and beauty.

Make this sanctuary your daily retreat. Commit to spending time here each day, engaging in quiet prayer, scriptural meditation, or reflective reading. Whether it's in the early morning, during a lunch break, or at the end of your day, let this refuge become more than just a place. Let it become a rhythm in your life, a sacred routine where you consistently meet with God. Over time, this practice will turn your sanctuary into a place where your soul finds comfort and your heart finds peace.

PRAYER

Almighty God, you are my ultimate refuge and rest. Help me to find refuge in your presence as I withdraw from the world to seek quiet moments with you. In this sacred space, renew my spirit and refresh my weary heart. May I always remember that my true home is with you, where I am fully known and eternally loved. Grant me the peace that comes from this divine assurance, and may I carry it with me every day, finding rest in the shadow of your wings. In Jesus' name, amen.

AFTERWORD BY LEONARD SWEET

The Sacred Rhythm of Rest

When Jesus' disciples returned from their first mission, brimming with intensity and excitement over what they had accomplished through the Spirit's power, Jesus responded with a surprising invitation: "Come with me by yourselves to a quiet place and get some rest" (Mark 6:31). This wasn't just physical rest he offered but a deeper sanctuary of renewal—an *aliyah*, an ascent into sacred space.

In Hebrew tradition, *aliyah* means "ascent" or "going up." It's used both for being called up to read the Torah and for moving to the land of Israel—a journey that is both geographical and metaphysical. What might look like withdrawal to the world's eyes is actually an upward movement, an ascent into deeper communion with God. This sacred pattern of withdrawal and ascent appears throughout Scripture: Elijah after Mount Carmel (1 Kings 9), Moses coming down from Mount Sinai, and countless others who found that our deepest encounters with God often require both movement and stillness, both striving and surrendering, both socializing and solitude.

The Greek word used in Jesus' invitation, *anapausasthe*, carries connotations of both physical and spiritual refreshment. It speaks to our need for holistic restoration. We all need harbors and havens where our whole being (mind-body-spirit) can be recharged for mission on the high seas of this noisy, perilous, threatening world.

This is why I refuse to use the word *retreat* for these sacred pauses. They are advances—strategic movements toward deeper communion with God. Like the marines who humorously say "We're not retreating, we're just advancing from a different direction," our moments of withdrawal are actually forward movement into God's presence. It is this advent adventuresomeness that was captured memorably by French mathematician Georges-Théodule Guilbaud, who introduced cybernetics into French academic circles: "Heads I win, tails we start again—on the other foot." This is why I call my hospitality oasis on Orcas Island (sanctuaryseaside.com) an "advance center" rather than a retreat center.

The ancient Pharaoh understood the power of denying people this rhythm. In Exodus 5:9 (ESV), he commands, "Let heavier work be laid on the men that they may labor at it and pay no regard to lying words." This strategy of drowning spiritual awareness in busyness remains potent today. Our phones ping endlessly, our calendars overflow, and even our "leisure" time becomes programmed to the minute. We become like Jesus' favorite chef Martha, "anxious and troubled about many things," when Jesus says only "one thing is necessary" (Luke 10:41–42 ESV).

The Hebrew concept of Sabbath wasn't just about physical rest. It was about creating sanctuary in time, a space where we could remember who we are and whose we are. Perhaps this is why the psalmist wrote, "Be still, and know that I am God" (Ps. 46:10).

The knowing comes in the stillness. The revelation comes in the rest. The clarity comes in the quiet.

This harmonious dynamic between engagement and withdrawal reflects the deeper truth of *aliyah*—that sometimes what looks like stepping back is actually stepping up. When we "come apart" for rest and reflection, we're not retreating. We're advancing upward, climbing to higher ground where we can gain perspective, find renewal, and hear God's voice more clearly. When we create space for rest and reflection, we're not withdrawing from life but advancing into a more meaningful way of living our story.

In a world that glorifies constant motion, perhaps the most courageous act is to stop running, as Terry Crist has outlined in this beautiful book *Now You Can Stop Running*. Not in defeat but in recognition that our ultimate refuge is found not in endless activity but in the sacred rhythm of renewal and rest. Here, in these sanctuaries of stillness, we discover that we're not just running from or running to but being held in the embrace of divine love.

—LEONARD SWEET, Orcas Island

NOTES

CHAPTER 0: CAN'T STOP RUNNING

1. Augustine of Hippo, *Confessions*, 1.1.5.
2. Paul Tournier, *A Place for You* (New York: Harper and Row, 1968), 15.
3. *HaMakom*, meaning "the Place," is one of the many names for God in Jewish tradition, reflecting profound theological concepts about the nature of God and his relationship with the world. While the name is not explicitly used for God in the Torah, the concept is derived from the Scriptures, where "place" (*makom*) is connected to divine encounters.
4. I have a friend who introduced me to the term *mind monsters*, and he has written a book by the same name. Kevin Gerald, *Mind Monsters* (Lake Mary, FL: Charisma House, 2012), 1.
5. Proverbs 18:10.
6. C. S. Lewis, *The Problem of Pain* (New York: MacMillan, 1962), 145.
7. Ecclesiastes 9:11.
8. Henry David Thoreau, *Walden* (Boston: Ticknor and Fields, 1854), 8.

CHAPTER 1: RUNNING NOWHERE

1. Romans 8:38–39.
2. For further study, see the works of Augustine, Martin Luther, and Karl Barth as cited in Matt Jenson, *The Gravity of Sin: Augustine, Luther, and Barth on Homo Incurvatus in Se* (London: T&T Clark, 2007). Additionally, Dr. Leonard Sweet reflects on this in *Designer Jesus: The Lifestory of a Disciple* (Orcas Island, WA: Salish Sea Press, 2024), 119, as does Rich Villodas in *Good and Beautiful and Kind: Becoming Whole in a Fractured World* (Colorado Springs: Waterbrook, 2022), 3.

3. Walter Brueggemann, *Genesis* (Atlanta: John Knox Press, 1982), 55.

4. Genesis 4:1.

5. Genesis 4:2.

6. Chad Bird, *Unveiling Mercy: 365 Daily Devotions Based on Insights from Old Testament Hebrew* (Irvine, CA: 1517 Publishing, 2020), 18.

7. Genesis 3:15–16.

8. Genesis 3:17.

9. Genesis 4:6–7.

10. Jordan B. Peterson, *Twelve Rules for Life: An Antidote to Chaos* (Toronto: Random House Canada, 2018), 52.

11. Genesis 4:15.

12. Dr. Leonard Sweet introduced me to this concept. Jewish and Christian interpretations of Cain's mark vary widely, from leprosy and horns to racial and antisemitic stereotypes. However, some of the most profound interpretations come from midrashic texts. One suggests God marked Cain's arm with a Hebrew letter as protection (Pirqe Rabbi Eliezer 21), transforming the mark into a divine symbol. Another midrash proposes that the word *Sabbath* was inscribed on Cain's face, following the Sabbath's plea for his forgiveness (Tanhuma Genesis 10). Additionally, a targum interprets the mark as God inscribing Cain with the tetragrammaton, YHWH, the most sacred name of God, signifying profound sanctity.

13. Brené Brown, *Atlas of the Heart: Mapping Meaningful Connection and the Language of Human Experience* (New York: Random House, 2021), 137.

14. Christopher Cook, *Healing What You Can't Erase* (Colorado Springs: Waterbrook, 2024), 61.

15. Daniel DeWitt, "The Difference Between Guilt and Shame," Gospel Coalition, February 19, 2018, www.thegospelcoalition .org/article/difference-between-guilt-shame/.

16. John 16:8.

17. The Greek word for *convict* is *elegcho*, and it means "to expose, convict or convince by proof."

18. Romans 8:1–2.

19. 2 Corinthians 5:21.

20. Hebrews 10:2.

CHAPTER 2: RUNAWAY THOUGHTS

1. Center for Substance Abuse Treatment (US), "Trauma Awareness," chap. 2 in *Trauma-Informed Care in Behavioral Health Services*, Treatment Improvement Protocol (TIP) Series 57 (Rockville, MD: Substance Abuse and Mental Health Services Administration [US], 2014), www.ncbi.nlm.nih.gov/books /NBK207203/.

2. *APA Dictionary of Psychology*, s.v. "intergenerational trauma," accessed May 20, 2024, https://dictionary.apa.org/intergenerational-trauma.

3. Some people have identified them as generational curses, which is theologically disputable. What is clear, though, is that we carry the weight of our ancestors' hopes and failures.

4. N. P. F. Kellermann, "Epigenetic Transmission of Holocaust Trauma: Can Nightmares Be Inherited?" *Israel Journal of Psychiatry and Related Sciences* 50, no. 1 (2013): 33–39. This paper discusses the potential for Holocaust trauma to be transmitted to the children and grandchildren of survivors, with a focus on psychological and biological perspectives.

5. A. Bombay, K. Matheson, and H. Anisman, "Intergenerational Trauma: Convergence of Multiple Processes Among First Nations Peoples in Canada," *Journal of Aboriginal Health* 5, no. 3 (2009): 6–47.

6. Genesis 12:16 notes that Abram received gifts from the pharaoh of Egypt, which included "male and female servants." While Hagar is not mentioned in this passage, she could have been one of the servants given to Abram during his time in Egypt, especially considering her Egyptian origin.

7. Genesis 16:2.

8. Genesis 16:4.

9. Genesis 16:5–6.

10. Genesis 16:10.

11. Genesis 16:11.

12. Genesis 16:13.

13. Genesis 16:13.

14. Genesis 16:14.

15. Matthew 28:20.

16. Deuteronomy 31:8; Hebrews 13:5–6.

17. Genesis 21:8–19.
18. Genesis 21:16.
19. Genesis 21:17.
20. Genesis 21:20.
21. Bessel van der Kolk, *The Body Keeps the Score: Brain, Mind, and Body in the Healing of Trauma* (New York: Penguin, 2014).

CHAPTER 3: RUNNING FROM YOUR SHADOW

1. Robert Alter, *Genesis: Translation and Commentary* (New York: Norton, 1996), 115n11, 131.
2. Genesis 24:1–66.
3. Genesis 25:23–26.
4. Genesis 17:5.
5. Revelation 2:17, emphasis added.
6. Genesis 25:27–28.
7. For more information on family systems theory, see "The Murray Bowen Archives Project," accessed May 1, 2024, www.murraybowenarchives.org.
8. Genesis 27:5–17.
9. Genesis 27:41.
10. Genesis 27:43.
11. For more information, see Peter Titelman, *Emotional Cutoff: Bowen Family Systems Theory Perspectives* (New York: Haworth Press, 1998).
12. Mark 3:21; John 7:3–5.
13. John 1:10–11 MSG.
14. Galatians 3:13; Romans 5:12–21.
15. 2 Corinthians 5:17–20.
16. Genesis 27:19–24.
17. Genesis 29:25–27.
18. Genesis 31:20–21.
19. Colossians 2:9–10.
20. Genesis 32:24.
21. David G. Benner, *Surrender to Love: Discovering the Heart of Christian Spirituality* (Downers Grove, IL: InterVarsity Press, 2003), 77.
22. Brené Brown, *Rising Strong: How the Ability to Reset Transforms the Way We Live, Love, Parent, and Lead* (New York: Random House, 2017), 4.
23. Galatians 5:16–26.

24. Matthew 23; Mark 8:34.
25. Thomas Merton, *New Seeds of Contemplation* (New York: New Directions, 2007), 34–35.
26. Henri Nouwen, *Reaching Out: The Three Movements of the Spiritual Life* (New York: Doubleday, 1975), 138.
27. David G. Benner, *The Gift of Being Yourself: The Sacred Call to Self-Discovery* (Downers Grove, IL: InterVarsity Press, 2004), 83.
28. 2 Corinthians 12:9.
29. Genesis 47:9.
30. Romans 6:11–12; 8:13; Ephesians 4:22; Colossians 3:5.

CHAPTER 4: RUNNING IN CIRCLES

1. Gary Chapman, *Anger: Taming a Powerful Emotion* (Chicago: Moody, 2015), 17.
2. Exodus 1:6–13.
3. Exodus 1:15–16.
4. Exodus 2:1–3.
5. Exodus 2:11–12.
6. Exodus 2:13–15.
7. Exodus 32:19.
8. Exodus 34:1.
9. Numbers 20:10–13.
10. My notion of loops and cycles draws on general principles from cognitive behavioral therapy (CBT), where cognitive loops are recurring patterns of thoughts, emotions, and behaviors that reinforce one another. While I have not drawn this concept from a single source, it is informed by a synthesis of CBT literature, habit-formation studies, and personal observations in ministry.
11. Numbers 12:3.
12. John 1:17.
13. Mark 11:11–19.
14. Matthew 21:14.
15. Luke 19:41–44.
16. John 2:13–17; Psalm 69:9.
17. Bret Hammond, "Jesus Cleansing the Temple Does Not Excuse Your Lousy Temper," blog post, February 27, 2022,

www.brethammond.com/2022/02/jesus-cleansing-the-temple
-does-not-excuse-your-lousy-temper/.

18. Jeffrey Gibbs, "The Myth of 'Righteous Anger': What the Bible
Says About Human Anger," Concordia Theology, October 19,
2015, https://concordiatheology.org/2015/10/the-myth-of
-righteous-anger-what-the-bible-says-about-human-anger/.

19. 2 Corinthians 12:20; Galatians 5:19–21; Ephesians 4:26, 31;
Colossians 3:8, 21. For further research read Thomas Winger,
Ephesians (St. Louis: Concordia, 2015), 522. Gustav Stählin,
"The Wrath of Man and the Wrath of God in the NT,"
TDNT 5, no. 421, comments, "In Eph. 4:26 . . . [the imperative
'be angry'] by no means has the full force of an imperative, for
it is a quotation (Ps. 4:4) according to the sense given by the
LXX. Thus it is better to translate, not: 'Be angry for my sake
but do not sin,' but: 'If you are angry, be careful not to sin.'
Anger is not called sin here, but there lies in the background
the thought that when one is angry sin crouches at the
door. For this reason there is added: ὁ ἥλιος μὴ ἐπιδυέτω ἐπὶ
παροργισμῷ ὑμῶν. The quotation is to be read in the light of the
saying five verses later (v. 31), with its repudiation of πᾶσα ὀργή
['all anger']."

20. Brant Hansen, *Unoffendable: How Just One Change Can Make All of Life
Better* (Nashville: Thomas Nelson, 2015), 6.

21. Hansen, *Unoffendable*, 94.

22. Dietrich Bonhoeffer, *The Cost of Discipleship* (New York:
Touchstone, 1995), 127.

23. James 1:20.

CHAPTER 5: RUNNING ON EMPTY

1. 1 Kings 18:16–40.

2. 1 Kings 19:1–2.

3. 1 Kings 18:46.

4. 1 Kings 19:3.

5. 1 Kings 19:4.

6. 1 Kings 19:5–6.

7. 1 Kings 19:7.

8. Rodney Luster, "How Burnout Is Changing Our Lives," *Psychology*

Today, March 20, 2023, www.psychologytoday.com/us/blog
/more-than-a-feeling/202303/how-burnout-is-changing-our-lives.
9. Ecclesiastes 4:9–10 NLT.
10. 1 Kings 19:4.
11. 1 Kings 19:10.
12. 1 Kings 19:11–13.
13. John 1:14.
14. Matthew 11:28.

CHAPTER 6: RUNNING HOT AND COLD
1. Genesis 3:10.
2. "Anxiety in College: What We Know and How to Cope," *Harvard Health*, August 27, 2019, www.health.harvard.edu/blog/anxiety-in -college-what-we-know-and-how-to-cope-2019052816729.
3. "Quick Facts and Statistics About Mental Health," Mental Health America, accessed January 18, 2024, https://mhanational.org /mentalhealthfacts.
4. "Mental Health Information Statistics: Any Anxiety Disorder," National Institute of Mental Health, accessed October 10, 2022, www.nimh.nih.gov/health/statistics/any-anxiety-disorder.
5. "New Data on Gen Z—Perceptions of Pressure, Anxiety, and Empowerment," Barna Research, January 28, 2021, www.barna .com/research/gen-z-sucess.
6. "Studies Show Normal Children Today Report More Anxiety Than Child Psychiatric Patients in the 1950s," American Psychological Association, December 14, 2000, www.apa.org /news/press/releases/2000/12/anxiety.
7. Eugene H. Peterson, *The Jesus Way: A Conversation on the Ways That Jesus Is the Way* (Grand Rapids: Zondervan, 2007), 79.
8. 1 Samuel 17:28.
9. 1 Samuel 17:29.
10. Psalm 6:2.
11. Psalm 6:3.
12. Psalm 6:6.
13. Psalm 94:19.
14. Psalm 6:2–3; 55:4.
15. Psalm 6:6.

16. Andreia Esteves, "What Personality Types Are Prone to Anxiety?" October 10, 2022, *True You Journal*, www.truity.com/blog/what-personality-types-are-prone-anxiety.

17. Gaius Davies, *Genius, Grief, and Grace: A Doctor Looks at Suffering and Success* (Glasgow: Christian Focus Publications, 2003). This book contains case studies on Martin Luther, John Bunyan, C. S. Lewis, and others.

18. 1 Samuel 16:23.

19. John of the Cross, *Dark Night of the Soul*.

20. Romans 8:26–27.

21. Olga Khazan, "Relieve Your Anxiety by Singing It," *The Atlantic*, April 13, 2016, www.theatlantic.com/health/archive/2016/04/relieve-your-anxiety-by-singing-it/477960/.

22. I am indebted to the insights of my doctoral mentor, Dr. Leonard Sweet, for his body of work on this subject. He has shared these ideas on the stage and on the page. For further reading, see Leonard Sweet and Frank Viola, *Jesus: A Theography* (Nashville: Thomas Nelson, 2012), 237–41.

CHAPTER 7: RUNNING WITH SCISSORS

1. Gregory Popcak and Rachael Popcak, "Overcoming Bitterness: Five Steps for Healing the Hurt That Won't Go Away," Patheos, November 20, 2013, updated October 19, 2024, www.patheos.com/blogs/faithonthecouch/2013/11/overcoming-bitterness-5-steps-for-healing-the-hurt-that-wont-go-away/.

2. Stephen A. Diamond, "Diagnosing Scrooge Syndrome: The Dangers of Embitterment," *Psychology Today*, December 23, 2012, www.psychologytoday.com/us/blog/evil-deeds/201212/diagnosing-scrooge-syndrome-the-dangers-of-embitterment.

3. 2 Samuel 11:2–16.

4. Whether Bathsheba seduced David, willingly engaged in a sexual relationship at his initiation, or was raped remains up for debate among scholars. There is no denying the inequity of power between a young woman and a king, and by today's standards, this is unquestionably rape. For further research, see Richard M. Davidson, "Did King David Rape Bathsheba? A Case Study in

Narrative Theology," *Journal of the Adventist Theological Society* 17, no. 2 (autumn 2006): 81–95.

5. 2 Samuel 14:25–26.
6. 2 Samuel 13:23–29.
7. 2 Samuel 13:21.
8. 2 Samuel 13:38.
9. 2 Samuel 14:1–21.
10. 2 Samuel 14:24.
11. 2 Samuel 14:27.
12. 2 Samuel 14:33.
13. 2 Samuel 15:2–6.
14. 2 Samuel 15:5.
15. 2 Samuel 16:21–22.
16. 2 Samuel 15:7–12.
17. 2 Samuel 18:1–8.
18. 2 Samuel 18:9–15.
19. 2 Samuel 18:33.
20. Hebrews 12:15.
21. The Greek word *pikría* conveys the idea of a pervasive bitterness or acridity that functions like a corrosive toxin, damaging relationships and spiritual well-being.
22. Romans 12:19–20.
23. 1 Samuel 24:12–13.
24. Luke 23:34.

CHAPTER 8: RUNNING RAMPANT

1. 2 Timothy 2:22 NLT.
2. A proper theology of pleasure begins with "God saw all that he had made, and it was very good" (Gen. 1:31). It affirms, "Everything God created is good, and nothing is to be rejected if it is received with thanksgiving, because it is consecrated by the word of God and prayer" (1 Tim. 4:4–5). We should embrace the belief that God "richly provides us with everything for our enjoyment" (1 Tim. 6:17), and that he "[fills] our hearts with food and gladness" through the blessings of rain and fruitful seasons (Acts 14:17 KJV). These Scriptures remind us of the inherent

goodness of God's creation and his intention for us to find joy in what he has provided.

3. Genesis 1:1, 27–31.
4. Jeremy Jernigan, *Redeeming Pleasure* (Franklin, TN: Worthy Books, 2015), 8.
5. Ecclesiastes 9:7.
6. 1 Kings 3:5.
7. 1 Kings 3:9.
8. Song of Songs 2:15.
9. The full quote is "Uneasy lies the head that wears a crown," from part 2 of William Shakespeare's play *Henry IV.*
10. First Kings 9:15–17 describes Solomon's use of forced labor for his numerous building projects, including the temple and his palace. Although he initially avoided enslaving Israelites, he did impose heavy labor requirements and taxes on them (1 Kings 12:4). This led to increasing dissatisfaction among the people, which came to a head after Solomon's death. When his son Rehoboam succeeded him, the people petitioned for relief from the heavy burdens imposed by Solomon, highlighting grievances over high taxes and forced labor (1 Kings 12:4–11).
11. Ecclesiastes 1:2.
12. Ecclesiastes 2:17 NLT.
13. A. J. Swoboda, *The Gift of Thorns: Jesus, the Flesh, and the War for Our Wants* (Grand Rapids: Zondervan, 2024), xxiii.
14. Augustine, *Confessions,* VIII.7.
15. Augustine, *Confessions,* I.1.
16. Thomas Aquinas, *Summa Theologica* II–II, Q. 35, Art. 4.
17. Martin Luther, *Table Talk,* no. 239.
18. C. S. Lewis, "The Weight of Glory," in *The Weight of Glory and Other Addresses* (New York: HarperOne, 2001), 30.
19. C. S. Lewis, *Mere Christianity* (New York: HarperOne, 2001), 50.
20. John Piper, *Desiring God: Meditations of a Christian Hedonist* (Portland, OR: Multnomah, 2011), 18.
21. Psalm 16:11 NKJV.
22. Leonard Sweet, *Designer Jesus: The Lifestory of a Disciple* (The Salish Sea Press, 2024), 403.

CHAPTER 9: RUNNING AGAINST THE CLOCK

1. Virginia Brasier, "Time of the Mad Atom," *Saturday Evening Post*, May 28, 1949, 72.
2. Terry Crist, *Loving Samaritans: Radical Kindness in an Us vs. Them World* (Grand Rapids: Zondervan, 2024).
3. Esther 1:4–8.
4. Esther 1:10–11.
5. Esther 1:12.
6. Esther 1:19.
7. Esther 2:2–4.
8. Esther 2:17.
9. Esther 2:15.
10. Esther 2:20.
11. Esther 2:21–22.
12. Esther 3:1–2.
13. Esther 3:5–6.
14. Esther 3:13.
15. Esther 4:1.
16. Esther 4:8.
17. 2 Corinthians 12:8.
18. Esther 4:14.
19. Esther 7:2.
20. Cara Feinberg, "The Science of Scarcity," *Harvard Magazine*, May/June 2015, www.harvardmagazine.com/2015/04/the-science-of-scarcity.
21. Feinberg, "Science of Scarcity."
22. Ecclesiastes 3:1–8.
23. Psalm 90:12.
24. 1 Samuel 9:1–2.
25. Sefaria, "Esther 2:5," accessed May 15, 2024, www.sefaria.org/Esther.2.5.
26. Esther 9:24. See also Emil G. Hirsch, M. Seligsohn, and Solomon Schechter, "Haman the Agagite," *Jewish Encyclopedia*, accessed May 15, 2024, www.jewishencyclopedia.com/articles/7124-haman-the-agagite.
27. 1 Samuel 15:3.
28. 1 Samuel 15:9.

29. Esther 3:13.
30. Esther 8:11.
31. Michael V. Fox, *Character and Ideology in the Book of Esther* (Columbia, SC: University of South Carolina Press, 1991), 3095 Kindle.

CHAPTER 10: RUNNING THE GAUNTLET

1. Thomas John Carlisle, *You! Jonah!* (Grand Rapids: Eerdmans, 1968), 27.
2. Jonah 1:17: the Hebrew word *dag* is best translated as "big fish" or "sea monster." In Matthew 12:40, Jesus uses the Greek word *ketos*, or "big fish."
3. The Hebrew letter *y* is transliterated as a *j* in English, which makes the pronunciation *Yonah*.
4. Genesis 8:8–12.
5. 2 Kings 14:23–25.
6. Described by Bruckner as "terror-mongering": James K. Bruckner, *Jonah, Nahum, Habakkuk, Zephaniah*, NIV Application Commentary (Grand Rapids: Zondervan, 2004), 28–30.
7. Timothy Keller, *The Prodigal Prophet: Jonah and the Mystery of God's Mercy* (New York: Viking, 2018), 39.
8. Chad Bird, *Unveiling Mercy: 365 Daily Devotions Based on Insights from Old Testament Hebrew* (Irvine, CA: New Reformation, 2020), 226.
9. 1 Kings 10:22; 2 Chronicles 9:21.
10. Isaiah 27:1.
11. Jonah 1:3.
12. Cyrus Gordon, "Tarshish," *Interpreters Dictionary of the Bible* (Nashville: Abingdon, 1962), 518–19, quoted in Eugene H. Peterson, *Under the Predictable Plant: An Exploration in Vocational Holiness* (Grand Rapids: Eerdmans, 1992), 14.
13. Peterson, *Under the Predictable Plant*, 15.
14. Peterson, *Under the Predictable Plant*, 11.
15. Jonah 1:3.
16. Jonah 1:5.
17. Jonah 1:15.
18. Jonah 1:17.
19. Psalm 139:7–10.

20. Jonah 1:4.
21. Jonah 1:7–8.
22. Jonah 1:15.
23. Jonah 1:15.
24. Jonah 1:17.
25. Keller, *Prodigal Prophet*, 17.
26. Romans 1:29.
27. Romans 2:17–18.
28. Romans 3:10–12.
29. Robert Solomon, *God in Pursuit: Lessons from the Book of Jonah*.
30. Peterson, *Under the Predictable Plant*, 101.
31. Jonah 2:10.
32. Jonah 3:1–3.
33. Jonah 3:10.
34. Jonah 4:1.
35. Jonah 4:10–11 ESV.
36. Jonah 4:11.
37. Bird, *Unveiling Mercy*, 351.
38. Hebrews 10:5–7 is the fulfillment of this messianic expression in Psalm 40:6–8.
39. Matthew 12:39–41.
40. Hebrews 4:15.
41. Matthew 12:40.
42. 2 Corinthians 12:9.

CHAPTER 11: RUNNING TO JESUS

1. John 20:2.
2. John 20:3–4.
3. John 20:4.
4. Matthew 28:8.
5. 1 Peter 1:3.
6. John 12:13.
7. Luke 23:55–56.
8. John 20:11–16.
9. Luke 8:2.
10. Luke 8:3.
11. John 19:25.

12. Mark 15:47.

13. John 20:1.

14. John 20:17.

15. Bruce Chilton, *Mary Magdalene: A Biography* (New York: Doubleday, 2005), 462 Kindle.

16. According to Josephus, Taricheae was a fishing village destroyed by the Romans during the rebellion and seems geographically situated relative to Tiberias as described in the Talmud.

17. Thomas F. McDaniel, "The Meaning of 'Mary,' 'Magdalene,' and Other Names: Luke 8:2," in *Clarifying Baffling Biblical Passages* (n.p., 2007), 338–39. McDaniel goes on to quote John Lightfoot, *A Commentary of the New Testament from the Talmud and Hebraica* (1658: 3:87, 375), where Lightfoot equates plaited hair with prostitution.

18. McDaniel, *Clarifying Baffling Biblical Passages*, 339–40. McDaniel also gives a few other possible meanings for *Magdala* in his book.

19. Matthew 16:18; Mark 3:17.

20. Luke 8:2.

21. Gregory the Great, "Homily XXXIII," in Richard J. Hooper, *The Crucifixion of Mary Magdalene: The Historical Tradition of the First Apostle and the Ancient Church's Campaign to Suppress It* (Sedona: Sanctuary Publications, 2005), 79.

22. Hooper, *Crucifixion of Mary Magdalene*, 81.

23. Ben Witherington III, "Mary, Mary, Extraordinary," accessed May 17, 2024, www.leaderu.com/theology/maryandjesus.html. Witherington writes, "Seven was the number of completion or perfection. We are meant to understand that she was particularly captivated by the dark presence in her life and required deliverance by an external power. Demonic possession controls the personality and leads to voices speaking through the person, fits, and acts of unusual power. Jesus delivered Miriam from this condition, which apparently prompted her to drop everything and follow him around Galilee."

24. Lamentations 3:19–24.

25. Psalm 42:7.

CHAPTER 12: FINDING SANCTUARY

1. Aaron Boxerman, "What We Know About the Death Toll in Israel from the Hamas-Led Attacks," *New York Times*, November 12, 2023, www.nytimes.com/2023/11/12/world/middleeast/israel-death-toll-hamas-attack.html.

2. Daniel Byman et al., "Hamas's October 7 Attack: Visualizing the Data," Center for Strategic and International Studies, December 19, 2023, www.csis.org/analysis/hamass-october-7-attack-visualizing-data.

3. Numbers 35:1–8; Joshua 21:1–42.

4. "Levitical Cities," *Encyclopedia of the Bible*, BibleGateway, www.biblegateway.com/resources/encyclopedia-of-the-bible/Levitical-Cities.

5. Joshua 20:1–8.

6. Exodus 21:13.

7. Numbers 35:6–34.

8. Sefer Hachinuch, mitzvah 408.

9. Talmud, Bava Batra 100b.

10. Levi Mendelson, "Cities of Refuge Demystified," Chabad.org, accessed May 6, 2024, www.chabad.org/parshah/article_cdo/aid/2684913/jewish/Cities-of-Refuge-Demystified.htm.

11. Jeremiah 29:11.

12. Matthew 11:28–29.

13. Eugene H. Peterson, *Under the Predictable Plant: An Exploration in Vocational Holiness* (Grand Rapids: Eerdmans, 1992), 130.

14. Matthew 11:28–30.

15. Luke 15:11–21.

16. Carol Lakey Hess, "Educating in the Spirit" (PhD diss., Princeton Theological Seminary, 1990), 214–15.

17. T. S. Eliot, "Little Gidding," *Four Quartets* (New York: Harcourt, Brace, 1943), 59.

18. James C. Wilhoit, *Spiritual Formation as If the Church Mattered: Growing in Christ Through Community* (Grand Rapids: Baker, 2022) 82.

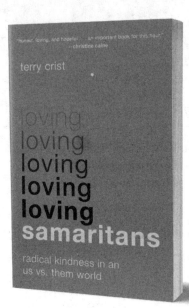

Loving Samaritans

Radical Kindness in an Us vs. Them World

Terry Crist

In a world defined by division, what would it mean to see people the way Jesus sees them?

As a pastor, Terry Crist is committed to building deep relationships with people whose experiences are different from his own—people whom much of society rejects. Why? Because those relationships are where we see Jesus at work.

It doesn't have to be one or the other; you can both love God and love your neighbor.

Drawing fresh insights from the story of Jesus and the Samaritan woman at the well, Terry shares how to trade judgment for grace, disputes for harmony, apathy for empathy, and hate for love. By the end of this book, you will be able to:

- Identify how you see the world and why it matters
- Recognize people on the margins who are right around you
- Reflect Jesus' love in your interactions with others
- Extend dignity to people who are suffering from mental illness, homelessness, and addiction
- Maintain healthy relationships, even when family members hold opposing views
- Serve as an ambassador of reconciliation in your community

We come close to Jesus when we love people society tells us we should hate. And that just might change everything.

Available in stores and online!